"Orlean takes readers on a whiz-bang tour of several dozen spots where locals whoop it up, workers rake it in, women hunt husbands, dieters binge, prisoners go on dates, and religious people convert. . . . Orlean's research is original and ambitious, and her findings wonderfully entertaining. . . . Orlean bucks America's obsessions with work and celebrity. Yet her characters become stars."

—*The Christian Science Monitor*

"A phenomenological journey of discovery . . . splendidly unscientific and witty."

—*The Economist*

"Orlean's high spirits and intelligence give her book the feeling of a good Saturday-night conversation. She approaches all her subjects with a sense of adventure and openness. . . . Her impressions are so rich and generous that I wanted to hear more of her speculations. . . . Her chapters are like beginnings of suspenseful novels, and if we look at ourselves on a Saturday night, we'll see action about to begin."

—*USA Today*

"Entertaining . . . a keenly observed slice of American life."

—*Atlanta Journal-Constitution*

"Orlean can turn a vivid phrase . . . . The more you read, the more you notice how various stories throw new light on what went before . . . . All in all, a pretty entertaining way to spend a Saturday night."

—*The Philadelphia Inquirer*

"Good, funny and drum-tight. Orlean has a knack for catching a scene at just the right moment."

—*Newsday*

ALSO BY SUSAN ORLEAN

Saturday Night

Susan Orlean

SIMON & SCHUSTER PAPERBACKS
New York   London   Toronto   Sydney   New Delhi

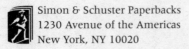 Simon & Schuster Paperbacks
1230 Avenue of the Americas
New York, NY 10020

First Simon & Schuster trade paperback edition August 2011

SIMON & SCHUSTER PAPERBACKS and colophon are registered
trademarks of Simon & Schuster, Inc.

For information about special discounts for bulk purchases,
please contact Simon & Schuster Special Sales at 1-866-506-1949
or business@simonandschuster.com

The Simon & Schuster Speakers Bureau can bring authors to your
live event. For more information or to book an event contact the
Simon & Schuster Speakers Bureau at 1-866-248-3049
or visit our website at www.simonspeakers.com.

Manufactured in the United States of America

10   9   8   7   6   5   4   3   2   1

ISBN 978-1-4516-6098-2
ISBN 978-1-4516-6101-9 (ebook)

For Jeff Conti

Contents

Introduction

Not long ago, I spent an interesting Saturday night in Elkhart, Indiana. I had gone there to write about a local imbroglio that pitted the mayor, a young man with conservative tastes, against a group of people who liked to spend their Saturday evenings cruising in fancy cars through downtown. The mayor saw the issue as a traffic problem; the cruisers saw his efforts to stop cruising in Elkhart as an infringement on their inalienable right to have fun on weekends. I saw it as a chance to see how seriously people take Saturday night.

I arranged to meet the cruisers at nine o'clock so I could ride with them on Main Street. At seven I got hungry, so I drove to an Italian restaurant someone had recommended to me. I was alone and it was Saturday night and I didn't want to feel out of place, so I hoped the restaurant would be a quiet hole-in-the-wall. It was not. It was the sort of place that attracts every birthday celebration, first date, last date, prom date, anniversary party, engagement celebration, and stag party within a two-hundred-mile radius. All around me were couples, people on dates, groups of friends, and a few family reunions; a big birthday party was under way at the table next to mine. It was a large restaurant, and there were no other single diners. I am not unaccustomed to being alone in a crowd, but this was the first time in my life I had dined alone at a restaurant—let alone a restaurant preferred by big, ostentatiously convivial groups of people—on a Saturday night. It was an uncommon and largely disagreeable sensation. I saw that I was being noticed by the people seated near me. It made me feel as if I had walked out of the house without any pants on. I decided that the best defense was to look busy, but reading the label on the aspirin bottle in my purse took only a minute. Next, I read the menu. Then I turned to the place mat, which had only a photograph of a beach on it—I never thought I would see the day when I would miss those place mats with puzzles on them, but this was it. I wondered whether I could leave without being too obvious, and if I left, whether I could get a more secluded dinner somewhere else.

My musing was interrupted by my waitress, a tall woman with curly brown hair, a high forehead, and a voice that could cut through drywall. Her name tag said MARIAN. She greeted me and asked if I was meeting someone. I said I wasn't. "Here on vacation?" she asked. When I said I was in town doing work, she gave me a long look full of pity and proceeded to take my order. At that point, all I wanted was to get a quick dinner and get out. I hoped that Marian would speed me on my way. Marian, however, dawdled. She tidied my place setting and filled my water glass. She eyed me. I looked away. She checked my salt and pepper shakers. I began to suspect that in her eyes I was a statistical freak—a Fourth of July snowstorm of customers. She dawdled some more. Another minute passed. Finally, just as she was walking away, Marian grabbed a waitress passing by, turned her so she could get a good look at me, and said in her loud, clear voice, "Just look at her! My god! All by herself and working on Saturday night!"

After that dinner, and after I had gone cruising, I was convinced: Saturday night is different from any other night. On Saturday night, people get together, go dancing, go bowling, go drinking, go out to dinner, get drunk, get killed, kill other people, go out on dates, visit friends, go to parties, listen to music, sleep, gamble, watch television, go cruising, and sometimes fall in love—just as they do every other night of the week, but they do all these things more often and with more passion and intent on Saturday night. Even having nothing to do on a Saturday night is different than having nothing to do on, say, Thursday afternoon, and being alone on a Saturday night is different from being alone on any other night of the week. For most people Saturday is the one night that neither follows nor precedes work, when they expect to have a nice time, when they want to be with their friends and lovers and not with their parents, bosses, employees, teachers, landlords, or relatives—unless those categories happen to include friends or lovers. Saturday night is when you want to do what you want to do and not what you have to do. In the extreme, this leads to what I think of as the Fun Imperative: the sensation that a Saturday night not devoted to having a good time is a major human failure and possible evidence of a character flaw. The particularly acute loneliness you can feel only on Saturday night is the Fun Imperative unrequited. But most of the time Saturday night is a medium of enjoyment. Observing different kinds of people in different parts of America who live in different sorts of circumstances at leisure on Saturday night seemed like a perfect opportunity to observe them in their most natural and self-selected setting—like studying an elephant romping in the Ngorongoro Crater as opposed to studying an elephant carrying an advertising sandwich-board in front of a used-car lot in Miami.

After my trip to Elkhart, I decided to travel around the country and spend Saturday nights with a variety of people in a variety of situations, with the intention not to define Saturday night but to illustrate it. What I wanted to know about Saturday night was not so much what is fun to do with your spare time as what, given some spare time and no directives or obligations, people find themselves doing. I wanted to know what determines how Americans spend Saturday night. Is it mainly regional? Is it a matter of age and marital status? Relative wealth? Urban versus suburban versus rural? Is there such a thing as a typical Southern Saturday night, or a middle-aged Saturday night, or a working-class Saturday night? Is there someplace everyone goes on Saturday night—that is, is there something that has sprung up to replace the vanished town squares and bars and bowling alleys where people used to gather when they wanted to get together and had no particular place to go?

This task had a few challenges. For one thing, many people, including me, often spend Saturday night with friends at home. For a reporter, this is a tough world to infiltrate and an impossible one to write about, and judging by many of the Saturday nights I've spent this way, their pleasures are too self-referential to bear description. So for the record, I will note here that a great many people across America spend a great many Saturday nights at home with their family or their friends. It is also true that in the era of disaster news, people have come to expect to be written about only when something exceptional or shocking takes place in their lives. When I showed interest in a subject people considered terribly ordinary—Saturday night in the life of a suburban baby-sitter, for instance—I had some explaining to do. All I could say was that I was looking for things that were neither exceptional nor shocking, and that would reveal what a typical Saturday night was like for somebody—say, an eighty-two-year-old woman who liked to dance, or an Air Force officer on Saturday-night missile duty, or a Park Avenue hostess with a reputation to maintain. Quite often, people would ask me to come back when the town was having its jazz festival or mariachi festival or rodeo. That wasn't what I was after. I had this notion that Saturday night itself was a good enough subject. I liked the idea of writing about people in a setting that had nothing to do with business or government or concession stands. I liked the contrariness of examining leisure in an era that is obsessed with work, and writing about average citizens in an era that celebrates celebrity.

Obviously, there are about two hundred million ways Americans spend their Saturday nights, and quite obviously I could not document any sizable percentage of them. I decided early on to be impressionistic rather than encyclopedic—to take a ride across the country, with stops along the way, rather than to attempt a door-to-door survey. Relieved of the impossible burden of comprehensiveness, I was drawn to certain themes (what it is like to work on Saturday night, for instance, and the too-common experience of Saturday-night murder); types of people (the Park Avenue maven, the recovering drug addict); places (the busiest restaurant in the United States); communities (the Louisiana blacks who have settled in Houston); classic Saturday-night situations (the life of a lounge band). I expected to report on someone on a date and never did (my belief in the Heisenberg Principle of the observer affecting the observed dissuaded me); I expected to spend no time whatsoever in churches and ended up in them three times. There is nothing exhaustive about my final results and I employed no quota system: I would give in to what seemed interesting, informed by a wish to throw as broad and engaging a net as I could.

There were a few things about Saturday night I wanted to figure out. For instance, even though Saturday night is itself a democratic occasion, I wondered if most people choose to spend it undemocratically—that is, to spend it around people just like themselves. Some Saturday-night situations don't appear to have any social parameters. One Saturday night, I hung around the emergency room of a large veterinary hospital in New York. I'd heard there were certain animal accidents (cats falling out of windows, especially) that seemed to happen mostly on Saturday nights and I wanted to find out why; I also wondered whether there was any similarity to the people who ended up at such a place on Saturday nights when they didn't have an emergency. Some flattened cats did come in (it was a hot night, and a lot of people probably left their windows open while they were out) but there were also a lot of people who just chose that Saturday night to get their dogs' teeth cleaned or to have their sick parakeet put to sleep. Except for sharing a somewhat unconventional notion of pet care, these people appeared to have nothing in common. The animal emergency center aside, I saw some white people at the black church social I went to, and some black kids and a few upper-middle-class white kids hanging around the white, blue-collar cruising crowd in Elkhart. But generally, it seems that Saturday night acts as a subset intensifier, and that most people stick with their own small social set when they are out on their own.

Distinguishing Saturday night from the rest of the week began around 7 B.C. with the introduction in Assyria of once-a-week "evil days," and it has remained constant throughout human history, including but not ending with *Saturday Night Fever.* That is a rather exceptional sweep: I don't know of anything else that has social significance spanning ancient Babylonia *and* Babylon, Long Island. The origin of Saturday night's distinctiveness was religious—one day each week set aside as sacred to contrast with the six others that were profane—and, over time, became economic (a day of rest versus days of labor). Before this century, days of rest were permitted mainly so that laborers could restore—"recreate," in Victorian terms—their strength and then return to another six days of hard work. Eventually, as affluence and easy credit spread through the American middle class after World War II, weekend "recreation" became an end in itself. Fun was viewed as an entitlement of the middle class rather than an exclusive right of the rich and elite. The satisfying life, after the war, included an imperative to have fun, and Saturday night was the center of it.

How is Saturday night different now from the past? There is no doubt that AIDS has quashed some of the abandon that Saturday night symbolized and contained—not just in gay nightclubs, but in all bars and clubs and parties. This was probably the most depressing truth that arose in my reporting. There are other ways social behavior and Saturday night have changed. A sex researcher told me that he believes many people used to have sex only on Saturday nights, in some cases because it was their only chance, and in other cases because an unconscious sense of guilt made them feel that it was improper on "regular" nights of the week. He ventured that sex on Saturday night was titillating for some people because it was only hours before they would have to go to church. Sexual liberation, this scientist concluded, has probably changed that.

Vidal Sassoon also was an agent of change. In 1964, in a fashion-press–packed ballroom of the Hotel Pierre in New York City, he demonstrated on girl triplets from Brooklyn the free-swinging, loose-falling haircut he had pioneered, a cut that could be washed and dried at home and would eventually eliminate for most women the ritual of the Saturday afternoon hair-setting at a salon. "We did for faces what Frank Lloyd Wright did for architecture," Sassoon says. "We're talking about freeing five, six hours a *week* for women.

And they would still look good for Saturday night. It was a big change for society. There were people in deep shock."

Then there's the effect of indoor plumbing on Saturday night: when baths were once-a-week events at the neighborhood bath-house, Saturday had the distinction of being bath night for most people, since it allowed them to get clean after a week of work and before a night of leisure. A man I know who founded a bath-accessories business named it Saturday Knight Ltd. to satisfy his Anglophilia and to commemorate his childhood ritual of Saturday-night baths. Some people I met still remember bath night fondly, but I have yet to meet anyone who thinks full-time access to hot water is something to regret.

Saturday night happens to be when most people take part in whatever is the current entertainment trend. One month, they might watch a break-dance contest, and a lip-synching contest the next, and a vogueing demonstration the one after that. I began to think of this aspect of Saturday-night culture as the Palace of Social Meteors. Every city I've ever visited seems to have a bar or nightclub called the Palace, the local showcase for whatever the current public di-version happens to be. I made a practice of avoiding all the Palaces and all study of Social Meteors. Bar life is certainly a constant of the American Saturday night, but the ancillary activities that take place in them, I'm convinced, are mostly new ways to get people to spend money on drinks, and their evanescence only proves that people get bored with the ways in which they keep busy in bars.

It's hard to think about Saturday night without realizing that chronological time itself is something of an anachronism these days. Schedules are less rigid now than in the past. Everything is open all the time. People work unusual hours. When I was a kid, grocery stores closed at six and were never open on Sundays. I still remem-ber the first time I went to a twenty-four-hour grocery store at four in the morning, thinking that something fundamental had changed forever. You used to be out of luck for money on the weekend if you didn't get to the bank by three on Friday. Now most people I know don't even know when banks are open and don't need to know because they use twenty-four-hour automatic bank machines. Most stores are now open every day, since in many places blue laws have been repealed. Saturday is still the busiest shopping day of the week, but the opening of stores on Sundays has made it less distinctively busy.

The way we perceive time changed when the American economy shifted from agriculture to industry. On a farm, the significant unit of time is a season. On an assembly line, though, you're inside all the time and you work all year round and you have no interaction with the natural physical world, so seasons no longer matter: what matters is the week, and you know that if you're annoyed to be back at work, it's probably a Monday, and if you just got paid and feel more cheerful, it's Friday, and if you're happy, it's the weekend. Now, as manufacturing with its regular hours and rigid schedules is displaced by a service and high-tech economy that runs incessantly, night and day, the convention of the five-day workweek and the two-day weekend is coming apart. Many workers have unusual schedules—swing shifts, night work, three-day weekends. They also have their pay deposited electronically, bank by phone, shop at midnight, and tape the *Tonight* show and watch it at breakfast. The idea of having to get to a bank by three on Friday to cash a paycheck or to watch Johnny Carson when he's on at midnight seems, in the late twentieth century, nostalgic. Murray Melbin, a sociologist at Boston University, recently wrote that we have run out of land to colonize, so we are now colonizing nighttime, operating businesses twenty-four hours a day, and setting up services (like the automatic bank machines) to obviate the importance of time. People will eventually work from their homes via computer workstations and modem hookups and won't have work schedules. The week as we know it won't mean anything. Some people see this as liberation. Other people—I'm inclined to include myself in this camp—think it sounds awful. Maybe it would eliminate the problems of getting to work on time, but that's only because it means you are *at* work all the time. And the more the structure of the week disappears, the less extraordinary and special Saturday night will be. I am not an enthusiast with regard to the seamless week. I think the Assyrians had it right when they decided it was comforting to divide infinity into comprehensible, repeating units of time with distinct qualities. In particular, I would consider losing the singular nature of Saturday night—one night set aside to be off-limits to obligations, when you don't have to work or visit your aged relatives or be cautious about money or be careful about what you eat or feel guilty about dancing in your church—kind of a shame.

I was happy to discover that—the possibility of a dateless, hourless, calendarless future notwithstanding—Saturday night still does have a distinct personality and effect on most people. People still act differently on Saturday night for no reason other than it's Saturday night. For instance, there are fewer long-distance calls made on Saturday night than on any other night of the week. What is it about Saturday night that inhibits the urge to make calls? Is it that so many people are out, or that anyone who happens to be at home assumes that anyone they want to call is out? Or does it just *feel* weird? (As a matter of fact, I am an enthusiastic long-distance phone-call maker, and I am often home on Saturday night, yet it rarely occurs to me to make a long-distance phone call on a Saturday night.) On Saturday night, there are also the fewest airplane flights, the most murders, most taped radio shows, fewest television viewers, most visits to the emergency room, fewest suicides, most incidents of cats falling out of Manhattan apartment windows, most scheduled showings of *The Rocky Horror Picture Show*, most people breaking their diets, most liquor sold by the glass, the fewest number of calls to businesses offering products on television, and the highest number of reported incidents of cow toppling in rural Pennsylvania. These might at first seem like weird specifics— informational dead ends, like knowing that 75 percent of all Iowans think Scotch tape is the best modern invention—but they really add up to a picture of what Saturday night in America is like. It is a time when people either aren't home to make phone calls or don't want to make them if they are, don't start or end trips, kill other people, listen to prerecorded radio shows, are too busy to watch television, have accidents, don't feel like killing themselves, go out for the evening and forget to close their windows and own curious cats with bad depth perception, feel like seeing campy movies, are in the mood to eat with abandon, drink in bars, aren't in the mood to order the five-volume set of Slim Whitman's greatest hits or aren't home to fall victim to the ad, and see cows sleeping in pastures and are inspired to tip them over just for fun. That does have the ring of truth. It's in keeping with what the Assyrians had in mind when they first established the seven-day week.

For the last few years, while working on this book, I kept two items posted over my desk. The first is a clipping from the Chicago *Tribune* wire service. It says:

LEISURE TIME SHRINKS BY 32%

Since 1973, the median number of hours worked by Americans has increased by 20%, while the amount of leisure time available to the average person has dropped by 32%. The difference between the rise in working hours and the drop in leisure time has been the time that people spend on work around the house and other responsibilities that do not qualify as work. The trend toward less and less leisure time has been steady and inexorable, according to a Harris Survey.

This I used for inspiration. If the law of supply and demand is universally true, the shrinking of leisure time could only serve to make Saturday night more valuable. In a world with 32 percent less leisure time, wouldn't a night imbued with pleasure and abandon remain an important and welcome tonic, no matter how irrelevant the conventional notion of time may come to be? Jane Champagne, whom I met at a Saturday night church social in Houston, put it more vividly. One afternoon she mentioned that she had to make a bunch of phone calls, cook the food, talk to the bank, clean up the church hall, feed her husband, cook dinner for the pastor, and change her clothes by nine o'clock, when the dance was scheduled to begin. "I'm so busy, busy, busy, *busy*," she said. "I get so tired! But then I just think about the church dance coming up, and I think about Saturday night, and then everything's all right."

The other item posted over my desk is something I found buried in a survey about leisure-time activity. It said:

—

Fifty-four percent of those surveyed have sex at least once a week but ranked it below gardening and visiting relatives as a regular activity.

For a year or so, I didn't really know why I was so taken with this piece of rather arcane data except for its innate comic value. After a while, I stopped wondering why I wondered about it. I went to spend Saturday night in a few dozen different places around the country. Time and time again I saw that Saturday night was indeed something special—a time when people are most at ease with themselves. Surveys and statistics of any sort began to seem less important once I realized that Saturday night is mostly mythic: larger than life, more meaningful the less closely it is examined, romantic in the purest way, more an idea than an event. At last I figured out why that survey seemed to have a particular connection to my interest in Saturday night. According to the survey, most people have sex less often than they garden or visit their relatives, but I'm positive that they still consider sex the larger, more mystical, more mythic, more important, more noteworthy experience. That is how I finally feel about Saturday night. It is a matter of quality over quantity. If you add them up, there are many more weekdays in our lives than there are Saturday nights, but Saturday night is the one worth living for.

Saturday Night

Cruising

Elkhart , Indiana

James Patrick Perron, who is twenty-seven years old and the youngest mayor in the history of Elkhart, Indiana, as well as the youngest mayor of any decent-sized town in the state, drives a navy-blue Buick sedan with four doors, plush seats, power brakes, and a big, squishy suspension that smooths out bumps in the road. The car is loaded with luxury options and has a lot of pep. It has a handsome paint job. Still, it is not the sort of vehicle that people in Elkhart who consider themselves judges of such things—and there are quite a few who do—would call a cruising machine or a piece of muscle-car perfection.

Mayor Perron is medium-sized and has brown bowl-cut hair, broad cheeks, a mild, toothy, genuine-looking smile, and an unaggressive chin. His skin is as soft-looking and unwrinkled as a child's, but he carries himself with the gravity of someone who would not wear a bathing suit with abandon. A lot of people who knew Jim Perron when he was growing up in Elkhart recall that the air of maturity—the air of a man who would drive a Buick—has always been rich around him. No one, including the mayor himself, remembers him experiencing adolescent spasms of girl craziness or car craziness or experimental self-destructiveness. At the appropriate moment in history—his and the world's—he did flirt with the concept of hippieness, but the flirtation exhausted itself with his reading of *The Whole Earth Catalog* and some discussions about conserving fossil fuels. He has always preferred light classical music to car horns that play the theme song from *The Godfather*. He ran for city council before he finished college. His earnestness about civic matters and his absolute solidness made the question of his age, or lack of it, irrelevant. In fact, anyone who expected that a young mayor would incline civic temperament in Elkhart toward frivolity would have to admit to having been confounded by Jim Perron.

I had come to spend a Saturday night in Elkhart, Indiana, for a reason not dear to Jim Perron's heart: I knew Elkhart was one of the nation's capitals of cruising, and cruising struck me as being what Saturday night in America is all about. Cruising in a motor vehicle is the contemporary equivalent of strolling, which is what Saturday night *used* to be all about. It is done at approximately strolling speed, so that cruisers can look at one another and tenderly insult one another's cars as they drive around in a big loop. The purpose of cruising is slow-going and social—it is more spectator than sport. It is an opportunity to get together and do nothing, but in a somewhat organized fashion. It feels silly and wasteful and independent, all of which is especially suited to Saturday night, when people like to do something that very specifically does not duplicate the purposefulness and productivity and obligations of the workday. If you are imagining something done at more than thirty miles an hour, you are confusing cruising with drag racing. If you are thinking of something that is a procession of vintage cars, you are confusing cruising with an auto meet. Some people do cruise in fabulous cars, but plenty cruise in beat-up station wagons with wobbly fenders and bad paint jobs. The car doesn't really matter. What matters is being out on a street, with friends, in some vehicle, with time on your hands, with nowhere in particular to get to, on a Saturday night— which has a way of making such simple things seem spectacular.

The folklore of cruising suggests that it arose in the 1950s, when many families had cars or second cars for the first time, and town squares made to walk around were being replaced by commercial strips you had to drive around, and the critical mass of people looking for something cheap and easy to do on weekends was reached. Cruising was the elegant solution. It solved the biggest challenge of Saturday night—that is, how to have fun when you don't have anything much to do. As such, it is especially suited to small towns. In Indiana, a state made up of small towns, cruising flourished.

Elkhart, the largest town in Indiana without mass transit, is the biggest city in the region and the natural magnet on weekends for people from neighboring towns such as Goshen and White Pigeon and Sturgis and Mishawaka. In the center of town is the wide, inviting roadbed of Main Street, and there is very little competition for the local entertainment dollar. It is also a town that has pleasure driving to thank for its economy: Elkhart is the hub of the recreational-vehicle industry, and more than half of its citizens have jobs building, servicing, selling, or outfitting mobile homes and fancy vans. In 1930, when Elkhart was still just a squirt of a town set among cows and farm stands in the northeast corner of this big, flat state, Skyline Motor Homes was founded by a local resident, and in time was joined here by Holiday Rambler and Coachman and Schult and trailer-top manufacturers and van converters and tinted-glass shops and paint-job outfits and rec-vehicle–accessory shops, and pretty soon Elkhart started to be known as the Detroit of the Recreational Vehicle Industry. The only other major business in town is an Alka-Seltzer plant. All of this appears to have inclined people in the area to having a super-developed appreciation of cars as entertainment units.

On Saturday nights for many years, hundreds of people from miles around converged on Elkhart's Main Street and traveled a loop that went from the railroad tracks through the McDonald's parking lot and back to the railroad tracks. In some places around the country, the cruising crowd is mostly adolescent; in Elkhart, it was diverse, made up of teenagers who had just discovered cruising and middle-aged adults with nicer cars and fond memories of their teenage cruising years. On Saturday nights, the cruisers on Main Street formed a considerable and interesting cavalcade. *Car Craft*, a performance-car magazine, has included Elkhart on its list of the ten best American cruising cities—something that has made Main Street regulars understandably proud, considering that Elkhart is not often on lists of the ten best American anythings, and considering that many other towns on the list are in California, where the length of the cruising season and the prevalence of convertibles provide an unfair advantage.

This equation remained intact for many years: a small city grateful for and dependent on the recreational-driving industry, where there isn't an overabundance of things to do with free time, raises to a near platonic ideal the classic American Saturday-night sport of cruising. Then into this was added James Perron, a young, sort-of-urban professional who drives a Buick and makes use of his turn signals all the time, and who pictures the Elkhart of the future with an expanded economy, more attractive boutiques, more tasteful entertainment, and fewer people who like to wear hats made out of beer cans.

"We're too dependent on the recreational-vehicle industry," Mayor Perron has said. "It's time for Elkhart to diversify. We should become the banking and high-tech center of the region." On cruising specifically, he has said, "I personally have no feeling about cruising, but it generates too much noise and trash and has made Main Street unusable for emergency vehicles as well as people who are not cruising. We should have all strata of people coming to Main Street to enjoy a variety of cultural and entertainment opportunities. Theater. Symphony. I tend to spend my Saturday nights at home with my wife, or we go out with friends. During election season, of course, I spend most Saturday nights at political functions. Elkhart is a growing metropolitan area. The trend here is community pride. That's what's important, not more cars and cruising."

Just before I came to Elkhart, the mayor did something about his displeasure with the standard Elkhart Saturday night: he enacted an executive order banning traffic from the center two lanes of Main Street after 8 p.m. Of course, traffic could continue as usual in the outer two lanes on Main. But without use of the center lanes, the cruisers, who considered hollering, waving, and peering into one another's cars the material points of the experience, had to cruise past one another at a fifteen-foot distance—something that had on the activity what legal minds might call a chilling effect. Suddenly, Saturday night—which probably had not been a matter of municipal concern in the past—became a matter of great emotional debate in town. When I told some people in Elkhart that I was coming to spend time in the cruising capital of the Midwest, they warned me that the mayor's order meant I would be cruising under reduced circumstances. I was also warned that some of the cruisers had banded together and were waging war against Major Perron.

When I first arrived in Elkhart, Mayor Perron met me at my hotel and suggested we drive down Main. I knew it was a symbolic gesture, but it was also a practical one: there is almost nowhere you can go in Elkhart that doesn't require a trip down Main. The street is as straight as a paper cut, and the town peels off on either side of it. Before it gets to the center of Elkhart, Main is a country road that runs past plowed fields and then fields that look as if they've been left fallow in anticipation of a future industrial park, and then past sparse neighborhoods, and then past patches of small businesses with gigantic parking lots festooned with plastic flags and marked with junky electric signs on three-wheeled trailers. Downtown, Main is lined with narrow sidewalks, parking meters, and low, flat-faced buildings with modestly ornate trim and stout dimensions. Some of the downtown storefronts have been remodeled in a style that probably looked snazzy and modern twenty years ago. The building materials are the sturdy, unspectacular sort you often find in old, solvent midwestern towns—brick, granite, some wood, and some aluminum siding—in muted shades that look as if they had been alternately bleached and frozen over the last several decades. Over the railroad tracks, Main peters out quickly, and a mile out of downtown, you feel as if you're on a country road again.

Mayor Perron drives with his hands in the eleven- and two-o'clock positions. He prodded the accelerator erratically, as if his foot had hiccups. At the first stoplight, he stomped on the brakes and then turned to me. "I want to make one thing clear," he said. "In spite of all that's gone on, I think people should know a few things about me. I think they should know that as a matter of fact, I like to drive. I really do. But as much as I might like to drive, I just don't think of driving as *recreation*. I think of it as transportation. I realize some people think of driving and cars and I suppose even cruising in their cars as a pastime. I imagine for them it's like a hobby. They probably view it the way some people view fishing or collecting stamps. But as far as I'm concerned, I just don't see the attraction in it. A car like this Buick is all I'd ever want." He smiled at me and patted the dashboard.

"This car takes me where I want to go, and that's enough for me," he said. "Personally, I just don't think of the automobile as a pleasure tool."

Around nine o'clock that Saturday night, I joined some of the people who do think of the automobile as a pleasure tool in a parking lot on Main Street called the Bucklen Lot.

Bucklen is the biggest parking lot downtown. The Bucklen Opera House, an imposing rococo stone structure built in 1884, used to stand on the site. In its day, the opera house was probably the swankiest recreational facility in town. After burlesque and vaudeville went out of fashion, the Bucklen showed movies, and then the movies moved out to the mall. No other use for the building cropped up. Eventually, it fell into complete disrepair and everyone gave up on it, so it was torn down. Some people in Elkhart consider the incident a shame, but as you might expect in a town of avid drivers, many others consider the parking lot a fine thing to have acquired in the deal.

Bucklen is now regarded as ground zero by the people who come to Elkhart to cruise, and by nine that night, even under these reduced circumstances, it was busy. Three monster trucks—pickups perched on giant tires—were parked along the north edge of the lot; a Mustang convertible, a Dodge classic street rod with tongues-of-flames decals on the hood, several different makes of muscle cars, a blue Pinto with a fuzzy doll hanging from the rearview mirror, a '69 Camaro, a '63 Impala, and one ratty station wagon were lined up inside. No one had pulled onto the street yet: this was the assembly period, and most people were just standing around chatting and smoking cigarettes.

The fainthearted, of course, were long gone. Center-lane–viola-

8

tion tickets were going at fifty dollars a pop, and as a reminder, the mayor had sent a phalanx of police with pencils and ticket pads to Main Street on the first several Saturday nights after the order had gone into effect. "It's too *expensive* to cruise now," one man who had been ticketed told me. "I can't afford to go out there and drive around for a few hours if it's going to cost me a fifty-dollar bill." Some cruisers had shifted their base of operations to Mishawaka, a nearby town with a cruising strip just beyond its city limits. A lot of Elkhart's cruisers don't like the Mishawaka strip because it is dark, dismal, runs past fields and parking lots (which make for a boring cruise backdrop), and has a lot of high-speed incidental traffic that makes the lollygagging pace of cruising a little dangerous. On the other hand, so far, no one in the Mishawaka town government seems to mind the cruisers being there. It may just be a matter of time before Mishawaka goes the way of Elkhart, since bans like Mayor Perron's are becoming increasingly popular around the country. In Goshen, Indiana—a little town a few miles east of Elkhart—Mayor Max Chiddester made a cruising ban one of his final official acts before retiring. In Portland, Oregon, the city fathers have imposed a $150 fine on anyone driving purposelessly past the same spot twice in an hour. Third time around gets the vehicle impounded. Officials in Allentown, Pennsylvania, have considered similar legislation. The standard complaints were trash, noise, the creation of an unattractive nuisance, and, by implication, greaser overload. "Why encourage this sort of activity?" one city council-man in Oregon complained. "Why can't these people find some-thing else to do with their weekends that doesn't include cars?"

For a while, it had looked as if cruising would be killed off by causes other than legislative ones. When the price of gas rose in the 1970s, it pushed cruising out of the category of cheap, fun things to do on Saturday nights, and the vogue for finless, chromeless, sub-compact stick shifts with pokey little engines made it seem silly— more like a cortege of bumper cars than a grand display. It became much more with-it and contemporary to spend Saturday nights barhopping or disco dancing or eating in brassy, ferny Tex-Mex restaurants than driving up and down a street engaging in an anach-ronistic cornball ritual that wasted gasoline.

9

In Elkhart, the downslide in pleasure driving had a one-two punch. The financial considerations that queered cruising did the same to the town's economy: once gas cost a dollar or more per gallon, Americans reconsidered the wisdom of the recreational vehicle. What followed in Elkhart was a powerful slump. The net worth of one rich man in town who owned some of the rec-vehicle companies dropped so much in a single day that it was recorded in the *Guinness Book of World Records*. Unemployment in Elkhart became an ordinary condition. For a while, according to some people in town, it felt as if the rec-vehicle business would never recover, and Elkhart would be left as enervated and useless as a roughneck town on a tapped-out oil well. "Luckily, people eventually got used to high gas prices," one resident told me. "They came back to the realization that mobile homes are a marvelous thing." Around the time Elkhart was getting back to speed, Main Street was repaved, and on each subsequent Saturday night, more and more cruisers returned to the road. "They came back right after we got Main Street into good shape, too," Mayor Perron recalls with dismay. "Before that, for a while, it had really been beautiful."

Pete Russell, the man generally acknowledged to be leading the Elkhart cruiser resistance, was standing with a large group of people beside his monster truck when I got to the Bucklen Lot. Pete's truck is a half-ton Chevy pickup, white as milk, named the Intruder. Car naming is as common in Elkhart as estate naming is in the Virginia hunt country. Pete is a lean, leathery man in his mid-forties with narrowed eyes and a set jaw—the aspect of someone who spends a lot of time on his back halfway under car chassis in the bright sun. He wears his hair, which is either platinum blond or prematurely white, in a long and lightly sculpted pageboy. Charley Rich, the country-western star who is sometimes known as the Silver Fox, used to have a similar haircut. It happens that Pete is fond of country music and doesn't mind the comparison. He is also fond of Elvis Presley, and keeps a life-size bust of him in his living-room window. He is less fond of Mayor Perron, who he considers a nervous youngster with yuppie aspirations and a secret disdain for what is sometimes cruelly described in these parts as "trailer trash"—that is, the people who work in the rec-vehicle business. Pete sells race-car trailers for a living. That night, he was wearing a silver vinyl jacket decorated with Valvoline Motor Oil insignias that made a faint crunching sound when he turned and glinted when it caught the streetlight at certain angles. He calls himself a race-car fan. When he is interviewed on television about the cruising controversy, he is identified as "Pete Russell—Cruising Advocate."

"Pretty quiet night," Pete said to me. He gestured around the lot. A few people standing within earshot murmured in agreement. "Actually, since the new rules, we haven't had a really big night here since fifty German band students who were touring the United States ended up in Elkhart. I don't know how they knew about cruising, but they wanted to do it. We put ten Germans at a time in the back of a pickup and cruised them up and down Main. They sang obscene German drinking songs and had a great time. They told us they liked cruising more than anything else they did the whole time they were in the United States. They spent the next two days walking around in a daze saying 'Big truck! Big truck!' " He shook his head. "Except for that night, though, it's not the way it used to be."

Someone laughed and said, "It's not the way it used to be, Pete, but then again, what is?"

"My wife looked up the definition of cruising in the dictionary the other day," Pete said. "You know what it said? The definition of 'cruise' is 'to meet.' As in, 'to meet people.' That's all we're trying to do here, and as far as I'm concerned, that's a pretty basic right. That's why we set up the Elkhart Cruising Association." He pointed to a bumper sticker on his truck that said ELKHART CRUISING ASSOCIATION, CRUISIN' USA, ELKHART INDIANA. "That's us against the mayor."

The fact is that until this point Jim Perron had been a very popular mayor. He'd brought attention to an interesting local groundwater problem and had presided over Elkhart's return from the depths of the gas crisis and recession. He proposed rehabilitating Main Street and the surrounding neighborhoods, and no one, including the cruisers, denied that Main Street could stand some rehabilitation. Some of its storefronts were empty and some were dilapidated; it looked droopy and outdated while everything snappy and new was out at the mall. The most exciting thing that had taken place on Main in recent memory was the murder of the man who owned the movie theater across from the Bucklen Lot. He was shot by one of his employees as he stood next to the popcorn machine.

It did appear that the mayor had a mandate to tidy up downtown, and he considered the cruising ban the foundation of the effort. He figured that his only liability might be some irritated motorhead kids. He hadn't counted on the Elkhart Cruising Association—a coalition of teenagers and adult cruisers that soon provided the sociological and political spectacle of the mayor alienating both people fifteen years older and fifteen years younger than himself.

The association was headed by Pete Russell and a couple named Judy and Mark Cooke, two other Elkhart natives who happened to have conducted their own courtship while cruising on Main Street some decades ago. Judy and Mark own a custom auto-glass business in town. Their seventeen-year-old son is also a cruiser. "I didn't know Pete before, but I saw him interviewed on television about the cruising rules, and I felt I had to do something about it," Judy Cooke once told me. "To me, cruising *is* Saturday night. I'd felt that since my adolescence. I felt the mayor was negating my adolescence. I didn't feel too great about that. I felt like, *hey*, that's my *youth* you're talking about."

A few cars were heading down Main Street. A police car drove by, slowed near the lot, and passed. A '69 Camaro pulled into Bucklen, swung around the Intruder, and parked. "Hey, everyone," the driver said. "Hey there, Pete."

"Looking good, Steve."

"It's *always* looking good, man," Steve said.

"Some car."

"You know, I once had a '69 Firebird," Steve said. "Years ago, I had a '69 Firebird and *I let it get away*. I wasn't going to let that happen again. My wife understands. When we were about to get married, I said to her, 'Honey, somewhere out there, there's a '69 Camaro and I'm going to buy it.' "

I asked him how long he had been cruising in Elkhart. "I grew up here, and I cruised here when I was a kid," he said. "When I came back from Vietnam, there was nothing going on. Then cruising came back. I was really pumped when I saw everyone back on the street. I don't know what the hell the mayor is trying to do. I'm still going to cruise, that's for sure. I'm not in it to show off. Okay, I've generated something of a reputation, but I haven't done anything. This is a three-fifty small-block engine, but I guess it's a hot car and people assume things about me because of it. Some of which are not true. Hey, if I don't come out and cruise, all I do is sit at home and watch TV with my wife. When I'm out cruising, I feel like it's Christmas."

"You're lucky you have a wife who is willing to stay home alone on Saturday nights."

He looked at me in surprise, and then said, "I wouldn't have married her if she wasn't."

Pete slapped the hood of the Intruder. "Let's get out on the street already," he said. "Can't waste a minute anymore when you're cruising on borrowed time."

I was dispatched into the car of one of the younger cruisers, a chatty, long-haired young man named Scott Longacre. His car was called Bad in Blue. At the time, Scott was a senior in high school in Elkhart, and he told me that after he graduated he hoped to go to college and then work toward becoming a vice president or general manager of a Fox Network affiliate. Bad in Blue was a funky, low-slung, creaky Pinto that had been unsubtly patched with Bondo, which showed through the paint the way a panty line shows under a cheap suit. "I don't know what I'd do if something happened to this car," Scott said, as he maneuvered out of Bucklen. "No, that's not true. I do know what I'd do if something happened to this car. I'd get sick." When we got onto Main, we were behind Pete. "I *love* the Intruder," Scott said, pointing. "It is so great."

Pete had roused nearly everyone out of Bucklen and onto Main, so within a few minutes, a few dozen people were cruising down the street. They were all driving with their windows down and their radios on loud, so each time we passed a car, I would hear an abrupt blurt of music that sounded like an industrial accident. No one drove on the center lanes, except occasionally. Scott's seat was pushed far back from the steering wheel. His arms were hyper-extended and his head was tipped back on the headrest—a position that made him look extremely relaxed. The streetlights on Main were twinkling. There was just enough wind to blow your hair back, car-commercial style.

"I hope Judy and Mark get down here soon," Scott said. "They are really cool." He honked and waved at someone driving by. We slowed at a light. At the end of the street we noticed a car driving backward. A few people lounging on the sidewalk were applauding. Scott kept up a running commentary on each of the cars we passed. He favored boat-sized vehicles over midget sports cars, and anything with a lot of chrome over anything without it. When we passed a glossy, chrome-ribbed Chevy, he sighed and patted his dashboard. "Okay, I know Bad in Blue is just a Pinto, but I've really fixed it up. Some people might think, Oh, it's just a Pinto. But I have a bunch of pretty neat sports-car features on it that I really don't need, and I have a bumper that's three inches over the legal bumper height. Seriously. I love this car. I spend all my money on it. I'd love to have a classic car, though. I have a friend who has a '57 Chevy, turquoise with a white interior. Plus, she has a Bel Air. Isn't that unbelievable?" He turned on the radio and turned the dial until he found a station playing a Platters song. "Oh, boy! Platters! All right!" He pounded his fist on the steering wheel in time to the song. After a moment of musical expression he said, "You know, I have this opinion that I was born thirty years too late. All the neat cars and all the neat music were made in the fifties. Cruising was really happening in the biggest way in the fifties. My mom told me that she cruised when she grew up here, in a '64-and-a-half candy-apple–red Mustang. It's not that my mom's so cool or anything, but that sounds very cool to me." He scratched his chin. "When I saw cruising was happening here, in my generation, on my Main Street, I thought it was just the neatest thing I had ever seen. They say that Elkhart is turning into a metropolis kind of a deal, but there's really nothing to do around here. If they get rid of cruising, there's really going to be nothing to do. Nothing."

We were approaching the turnaround at the McDonald's on the end of Main, passing a balloon shop, several shoe stores, a knit shop, and Flytrap's Bar and Grill, the only business open at this hour. The street looked gray and empty except for the stream of cruiser cars. Scott slowed down. We talked for a minute about how little he likes parties and movies compared to cruising. "I sort of have a girlfriend or something like that," he said. "I don't hang out with her, exactly. I feel out of place everywhere but here. I mean, I feel like this is where I fit in. The cruisers are a weird mix of people, but it works. There are the older people, who I think are really neat, and there are the richer kids with the nice sports cars, and rougher kids with cars like souped-up Novas, and some cool, smart kids who usually drive their parents' cars, and a nerd or two, and the street urchins who just hang out on the sidewalk. Everyone is welcome here. The idea of not cruising, man, I just don't understand that. I live for it. That's it for me. The week is just something I get through until Saturday night."

As we pulled into the McDonald's lot, Scott thought he saw the car he'd mentioned earlier, so he wanted to stop. A powder-blue '56 Bel Air with whitewalls, bright chrome trim, and blue upholstered seats with white piping was parked near the drive-through window. The car was shiny and bulbous and looked like a toaster. A chubby girl with a sulky face was sitting in the car ratting her hair with a long comb and eating a Ho-Ho. As soon as she saw Scott, she dropped her comb, finished the Ho-Ho, and got out.

"I thought that was you," she said to him. "You know what? It was so neat—some people who don't know my car just came over to say hello to me. I think it's great when they say hello to the person and not just the car."

Scott had gotten out of the Pinto and was fingering the chrome on the Bel Air. He was totally absorbed, as if he hadn't heard her. She fell silent. Then he looked up and said, "Where's the Chevy?" She said it was being repaired. Scott shrugged and started to walk away.

"Isn't it neat, though?" she said to him. "I mean, about people saying hello to me and not just the car?"

We got back into Bad in Blue, made two loops of Main, listened to the radio, avoided the center lanes, waved at a lot of cars, honked at groups of people standing around on the sidewalk, tried to find a girl named Candy Rodriguez on the citizens-band radio, waved at more cars, got into an argument on the CB with someone who thought we had insulted Candy Rodriguez, yelled "Ouch!" at a Pontiac Grand Prix with wire wheel covers, saw someone breaking a beer bottle against a wall, honked at a girl in a tube top on a skateboard, made another loop, passed Pete in the Intruder, stopped and got a Coke and french fries at McDonald's, got back in the car, yelled "Are you listening to Super Gold radio?" at several cars we passed, and then headed over to Bucklen to take a break. Scott had pointed out many cars to me by name: Wheels of Steel, the Orange Blur, Smog, Jealousy, Shadow of the Night. "I love naming cars," he said. "The greatest thing about cruising is that we do whatever we want. It's the only time of the week you do whatever you want. That's part of the point. In Elkhart, people work all week, and they want some freedom on the weekend. That's why the stuff with the mayor is so screwed up. I do have a lot of rules when I cruise, actually. The first one is: Be yourself. That's very important. Second: Don't be on someone's butt all the time. By that I mean tailgating. Three: Be cool in front of the old-age home on Main Street. Four: When there are people walking down the street to a nice restaurant, watch your language. Five: Go to Bob Evans's Farm Restaurant for breakfast when you're done cruising. I guess that one's not really a rule, but we do it every weekend so it's become just like a rule."

Steve was idling in his Camaro in the parking lot when we got back. He said he was going home a little early but that he'd be back next week. "The wife," he said, rolling his eyes. Then he gunned the motor and drove off. Judy and Mark Cooke had showed up, and they came over to Scott's car. Judy is pixieish; Mark is tall and deliberative. They had driven over in their van and were spending most of the evening in Bucklen talking to friends and watching the action on Main Street. Judy was telling someone how she had been organizing her high-school reunion at the time the center-lane rules were enacted. One of the reunion events was supposed to be a nostalgic cruise on Main Street. Instead, Judy called Pete and spent the next few weeks printing bumper stickers, T-shirts, and organizing a boycott of downtown merchants whom they suspected had pressured the mayor into the ban. The consensus in town was that the boycott didn't amount to much economically, but it did convey a seriousness. Judy, Mark, and Pete were on the local TV news almost every night. "I wasn't looking to get on TV," Judy said. "I just felt someone had to speak out. It was a class thing. Perron is trying to get rid of people like us in Elkhart."

The mayor had responded by setting up open meetings at city hall and establishing an advisory panel. The open meetings took on an unusual form when dozens of high-school students attended and walked out in protest at a prearranged signal from Pete and Judy. The walkout was the lead story on the evening news. Then the Elkhart Cruising Association made news again by endorsing the mayor's opponent—a gloomy-looking man who was head of the local license-plate bureau. Sentences that used to begin "James Perron, the youngest mayor in the history of Elkhart" now, quite often, began "James Perron, the mayor who wants to get cruising out of his town." Judy then wrote to one hundred local recreational-vehicle businesses asking for support. "I got back one hundred and sixty letters from people at the companies," she said. "They all wrote about how they had cruised when they were young, and how much cruising had meant to them as kids, and how they hoped it could be kept alive."

At this point, it was close to midnight. The stream of cars on Main Street was breaking up. Many of the cars in Bucklen were pulling out on the street and driving off with a purpose. The few people left stood together near the Cookes' van. Scott was back at his car, looking at the paint job. "Are we done for the night?" Mark asked.

Judy nodded. "Not a bad turnout, considering." Just then, Pete drove into Bucklen and parked nearby. He greeted Judy and Mark and said, "Ready for a little breakfast, outlaws?" Pete said to meet at Bob Evans's in ten minutes. I got back in Bad in Blue with Scott and we went out Main to Cassapolis Street. We weren't cruising; we were going somewhere. We passed Vans & RV Stuff, RV America, Jack's Mobile Homes, Bob's Mobile Home World, Tom's RVs, Holiday World RV Country, and Michiana Easy Livin' Country RVs. Eventually we got to Bob Evans's. There were nine of us—Scott, Judy, Mark, Pete, and some of their friends. The rest of the restaurant was empty. Everyone ordered breakfast, and Scott ordered breakfast and a milk shake. The waitress did not register surprise.

"This is what I call fun," Scott said. "Although you should have just seen it last summer."

"Hundreds of people," Judy said. "Literally hundreds. It was really fun. It was relaxing. It was a nice way to get together without a fancy plan. That's exactly what's great about cruising."

Pete leaned forward and said, "Anyone who knows anything about how to have a good time would see that this is a healthy, lawful way to have fun. For godssake, there's nothing else to do in this place! Especially for kids! It makes you wonder about people who can't understand that, you know?"

Scott started playing drums with his silverware. "You know, that's the real problem," he said. He folded his hands on his lap and got solemn. "The problem is that the mayor never cruised. When he was growing up he spent all his time worrying about Vietnam and everything. He never knew how to have a good time."

Actually, Mayor Perron has admitted to having cruised once. He said to me not long ago that his first car was a '69 Plymouth and that he did once spend a Saturday night driving it around. "I liked that car," he said. "I liked it a lot. But I never exactly cruised in it." Then he stopped himself and said, "Oh, well, *maybe* I cruised once with some friends, but we found it kind of . . . *weird*. See, cruising was very hot in Elkhart then, in the late sixties and early seventies, but I was not into it. I just didn't get it. At that time, I was very back-to-earth. I was starting to listen to the Mother Earth News and worry about fossil fuels and read the *Foxfire* books. I just didn't see what the attraction of cruising was. I don't know why I even tried it that once. I suppose I was just curious."

A few months after I was in Elkhart, Mayor Perron was returned to office by a comfortable margin. He promised to devote his new term to solving the groundwater problem and to attracting new banking and computer concerns to Elkhart. He told me he was "not dissatisfied" with the cruising situation as it stood. A few months after that, the Bucklen Lot was closed at night at the mayor's request. It had been reported that on Sunday mornings, the place was full of trash and was creating a nuisance. Not long after, it was discovered that the original executive order restricting the center lanes hadn't been enacted properly. Anyone who had been fined for a center-lane violation got his or her money back. For the next few weeks, before the Bureau of Public Works received the redrafted rule, cruising was restored on Main Street. It was as if the Hoover Dam had been dismantled. Hundreds of cars and people from all over the region came to Elkhart and ran the circuit all night. Within the month, the center-lane rule, now properly enacted, was back on the books. The mayor did make one concession: instead of starting at 8 p.m., the restrictions began at 9. Even so, most cruisers were discouraged and eventually dispersed to White Pigeon or Mishawaka or just went home. Judy, Mark, and Pete, who had come to think of themselves as stewards of Elkhart's cruising legacy the way folklorists consider themselves responsible for a particular branch of indigenous culture like, say, fish spearing or tattooing, each told me that they planned to keep at it. "We'll keep cruising, and we'll keep up the campaign to get Main Street back to the people," Judy told me. "If not, I'll never be able to feel the same about this town again."

Our conversation reminded me of a sign I noticed as I was leaving Elkhart. I was driving my rental car through town, down Main Street to Cassapolis to the Indiana Turnpike. Beside the ramp, a cluster of signs welcomed visitors to town and urged shoppers to visit Elkhart's various recreational-vehicle worlds, villages, and universes. Another sign was hand lettered and set off by itself. None of the cruisers ever mentioned having made it, but it struck me as something any one of them would have been proud to say:

DAYS ARE FOR WHAT YOU GOTTA DO
NIGHTS ARE FOR WHAT YOU WANT TO DO

Riding

Wellesley, Massachusetts

One thing worth knowing about the Wellesley bus—that is, the bus that carts Wellesley College students to Harvard and MIT every Friday and Saturday night to look for entertainment—is that it's nowhere near as nice a bus as the one that carts these same students twelve miles to Harvard and MIT during the week in order to further their education. The Wellesley women ride the regular weekday bus if they take exchange classes at the other schools. Wellesley College pays to lease it: the seats are cushioned, the windows are tinted, the air is sweet, the pursuit of knowledge is richly anticipated, the drivers are usually clean shaven. On the other hand, the Wellesley Student Senate pays to lease the weekend bus, and it's an old clunker with hard seats and sticky windows and someone with attitude at the steering wheel. Even the biggest fans of the weekend bus will admit that its sole attractive quality is its destination. On Saturday night, if you are a college student in the Northeast, you want to be in Harvard Square. Discoursing upon the nature of the buses, a Wellesley student said to me recently, "The students can't afford a deluxe bus. But the way most of us feel is that in the student senate bus, you're going somewhere a whole lot better than classes, so you don't mind as much that it's not as nice a vehicle."

Another thing I recently learned about the student senate weekend bus is that in Wellesley-Harvard-MIT idiom, it is often called the Fuck Truck, as an alternative to the more pedestrian "weekend bus," "senate bus," or "night bus." The names can be used interchangeably, as in "I took the [senate bus/night bus/weekend bus/Fuck Truck] into town last Saturday and met a really lovely guy at a B-School mixer." In spite of its charm, the use of the term "Fuck Truck" has fallen in and out of favor over the years, the outs being those times when word gets around that Harvard men are avoiding Wellesley women because they think they have wedding bells on the brain. Then the bus is just called "the bus." When relations return to normal and all goes as it is supposed to go in the northeastern collegiate corridor—which means constant weekend gatherings with the objective of exposing bright young people to one another—the more colorful name prevails.

The nature of Saturday night owes a great deal to the powerful effect of anticipation. That is, getting dressed and doing your nails and doing your hair and choosing your clothes and riding to your destination often ends up being more entertaining than the entertainment. As I learned in Elkhart, cruising is probably the highest expression of this—all it entails is getting to and from, and it skips over everything else. I came to Wellesley because I was under the impression that the senate bus provides the same sort of thrill. Not long before I spent a Saturday night riding the bus, I spent an afternoon on campus trying to find out when weekend bus service had begun. This struck me as important to know. Many Wellesley students consider the Fuck Truck a source of personal growth and a symbol of feminist liberation, and will often mention how weird it is to think that there was a time *in this century* when the senate bus did not exist and Wellesley women were confined to campus on weekends unless they had a note from home. Pinpointing the moment of the weekend bus's conception would reveal the exact moment in time and manner in which the Wellesley coed became a full participant in the modern weekend. I talked to some administrators, and none of them could remember, so the day before I rode the bus,

I went to the campus library and read through old student senate minutes in hopes of putting the Fuck Truck in precise historical context. I found some interesting facts—for instance, the 1967 Student Handbook advised new students to budget twenty-five dollars a year for Kleenex—and evidence of Wellesley's pro-entertainment spirit (the 1967 Student Handbook: "Wellesley is not all study! . . . If you are wondering where the dates come from, the first few weeks at Wellesley will provide the answer . . ." although students were limited to twelve "overnight permissions" freshman year, if accompanied by a note from parents or proof that they would be staying in "reputable accommodations"). But information about the bus was scarce. In 1966, a committee was set up to consider running a bus to Harvard Square on weekend nights; in 1967, a senate member observed that these buses were "developing into a more established part of the Wellesley community." That was it. No mention of shackles being thrown off or frenzied celebrations being held. This says more about the imprecise way social history is recorded than it does about the bus, because even though its existence came about without great notice, the Wellesley bus is a revered weekend institution of consequence in the greater Boston metropolitan area. Most importantly, it is the perfect way to get from the Wellesley campus, which is sedate most of the time, and the town of Wellesley, which has been dry for as long as anyone can remember, to keg parties and mixers in Harvard Square on Saturday nights.

"This is a really big college area, but Wellesley is kind of stuck out of town," a student at the college said to me after I finished my work in the library. "It's not easy to get from here to anywhere, and most students don't have cars, so you really do get antsy on the weekends. Plus, there's the issue of *men*, of which there are none at Wellesley. There used to be no decent way to get off campus and into town, and then the weekend bus was instituted. It changed the life of the Wellesley student by giving her freedom. It is now sort of a tradition, like hoop rolling, which is a ritual we have here in the spring, when the students perform with large wooden hoops."

I said to her that everyone seemed to like the bus.

"Well, obviously, the guys at Harvard and MIT think it's pretty great, and a lot of the students here live for it." She stopped and shook her head. "Sometimes, though, just *hearing* the name 'Fuck Truck' reminds me of what it was like last year when I was a freshman, and I was always dying to get off campus and meet men. Now that I'm a sophomore, I really appreciate staying on campus with my women friends on weekends and *talking*. I don't *always* need to ride into town the minute I can and go straight to some MIT party or whatever, and then ride back to campus in the middle of the night on the last bus run, at two in the morning, just for the privilege of having some drunken freshperson barf on my shoe. I still ride the senate bus on a lot of weekends, since I often feel the desire to get into town on the weekend and be part of the world. But I've outgrown some aspects of the senate bus. All the barfing and the giggling, for instance, is sometimes just too much. Occasionally, it can get pretty gross. I think most adults would be able to relate to that."

The Saturday night I rode the Wellesley bus was dry and cold. It was early in the fall. The first leaves to drop had formed piles on the side of the road like dark snowdrifts. Boston was still under siege by the three-ring binder sales and freshman orientations that accompany the beginning of the school year. Wellesley College occupies most of the rolling land west of the town of Wellesley, a patrician enclave west of Boston that maintains the fiction of small-town life even though it is now mainly a suburb of Boston. The college has a gorgeous, green campus with broad lawns and winding lanes and big brick buildings and healthy-looking shade trees; during the quiet summer months, it has the ambience of a fiscally sound Presbyterian rest home. Occasionally students venture to downtown Wellesley, and some students live in Boston, but mostly they stay within the low stone walls that mark the campus until the weekend, when they head for Harvard Square.

On Saturday, I drove from Boston to Wellesley and then pulled into the campus and made my way along the tangle of lanes. On either side of the road, young women in blue jeans were heading in the direction of Schneider Hall, the student center on the north end of campus. The senate bus tickets are sold at a booth in Schneider; it is also where many Wellesley students who have nothing else to do can be found on Saturday nights, trying gamely to look busy.

One sophomore had described the role Schneider played in Wellesley social life a few days earlier. "On Saturday night, if you're not on a date, and you're not on the bus," she said, "you're probably reading old copies of *Vogue* in Schneider." I parked under an oak tree and followed the students into Schneider, walked past the cafeteria, past a sign near the staff cloakroom that said THE KEYS TO PROFITABLE FRYING, and down the hall to the booth where student volunteers take turns doling out the dollar-and-a-half senate bus tickets. The worst Saturday night, in Wellesley legend, is to end up volunteering in the ticket booth. That night, the big loser was a small woman with short blond hair, red polished fingernails, and a baleful look on her face. I told her that I wanted a ticket. She glanced up at me. "Dollar and a half," she said. She sounded as though she meant it as an apology. "Boy, what a miserable job this is. Everyone's always complaining to me. I can't help what the bus drivers do, you know? Not to mention that I'm the one who's missing everything tonight, right?" She bit her nails slowly and then pushed a ticket across the counter at me. "Don't ask when the next bus is, because I don't know."

As she was talking, several ticket buyers lined up behind me— chic, leggy, brittle blondes with major-statement moussed hair. They started whispering in loud voices. "Could you hurry, please?" one of them finally said to me. "I mean, we're trying to get dinner in a hurry so we can make the nine o'clock."

According to the latest wisdom about contemporary behavior, formal social habits are back in vogue—fear of AIDS has tempered intemperate social appetites and post–sexual-revolution habits have run their course, replaced by the ceremony, custom, and restraint that characterized social life of the past. In such an atmosphere, Saturday night naturally emerges as the signal event. Having attended college at a time that didn't celebrate ceremony, custom, and restraint, I had the impression that college life was immune to these sorts of changes. After a short time at Wellesley, though, it was obvious that it is not. Most of the students I met were ferocious about keeping a sober social calendar. Many of them studied without a break during the week and celebrated without restraint during the weekend. They liked to talk very solemnly about their majors and follow that with an in-depth discussion of who passed out on the bus. There was almost no overlap between the two activities. I asked a few of them whether they wished the night bus ran every night of the week and got responses like "What for?" and "To go where?" Practically all the parties, especially MIT fraternity parties, are scheduled on Saturdays. A couple of days before my ride on the bus, I had checked the bulletin board in Schneider. There were ads for apartment shares, beanbag chairs, student-rate magazine subscriptions, volunteers for psych experiments, cheap tickets to San Francisco, lesbian folk-singing groups, and Luxo lamps, and there were party invitations. An MIT fraternity was inviting Wellesley students to attend a party being hosted by "the Evil Twin/the Son of Rasta Punk from Hell" and promised "free high-impact plastic cups after 9 p.m., dancing, socializing, and babies in funky clothes." Another MIT fraternity was pitching its toga party. Both of these galas were scheduled for the coming Saturday.

I was prepared for my ride by a Wellesley student named Eve Waterfall, a theater major who was Student Senate Director of Transportation that semester, which meant that she was responsible for managing the weekend bus. I figured it to be a prestigious job, considering how popular the bus is. She corrected me. "It's an *awful* job," she said. "Don't let anyone kid you. Everyone wants the bus to be perfect, and I've got to deal with all the headaches." Eve and a friend of hers named Meg Bogdan met me one afternoon a few days before I planned to spend the night at Wellesley. They had ridden to the Square on the nice bus—the Exchange Bus—and had about an hour to talk before they had to catch the last bus back to campus.

Eve: "You're going to see a lot of different kinds of people on the bus. Naturally, there are jocks. They live in the quads. Jockettes, I guess you'd call them."

Meg: "There aren't all that many of them, though. Then you have the girls who are called 'Wendy Wellesleys,' who come with pearls and BMWs. They don't ride the bus, of course, since they have their cars from Daddy."

Eve: "Right. There are a lot of people at Wellesley who are, you know, pretty smart and pretty normal. Then you have fringe-y people—the eccentrics, the partyers, the druggies. There aren't that many of them, but Wellesley *does* have a fringe, even though people don't think of it as a fringe kind of place."

Meg: "Also, there are the first-year students, typical freshpeople who don't know what they're doing yet, and they are the ones who especially love the weekend bus. A lot of plain weirdos also don't know what they're doing."

Eve: "We also have cooperatives. That's where the politicos, the super-feminists, and the coop-hippies are. There are actually a lot of those."

Meg: "Give me a break."

Armed with this scouting report and my bus ticket, I killed an hour in Schneider. The line for the products of profitable frying snaked through the little kitchen and into the hall. I ate something and then got to the bus stop outside Schneider in time to catch the nine o'clock to Harvard Square. The senate bus runs on the hour each Friday and Saturday night, starting at six. The last bus back to Wellesley leaves Harvard Square at twenty minutes before three. The buses of choice going into Cambridge are at nine, ten, and eleven o'clock. Anyone who goes into town on the six-, seven-, or eight-o'clock buses, according to my sources, is probably going to a movie, to dinner, or is simply outside the social loop. Anyone who returns before the one-forty or two-forty buses is presumed to have had a bad evening.

It had gotten colder; the streetlights along the lanes had snapped on and were throwing out splintered circles of light. A few people were walking between the buildings. The campus was quiet and gloomy—like a New England town emptied out by a storm warning. The moussed blondes who had bought their tickets after me were the first in line at the bus stop, followed by more women with blond hair and feline auras. Behind them was a short woman with a long-suffering look on her face, accompanied by someone whom I guessed was her mother; a woman in a kilt with a date in a sport coat; and about a dozen women whom Eve and Meg might have called "normals." Everyone was stamping her feet, looking at her watch, and not talking. After a moment, the bus came around the corner into view.

It is considered an indignity that the weekend bus, which embodies the notion that the Wellesley college student is the master of her destiny and the captain of her fate, the bus that changed her life by giving her freedom—the bus that might, although no one exactly counts on it, convey her from the gracious confines of the Wellesley grounds into the arms of a suitable mate—is one of those big yellow school buses that little kids ride to kindergarten. This is the high cost of freedom. As Wellesley women learn early on, if you want a nice, sleek-looking machine, try the Tuesday noon shuttle to the Harvard library. When the big yellow bus pulled up, the driver swung the door open, revealing his Burger King bag, his smoking cigarette with its inch-long ash, and his blaring radio.

"Lovely," one of the blondes muttered.

"Come oooon," the driver said, in a high, musical voice. "Let's gooooooo." We stepped in and began sorting ourselves into the seats. The driver, who told me later that his name was Richard, had long, wavy brown hair in a halfhearted pigtail, a long thin face, knuckly hands, and stooped shoulders. He was wearing a plaid flannel shirt, faded blue jeans, and black boots. He sat forward in his seat, as if he were trying to check his headlights. As the students stepped into the bus, he twisted around and grinned at them through his sandwich. "Oh, look, you girls are greeeaaat," he said. "Oh, I love this route. Not too much steering, which is good, because this thing doesn't have power steering." I sat a few seats behind him. "I sell real estate for my real money, and this I do for fun," he said, when I asked him how he got connected with the weekend bus. "Really, only one time has it gotten really bad, when I had six drunks—six girls—all at once in the back of the bus. They were singing songs, but I just let them go ahead and sing. Otherwise, the girls are great."

One of the blonde women, seated across from me, said in a low voice, "Boy, this driver is the worst, I think."

"Really," Blonde Two said. "Are you going to do anything about it?"

"Okay, look," Blonde One said. "As a Wellesley woman, I've been taught to be assertive. If the driver is grumpy or late, I complain about it. If he's gross, I'm going to complain about it, too. I don't want to get to the party smelling like Burger King, for one thing."

"Melissa, shut up, would you?" Blonde Three said. "You're not going to smell like Burger King. Maybe he's hungry, okay? Anyway, you guys, listen, they just finished filming a commercial at my parents' house. Around their cabana. I'm not kidding. I thought that was pretty neat. By the way, is this a cocktail party we're going to?" The other two nodded. "That's so out of *control*," she said. "Anyway, I wish I'd been in the commercial."

"Sounds great," Blonde Two said. "You'd be great in a commercial. Anyway, listen, I'm really worried about Doug."

"What do you mean?" Blonde Three said. "He's so great."

"I'm just sort of worried. I don't know if he's as well-rounded as I think he should be."

Richard crumpled his food bag and started to shut the door. Two more women ran toward the bus from Schneider, screaming and waving. He flipped the door open again, and they climbed in, flashed their tickets, and collapsed into the front seats. They surveyed the rest of the riders and then huddled in a conspiratorial clinch. "Look, I don't *know* where it is," I heard one of them say. She sounded annoyed.

"Well, I don't either, so what are we going to do?"

Pause. "Does anyone know where the Phi Sig party is?" the first one called out. After a long silence, someone in the back said, in a loud voice, "That's where everyone's going, you know? I mean, you can just follow anyone there." Just then, the bus lurched forward, and a woman with long dark hair who had been polishing her fingernails pitched forward with the bus. Her bottle of nail polish pitched backward. She slapped her forehead. "Oh, geez," she yelled. "Could somebody *please* save me? Grab that polish."

"Maybe," someone behind us said. "Tell me what color it was first."

Someone retrieved the polish. We bounced along the campus

—

roads and through Wellesley and down the turnpike, crossing the Charles River and idling for a long time at a stoplight on the edge of Harvard Square. Behind us was a billboard from Boston College saying "The Terriers Are Mad!" Ahead of us was a row of Harvard buildings—stout brick structures that taper into filigreed white bell towers. People were jostling along the sidewalks leading to the square.

The blondes were the first off at the bus stop. The nail polisher went next, muttering something unkind as she passed the bus driver. The mother-and-daughter team was the last to go, and as they walked past me I could hear the mother start a sentence with the phrase, "When I was your age . . ." I got off and walked around the Square, figuring I'd wait awhile for another bus back to campus. Across the street, the blonde women were in line at a huge automatic bank machine installation in the Square. The whole bank lobby was filled with students in a festive mood. Some were in line to use the machines and others were just hanging around talking. This installation of teller machines is said to be the second busiest in the country, right behind the machines at Walt Disney World.

The cement island that is the hub of Harvard Square is a well-traveled place as well as a destination. It is a subway station and a bus stop. Students from Boston University can ride their subway line to this station. Brandeis runs a weekend bus like Wellesley's that drops students in the Square. Local transit buses converge here. There are always several cars idling illegally at the curb. Despite millions of dollars spent to beautify it, it is not a beautiful place, but it is busy. I stood in the Square for a few minutes, just watching. There were couples strolling; packs of boys pursuing packs of girls; girls in clusters. A few solitary people walked by, looking rushed. On the brick wall along the Harvard Yard side of the Square, about a dozen kids were lined up, kicking their heels into the mortar and arguing listlessly. A short guy in a duffel coat, who looked as if he were trying to intersect with a blind date, stood a few feet away, smoothing his hair every few moments and breaking into a weak smile each time a girl veered in his direction, then, as she veered away, smoothing his hair again and frowning. To me, it looked exactly like a very active town square on a Saturday night in a mythical town where everyone is nineteen and a half years old, is full of great expectations, and wears Guess! jeans.

I caught the next bus back. I was surprised that there was anyone on it—by Saturday-night standards, it was rather early to be calling it quits. We arrived at Wellesley, picked up about twenty women, and headed to Harvard Square again. Except for Richard the Bus Driver, who kept whistling something that sounded like the chorus to "We Are the Champions," the bus was quiet. I finally asked the woman in front of me whether the ride was usually this subdued, and she shrugged and said, "Oh, I don't know, I guess we're just all storing up our energy for more important things."

The next loop was noisier, and the midnight loop positively jaunty. Most women were in groups of five or six and involved in high-decibel conversation. Someone passed around a bottle of peach schnapps. After midnight, Richard stopped whistling and turned his radio up so loud that the bus's dashboard was vibrating. As he was driving, he twisted the dial back and forth between a World Series game and a rock station. "Here we go, girls," he called out. He tuned in to a Supremes song. Someone in the back of the bus whooped. "Oh, you girls are really great," Richard said. We came off the turnpike and turned toward the Square. The traffic moved in spasms. "Go get 'em, now, girls!" Richard said to no one in particular when we pulled up to the bus stop. "Have fun, but not too much fun, okay? Last bus is twenty of three, or you're stuck here, okay? It's going to be a good one tonight, huh?" The women waiting to ride back to Wellesley started to board. Two women turned back just before getting on the bus and commenced misty farewells to two young men standing nearby, both wearing rugby shirts and Topsiders patched with electrician's tape. Richard looked at his watch. The farewells continued. He shut the door and put the bus in gear. A few riders made protesting noises. "Girls, come on," Richard said in a stern voice. "Girls, I'm all for love, but I'm on a schedule here, you know? I don't have all night."

I stayed on for a few more round trips. The last bus of the night pulled into the stop near MIT at twenty before three. The word in the bus was that the Phi Sig party had gone well, the toga party was a bust, and there were an unusually large number of Harvard Business School students—the *rara avis* of the Saturday-night scene. The first people to board the last bus were six Japanese students who were singing Japanese pop songs in wispy voices. One, a woman wearing a blue parka and large, black-rimmed eyeglasses, asked Richard, "Does this bus go to MIT?"

"This is MIT, dear," Richard said, looking bemused.

"Okay, does it go to MIT?"

"You're already *there*. We're here, I mean, this is MIT." He shook his head. "Just sit down. I'll get you there." The singing resumed.

Next, two women in early-fifties Greenwich Village uniforms (black turtlenecks, black miniskirts, black baggy raincoats) sat down near me in the middle of the bus. "Can you believe all the weekends we've had since the beginning of the year?" one said. "It's like all these strange episodes."

"It's so strange," her friend responded. "And tonight, those guys who thought they were so cool. I think they thought we were twenty-two or something."

"They were total fools. Hey, do you know Tracy? You know, at first she's really okay. Then at second glance, she's an obnoxious bitch."

"Tracy? Yeah? God, I can't get over those guys. I really thought the party was okay if you're into pure bullshit. We've got to remember that the boathouse is the place to meet grad students. This was so great tonight! We didn't meet a single undergrad!"

Her friend nodded and then said in a low voice, "Well, unless those guys were lying."

A thin brunette, whom I recognized from the nine o'clock, stumbled up the stairs, yelling over her shoulder to someone, "What are those drinks called? With the long straws?"

The woman behind her said, "Scorpions. They are *great*. I had about six, maybe. God, I'd love to call Aaron right now, but I think he's tripping tonight. He's into doing LSD about three times a year." The two of them walked down the aisle, bumping back and forth against the seats. Finally they sat down in the back. A few minutes later, three women looking meek and flustered stepped in and sat down near the front.

"Nice night, ladies?" Richard said. "Huh?" They ignored him. "I just drank ginger ale," one said, and the others nodded.

Another one said, "Me, too. I drank ginger ale until they ran out. Then I drank water. I don't even know what we're doing here."

Richard snapped his radio on as another dozen riders got on. The musty smell of flat beer and cigarettes began to take over. After several hours riding the bus, I had had a snootful of exhaust fumes and welcomed the bouquet of Amstel Light and Newports. The Japanese singing continued, although it was soon overwhelmed by the two Scorpion drinkers, who began singing a ballad by John Cougar Mellencamp. They were joined a few minutes later by several women who also had been drinking Scorpions. I changed seats and realized, after a moment, that I was sitting on a piece of paper on which someone had written "I WILL NOT WRITE OR DRAW ON THE BUS WALLS OR SEATS" twenty-five times. Two women wearing army pants and heavy boots climbed aboard, sat down, and after a minute began reading in unison from *Saint Jack* in exaggerated theatrical voices. A woman behind me started applauding and pounding the back of the seat. Someone yelled "Ick!" and threw a copy of a Susan Sontag book across the aisle. While it would not be fair to describe it as a riot, the atmosphere became highly stimulated.

"Girls," Richard said, to no one in particular. "Keep it together, girls."

Just then, a young man in a tie and tan windbreaker ran up to the bus, banged his fist against a window, and yelled, "Anyone in there want a quickie?" For a second, everything stopped. He smiled. One of the women behind me said, "God, if he weren't such a gross jerk, I'd think he was kind of cute." As we all started laughing, Richard shut the door and cranked the bus into gear. We headed out of Cambridge and down the highway with the radio blaring. More impromptu choruses formed and the *Saint Jack* reading continued. After about ten miles, a couple of riders fell asleep, but rather than dampening anyone's spirits, this was seen as an opportunity to shove them aside and give the rest of us more room.

"God, Cambridge is so *cool*," one woman said as she pushed the

—

woman sleeping next to her toward the aisle. "I don't know, I guess sometimes I wish I were in school there."

The woman across the aisle turned and said, "Not me. I could never get anything done. This way we can come in and leave and get back to work during the week."

The first woman shrugged. "Yeah, I guess. I guess so. In that case, at least we have the bus."

As we got closer to the Wellesley campus, two women in the seats in front of me started polishing their nails, which I have come to understand is business as usual on the bus. One of them was saying that she had chipped hers opening a bottle at the party. "Nails suck," her friend said, nodding sympathetically. "But I do love this color. It's called Lucifer." Just then, Richard, who had drifted into a private, reflective mood, stepped on the brakes. The bus jolted to a stop. One bottle of nail polish tipped over. "For *godssake*, my polish!" the woman yelled over the din. "God, I can't believe this." As she got out of her seat and began scrambling for the bottle, Richard put on the emergency brake, stood up, announced that he was going to get a cup of coffee, and walked off the bus. We were on a side street near the Wellesley campus. It was close to three in the morning. For a few minutes, everyone kept chatting and singing, but eventually the bus grew quiet.

"Did this guy just, like, leave us here?" one of the *Saint Jack* readers asked. She wiped her window and looked out. Richard was nowhere in sight. After a minute there was a rustle behind me. One of the Scorpion drinkers at the back of the bus stood up.

"Shelley," someone next to her said. "Just sit down. You'll be fine."

Someone in the front of the bus groaned. "Oh, God, is she going to puke?" Shelley drifted up the aisle. "Oh, somebody get her out of here, okay?" Two more Scorpion drinkers got up and hustled Shelley to the front of the bus. The door wouldn't open. They started pounding on it and yelling for Richard. Shelley started listing to one side. Four more people got up and started pushing at the door. The latch squeaked and the door finally opened. Shelley stumbled down the stairs and was positioned in the street by three women, who held her by the shoulders, turned their heads away, and started to laugh.

"Another beautiful senate bus ride," a woman behind me said, sounding as if she had had her sense of propriety dislodged several times on this route. Richard still hadn't come back, but for the moment he seemed to have been forgotten. Everyone on the bus was gazing out of the windows at Shelley.

"Talk about justice," I heard someone say. "Shelley just barfed on a Dodge Colt with a Wellesley College window decal."

Debuting

Phoenix, Arizona

Azteca Plaza, the biggest formal wear shopping center in the world, is on a skinny strip of sandy, cactus-studded Arizona real estate, a few miles east of downtown Phoenix, in a neighborhood that does not yet illustrate the vitality of the Sunbelt economy. There used to be nice small houses in the area, but in the last few decades they became unfashionable and then funky and finally abandoned. Azteca Plaza, in the meantime, did nothing but grow. When it opened in 1962, the plaza was just one shop with an inventory of three wedding gowns and five bridesmaid outfits. It is now a complex of forty thousand square feet with a florist, an invitation shop, a tuxedo annex, a bridesmaid wing, a veil wing, parking for two hundred, and a wedding-gown center the size of a suburban roller rink, with dozens of dress racks and yards of satin, netting, and peau de soie billowing all over the floor. Azteca Plaza has the corner on the greater metropolitan Phoenix prom-dress trade. It also does a brisk business in the fancy ball gowns Hispanic girls wear at their *quinceañeras*, the ceremony that takes place when they are fifteen years old—*quince años*—to celebrate their passage into womanhood, commitment to Catholicism, and debut into society. In the last decade, the number of Hispanics in Phoenix has grown by 125 percent. The *quinceañera* business at Azteca Plaza has enjoyed a corresponding upswing.

Azteca Plaza is just a few blocks away from Immaculate Heart Church, a boxy stucco-colored structure that serves as a central parish for the Hispanic community in the Phoenix diocese. Immaculate Heart was built in 1928, fourteen years after it was revealed that the priests at the main basilica in Phoenix, St. Mary's, had been obliging their Mexican parishioners to hold their masses and weddings and *quinceañeras* in the basement rather than on the main floor of the church. It used to be common for certain churches to serve an ethnic group rather than a geographical area—in most American cities, there would be French, Hispanic, Polish, Irish, and German Catholic churches. The practice is rare these days, and Immaculate Heart is one of the few such ethnic parishes left in the entire country. Someone in Phoenix, recounting for me the history of Hispanic mistreatment at St. Mary's, credited the continued existence of a national parish in Phoenix to the dry Arizona desert air, which, he claimed, had preserved the unpleasant memory of bargain-basement weddings at the basilica in many Hispanics' minds. Hispanics in Phoenix now regularly attend the churches in their immediate neighborhoods, but for sentimental and historical reasons they continue to think of Immaculate Heart as the mother ship. Not coincidentally, Immaculate Heart was for years the site of most of Phoenix's many *quinceañeras*—that is, the site of the mass when the girl is blessed and is asked to affirm her dedication to the Church. The party in which she is introduced to society and celebrates her birthday is held after the mass at a hotel or hall. For a while, there were so many *quinceañeras* at Immaculate Heart that they outnumbered weddings. For that matter, there were so many *quinceañera* masses and parties that they were a standard Saturday-night social occasion in town.

In early summer I was invited to a large *quinceañera* in Phoenix at which sixteen girls were to be presented. The event was being sponsored by the girls' parents and the Vesta Club, a social organization of Hispanic college graduates. In the Southwest, constituents of this subset are sometimes known as "Chubbies"—Chicano urban professionals. Chubbies give Azteca Plaza a lot of business. The girls' fathers and the sixteen young men who were going to be escorts at the *quinceañera* had rented their tuxedos from Azteca Plaza and would be picking them up on Saturday morning. The girls, of course, had gotten their gowns months before.

The traditional Mexican *quinceañera* gown is white or pink, floor length but trainless, snug on top and wide at the bottom, with a skirt shaped like a wedding bell. But like most traditions that migrate a few hundred miles from their point of origin and make it through a couple of generations in this country, *quinceañeras* have yielded somewhat to interpretation, and the gowns that the Vesta Club girls were going to wear demonstrated the effects of Americanization on taste as well as a certain American-style expansiveness in price. All of the gowns were white and full-length but otherwise they were freestyle—an array of high necks, fluted necklines, sweetheart neck-lines, leg-o'-mutton sleeves, cap sleeves, cascade collars, gathered bodices, beaded bodices, bustles, and sequins; one had a train and one had a flouncy peplum and a skirt that was narrow from the hip to the floor. Further Americanization has taken place with regards to scheduling. In Mexico, *quinceañeras* traditionally take place on the day the girl actually turns fifteen. In the United States, *quinceañeras*—like many important ceremonies in American life— take place on Saturday nights.

When I first mentioned to a woman I know in Phoenix that I wanted to attend a *quinceañera*, that I thought they seemed like interesting ceremonies and great displays of community feeling and a good example of how ethnic tradition fits into American Saturday nights, she clucked sympathetically and said she was very senti-mental about her own *quinceañera* but had become convinced that they were now going the way of many other ethnic ceremonies in this country—changed beyond recognition, marketed like theme parks, at the very least irrelevant to assimilated youngsters who would rather spend Saturday nights at keg parties than reenacting an old-world ceremony. An inevitable pattern transforms such things: immigrants gather in their leisure time so that they can bolster one another and share their imported traditions, their chil-dren tolerate the gatherings occasionally because they have a likeable familiar ring, and then the children of *those* children deplore them because they seem corny and pointless, and finally there is a lot of discussion about how sad it is that the community doesn't get together anymore.

That is partly what has become of *quinceañeras* in Phoenix, but the real problem, ironically, is that they have been too popular for their own good. A few years ago, the bishop of Phoenix, a slight, freckle-faced man from Indiana named Thomas O'Brien, started hearing complaints from some priests about *quinceañeras*. According to the bishop, the chief complaint was that *quinceañera* masses were beginning to dominate church schedules. This would surprise no one with an eye on the city's demographics: three-quarters of the Hispanics in Phoenix are under thirty-five years old and a significant number of them are girls—all potential subjects of a *quinceañera* mass and party. The priests complained that some girls came to their *quinceañera* mass without the faintest idea of its religious significance, never came to church otherwise, demanded a mass even if they were pregnant or using drugs or in some other way drifting outside the categories usually in good stead with the religious community, and badgered their families—some Chubbies, but many not—into giving them opulent post-mass parties. Some *quinceañera* parties in Phoenix were running into the high four figures and beyond. Many families could hardly afford this. In response to these concerns, Father Antonio Sotelo, the bishop's vicar for Hispanic affairs, surveyed the diocese's priests and then wrote a guidebook for *quinceañeras* similar to ones circulated recently in a few other American parishes with large Hispanic populations, advising that girls take five classes on Bible study, Hispanic history, *quinceañera* history, and modern morals, and go on a church-sponsored retreat with their parents before the event. He also recommended that *quinceañeras* be held for groups of girls rather than for individuals, in order to offset the queen-for-a-day quality that many of them had taken on, and so that the cost could be spread around.

One morning before the Vesta Club *quinceañera*, I stopped by Father Sotelo's office at Immaculate Heart. Besides being vicar for Hispanic affairs, Father Sotelo is the pastor of Immaculate Heart. His small office in the back of the church is decorated with pictures of his parishioners and dominated by a whale of a desk. Father Sotelo is short and wiry, and has rumpled graying hair, an impish face, and a melodious voice. His manner of address is direct. He is known for holding and broadcasting the opinion that anyone who wears shorts and a T-shirt to church should be escorted out the door, and that the men in his congregation who walk with a sloppy, swinging, barrio-tough gait look like gorillas. Father Sotelo grew up in San Diego. His heritage is Mexican and American Indian. He says that he considered the *quinceañera* issue a simple matter of facing reality, and he doesn't mind that the requirements have discouraged many girls from having *quinceañeras*. "We knew perfectly well that most girls were only thinking about the party," he said. "It was a big dream for them. Everyone wants a fancy *quinceañera* party. Unlike an American debutante ball, *quinceañeras* are not limited to the upper class. Any girl can celebrate it. But there are spoiled brats in every class. Many of these girls were demanding that their parents spend thousands of dollars on them whether they could afford it or not. People at the lower end of the economic scale cling to tradition most fervently, so they were most determined to have a traditional *quince-añera*, and their daughters would have the most expensive dresses and parties. And when these girls would walk down the aisle with their parents at the mass, you could tell that quite often the girls and their parents couldn't stand one another. It was an empty cere-mony. For what they were getting out of the church part of the *quinceañera*, they could have gone out and done the whole thing in the desert and had someone sprinkle magic pollen on their heads."

After the guidelines were circulated around the diocese, a few churches, including Immaculate Heart, set up the *quinceañera* classes and retreats. But to the enormous displeasure of parishioners who enjoyed spending Saturday nights at their friends' daughters' *quince-añeras*, and who imagined that on some Saturday night in the future their own daughters would be feted at a mass and nice reception of their own, many priests in Phoenix announced that they agreed with Father Sotelo but they lacked the time and facilities to run classes and retreats. Therefore, they declared, they would no longer perform *quinceañera* masses at all.

The one priest who took exception was Frank Peacock, the pastor of a poor church in a scruffy South Phoenix neighborhood. Father Peacock made it known that he thought the guidelines were too strict, and that they inhibited the exercise of a tradition that rightfully belonged to the people, and that as far as he was concerned, anyone in any condition or situation who wanted a *quinceañera* could come to him. "We get calls here all the time from people asking very meekly for Father Peacock's number," Father Sotelo said to me, looking exasperated. "They're not fooling anyone. I know exactly what they want."

A few weeks before I got to Phoenix, a small yucca plant on the corner of Twelfth and Van Buren, about a half mile down the street from Immaculate Heart, sprouted a stem that then shriveled up into an unusual shape and was subsequently noticed by a passerby who thought it bore a striking resemblance to Our Lady of Guadeloupe. The yucca stem was never certified as a genuine miracle by church hierarchy, but for several weeks, until someone shot at it with a small-caliber handgun and then two artists took it upon themselves to cut it down with a chainsaw as the climax of a performance piece, it attracted large crowds of people who came to marvel at it and pray.

Our Lady of Guadeloupe, the vision who appeared to the Mexican Indian Juan Diego on December 9, 1531, and who was so awe-inspiring a sight that she more or less nailed down the entire country of Mexico for the Catholic Church, has appeared in other places as unlikely as the corner of Twelfth and Van Buren. For instance, Our Lady of Guadeloupe also happens to be spray-painted on the trunk of at least one souped-up low-rider car in Phoenix, which I noticed bouncing down the street one afternoon when I was in town. Father Peacock had seen this same car and says he finds it remarkable. The day before the Vesta Club Ball, he and I had gotten together so he could show me videotapes of some of the outlaw *quinceañera* masses he had presided over at Our Lady of Fatima. Before we started the tapes, I said that Father Sotelo had pointed out that people were perfectly entitled to have *quinceañeras* that cost ten thousand dollars and celebrated fifteen-year-olds with heavy marijuana habits, but that the Church shouldn't necessarily endorse them or hold celebration masses for them. "People have a right to enjoy things that the Church doesn't endorse," Father Peacock said. "We don't endorse low-riders, do we?" He interrupted himself. "Actually, I endorse low-riders. I love them. Have you ever seen one? Oh, they can be gorgeous, really beautiful. Did you ever see the one painted with Our Lady of Guadeloupe?"

Of Father Peacock, Thomas O'Brien, the Bishop of Phoenix, says, "My druthers are that he conform. I haven't come down on him because I think he's well intentioned." Of Bishop O'Brien, Father Peacock says, "Oh, he's a good guy. I was a priest back when he was just a young novitiate, so I've seen him come through the ranks. We have a playful relationship, really a nice rapport. I kid him around. If he asked me to stop what I'm doing, I'd swear backwards and forwards that I would stop, and then I'd run right out and keep doing it. He knows that, and he lets me keep things in my little parish my way." Although there is a gulf between their positions on how lenient the Church should be with its supplicants, there is genuine goodwill between Father Sotelo and Father Peacock. Father Sotelo told me several times that he feels quite fond of old Frank. Father Peacock, that afternoon, said he is very fond of old Tony. Both of them mentioned that the other is the only other priest they ever see at political rallies and marches for the United Farm Workers or nuclear disarmament. Father Peacock, who is in his mid-sixties and is balding and tall, with a long oval head, high Yankee coloring, a beaked nose, and a jittery, nerve-racking way of walking, sitting, and talking, did remark that he thought Father Sotelo was most unfortunately under the impression that *quinceañera* masses were followed by wild beer parties and sexual escapades. "There definitely is *beer*," Father Peacock said. "Things are pretty lively. They are good parties. That's part of the tradition. Sometimes there are fistfights and so forth, but that's the way good parties are, isn't it? But I honestly think Father Sotelo thinks that these *quinceañeras* are orgies or some such thing. You know, if I were a married man and someone suggested that about my daughter's *quinceañera*, I'd sue him for libel." He chuckled and then said, "We have a good time at Our Lady of Fatima. We're just a little more savage than at the other churches. We're . . . noisier. We're more natural."

Some of the people who come to Father Peacock for a *quinceañera* are poor, or are recent immigrants who are still attached to the traditional Mexican style of the ceremony and resist what they could well consider pointless time-consuming requirements or irritating Americanizations. Quite often, Father Peacock is approached by affluent Hispanics as well, who tell him they want their daughters to have their own celebrations, not *quinceañeras* with a group of other girls, and that they want to go all out with the six-tiered *quinceañera* cake and the rhinestone crown and the catered sit-down dinner for three hundred and the mariachi band and the lavish gifts from the godparents and the fifteen boy escorts and fifteen girl attendants in matching outfits who traditionally accompany the *quinceañera* girl. Father Peacock says he has given *quinceañera* masses for daughters of state senators as well as for girls whose parents are illiterate. Most of the time, he begins his address at the mass by asking for forgiveness for his failures and then says, "You have asked us to take care of a fifteenth birthday celebration and we say no—this is one of our failures." Sometimes the people at the altar look bored or are wearing dark sunglasses and conspicuous amounts of jewelry and can't even remember the words to the Lord's Prayer when Father Peacock recites it. "That is one of my motivations," he says. "This might be the only chance I have to get that sort of person into church and try to reach them." Some of the families have experienced child abuse, sexual abuse, divorce, separation, or a combination of all four, and Father Peacock says he loves seeing such families together at the occasional happy affair like a *quinceañera*. Some of them take out loans to pay for their daughters' gowns. Father Peacock usually urges the poorer families to hold their parties at South Mountain Park, a city facility with a hall that can be used for free, but he says he can understand if they prefer a fancier place. On this point, he always says something in the homily like, "Through self-sacrifice we get our pleasure," and has said many times that he would rather that people go into hock for a traditional, ethnic, religious occasion—no matter how marginally religious it might turn out to be—than for something like a car or a boat. "A *quinceañera* costs a lot of money," he says. "But it's worth a lot of money. Anyway, I don't try to change people. I like to meet them in their own way."

In 1987, Father Peacock performed 10 percent of all the baptisms in the Phoenix diocese. There are sixty-one churches in the diocese, so that is an extraordinary percentage. Unlike other priests, Father Peacock will baptize the babies of unwed mothers or unreligious mothers—essentially, anyone who asks and who might get a lecture and no baptism elsewhere—so he is in high demand. He seems to be amazing himself when he mentions his baptism statistics. "Ten percent," he says. "Oh my! Ten percent of the whole diocese. That's a *lot*." His explanation is that he wants people in the church, and sometimes baptizing a baby with muddled origins is the only way to do it. His *quinceañera* schedule is also busy: usually at least two for every Saturday night in the year. Once, he did seven *quinceañera* masses on a single Saturday night.

"'Father Peacock will do anything," a young woman named Alice Coronado-Hernandez, this year's chairman of the Vesta Club *Quinceañera* Ball, said to me one afternoon. "Everyone knows that about Father Peacock, so everyone calls him." At the time, I was having lunch at a bad Mexican restaurant in a good part of Phoenix with Alice, her mother, Caroline, and Mary Jo Franco-French, a physician who helped found the Vesta *quinceañera* fifteen years ago. When she was organizing that first *quinceañera*, Mary Jo had just finished medical school and was pregnant with her daughter Laura. This year, Laura was going to be one of the girls up on the stage.

The Vesta Club is not going to be calling on Father Peacock anytime soon. "We're really happy with doing our *quinceañera* the way Father Sotelo has suggested," Caroline said. "We felt the classes and the retreat were really good for the girls. We saw what was going on with the *quinceañeras*—we saw the problem out there. Even if we could afford it, we knew it wasn't good to continue the old way."

Alice said, "It was crazy what people were spending. When I was that age, the girls were really competitive about their *quinceañeras* and about how nice they would be." Caroline nodded. My *quinceañera* was at the first Vesta Club Ball," Alice went on. "That year, I must have been invited to *quinceañeras* for friends of mine just about every weekend, so it was a pretty regular Saturday-night activity for me. But even then I could see how some people got very extravagant about it."

"They were hocking their souls for the fancy private *quinceañera*," Caroline added. "The diocese could see that it was becoming detrimental to the economy of their parishioners."

The three of them spent some time talking about last-minute details of the Vesta *quinceañera*. After a mass at Immaculate Heart, there was going to be dinner for the four hundred and fifty guests at Camelback Inn, an elegant resort north of the city, and a short ceremony in which each girl would be presented by her father. Then the girls and their escorts would perform a *quinceañera* waltz—a complicated dance to the "Blue Danube" which the kids had practiced once a week for the last three months. "The waltz is such a beautiful tradition," Mary Jo said. "It's what we have that makes the event really special. That, and having them learn about their Hispanic heritage. The kids have worked so hard at that waltz. They've really practiced, and they've really gotten good at it."

"They *have* gotten good at it, haven't they?" Caroline said, nodding. "It's hard to believe that some of them had never danced a step before they started to learn."

The Fifteenth Annual Vesta Club *quinceañera* Mass began at five o'clock with a procession of the sixteen girls up the center aisle of Immaculate Heart. I sat on the left side of the church, a row behind Mary Jo Franco-French and her husband, Alfred, an eye surgeon of Gallic extraction who has a large practice in Phoenix. Beside me were four cousins of Mary Jo's who had flown in from Juarez, Mexico, for the event. The day had been dry-roasting hot, and at five, the long, dusty southwestern dusk was just beginning and the light was hitting the city at a flat angle and giving everything a yellowy glow. The *quinceañera* girls in their white dresses had been standing on the sidewalk outside the church when I walked in, and each time a car drove down the street in front of the church, the updraft would blow their big skirts around. Immaculate Heart is a bulky, unadorned building with dark wooden pews, a vaulted ceiling, some stained glass, a wide altar with simple lines, and a pail hanging just outside the side door into which parishioners are advised to deposit their chewing gum. After I sat down, I noticed Father Sotelo and Bishop O'Brien seated together at the altar. The Vesta Club *quinceañera* is the only one in Phoenix at which the bishop celebrates the mass. He told me that it is the only one he attends because he liked the seriousness with which the club approached the spiritual content of the ceremony, and also because no one else having a *quinceañera* had ever invited him.

Father Peacock had mentioned that he was going to try to make it to Immaculate Heart for the Vesta Club *quinceañera* because he likes to go to as many *quinceañeras* as he can, but that he might not make it because he was supposed to celebrate a *quinceañera* mass at his own church for a girl from a poor family. The family didn't have a phone, and as of Friday, he hadn't heard from anyone, so he wasn't sure if they were still planning to come. He mentioned that he didn't know any of the particulars of the event except that the party was going to be at a social hall in South Phoenix and that the family had hired a video crew to film the whole thing. *Quinceañera* videos, with title sequences and soundtracks and sometimes introductions showing the girl's baby pictures, are getting to be big business in Phoenix. I glanced around the church and saw about two hundred people. Everyone was wearing tuxedos or formal gowns. I didn't see Father Peacock. I believe that even in such a big crowd he would have stood out. On the occasions I spent with him, he wore a priest's black shirt and white collar; baggy, faded black jeans; and scuffed-up Birkenstock sandals. In all the photographs he showed me of himself standing with girls he had just blessed at the *quinceañera* mass, he was wearing a rough version of a priest's cope that he had made by cutting up a Mexican blanket. "Some of the people at my church don't like when I wear it because they think it's too ratty-looking, but oh, gosh, it was such a beautiful blanket," he had said, gazing at the photographs. Then he stroked his chin and looked contemplative. "Actually," he said, "maybe it was a tablecloth."

After a few minutes, the organist hit a chord and the procession began. The Vesta Club girls walked in, trailing satin and netting. The gowns were a spectacle: each one was bright white, with different structural embellishments and complicated effects. I noticed the girl wearing the dress with the little train and the one with the narrow skirt. "Wow," whispered Carmen Gonzalez, one of Mary Jo Franco-French's cousins, who had celebrated her own *quinceañera* a few years ago at a country club in Juarez. "Pretty nice dresses. These girls look so *grown-up.*"

"The third one down is my niece Maria," the woman behind us said. "Fifteen already, but I still think of her as a baby. I think her mother's praying that Maria keeps her figure so she can wear the dress again when she gets married."

The procession took several minutes. Then the girls sat down in two rows of chairs at the altar, and the bishop made his greetings and began the mass. After a few prayers, he announced that it was time for the parents to bless their daughters individually. He turned and nodded at the dark-haired girl at the end of the row. She stood up cautiously, walked to the center of the apse and down the three steps, turned around and knelt down, partially disappearing in the folds of her dress. Her parents stood up in their pew and walked over to her, leaned down and made the sign of the cross on her forehead, kissed her, whispered something in her ear, and then returned to their seats. The girl rose up and walked back to the altar. Someone in a pew behind me sobbed lightly and then blew loudly into a handkerchief. A faulty key in the church organ stuck and started to squeal. The next girl stood up, smoothed her huge skirt, stepped down, knelt, was blessed by her parents, and returned to her seat. Laura Josefina Franco-French, a tall and elegant-looking fifteen-year-old with long dark hair and a serene expression, came forward and was blessed by Alfred and Mary Jo. Then the girl who was wearing the tight skirt stood up. We all sat forward. She walked in tiny steps across the apse, eased herself down the stairs, turned around, and then, with the agility of a high-school cheerleader at the season's big game, she folded her legs beneath her and knelt without straining a seam.

There were still some golfers on the greens at Camelback Inn when the Vesta Club partygoers arrived. The ballroom wasn't ready for us to be seated, so everyone milled around the pool having drinks and talking. I wondered if the golfers were curious about what we were doing—four hundred well-dressed people, mostly adult, and sixteen girls in formal white gowns. It might have looked like a wedding, except there were too many young women in white, and it might have looked like a prom, except no one has parents at her prom. It felt mostly like a community reunion. "It's a big group, but it's a small world," said a woman in a beaded lilac gown standing beside me at the bar.

"Relatives or friends?" I asked.

"Both," she said. "About half of these people were at my daughter's *quinceañera* last year." I must have looked surprised, because she started to laugh, and then said, "Some of these families even knew each other in Mexico. You could say that we're just keeping the chain or circle or what have you, intact. I had my *quinceañera* longer ago than I'm happy to say. It's an old-fashioned event but I love it." She took her drink and joined a group of people nearby who were talking about an expensive shopping center just opening in Scottsdale. One of the men in the group kept sweeping his hands out and saying "Boom!" and the woman beside him would then slap his shoulder playfully and say "For godsakes, come on, Adolfo!" Alfred Franco-French III, who was escorting his sister Laura, walked past the bar and muttered that he hoped he would remember the waltz when it came time to waltz. The patio got noisier and noisier. No one was speaking Spanish. One of the girls' fathers started a conversation with me by saying, "There are plenty of bums in the world out there, sad to say," but then he got distracted by someone he hadn't seen in a while and walked away. I had driven out to Camelback with one of Laura Franco-French's school friends, and after a few minutes we ran into each other. She said she was impressed with the *quinceañera* so far. She talked about how there was usually never anything to do on Saturday nights in Phoenix, and then she talked about how favorably Laura's involvement in a formal event, in particular one that required the purchase of a really nice fancy dress, was regarded by other students at their largely non-Hispanic private school. It happened that this girl was not Hispanic and had never been to a *quinceañera* before and had also never before considered what advantages ethnicity might include. She looked across the pool where the debutantes were standing in a cluster and said, "I never thought about it one way or another. But now that I'm at one of these *quinceañeras*, I'm thinking that being Hispanic might be really cool." I walked to the far side of the pool, where I had a long view of all the people at the party, in their fresh tuxes and filmy formals; with their good haircuts and the handsome, relaxed posture common to people whose businesses are doing well and to whom life has been generous; who were standing around the glimmery pool and against the dark, lumpy outline of Camelback Mountain, holding up light-colored drinks in little crystal glasses so that they happened to catch the last bit of daylight. It was a pretty gorgeous sight.

Finally, Alice Coronado-Hernandez and Caroline Coronado sent word that the ballroom was ready. The doors of the Saguaro Room were propped open. The patio emptied as the crowd moved inside. At one end of the ballroom, a mariachi band was ready to play. Around the dance floor were fifty tables set with bunchy flower arrangements and good china. I had been seated with Alice Coronado-Hernandez and her family. At the tables, each place was set with a program printed on stiff, creamy paper; it listed the Vesta Club officers, last year's *quinceañera* debs and escorts, and this year's debs and escorts, and had formal portraits of each of the girls. This was similar in style to the program for the St. Luke's Hospital Visitors' Society Cotillion—Phoenix's premier society event—at which the girls being presented are far more likely to have names like Bickerstaff and Collins than Esparza and Alvarez. I had seen the 1988 St. Luke's program when I had dinner one night with the Franco-Frenches. Laura had been studying the program so energetically that some of the pages were fingerprinted and the binding was broken. In the time since Mexicans in Phoenix were forced to hold their masses in the basement of St. Mary's, a certain amount of social amalgamation has come to pass: Laura Franco-French, half-Mexican in heritage and at least that much in consciousness, will also be presented at St. Luke's in a few years. Similarly, there was a Whitman and a Thornton among the debutantes at the Vesta ball.

I was reading the Vesta program when Father Sotelo came over to the table. "It's a wonderful event, isn't it?" he said, breaking into a huge smile. He gave Alice a bountiful look. She gave him one back and then got up and hustled off in the direction of the kitchen. The tables around us were soon filled and the conversations bubbling. "It's such a happy occasion for all the families," Father Sotelo said. He ran his finger around his collar. "This is a wonderful, wonderful thing. It's one of my favorite events. These girls are going to remember this forever. If you just do it the old way, with no effort to have it mean anything, it's just like giving candy to a baby. You're just trying to please people. This way, it's something that has significance." Laura Franco-French drifted past our table. Father Sotelo stopped her and told her she looked wonderful. She gave him a dreamy smile and then drifted on toward her family's table. Father Sotelo nodded after her and then crossed the room to his table.

After a moment, Alice came back and dropped into her seat. "They don't have enough prime rib, so some people will have to have steak," she said.

Her husband, Joe, shrugged, sighed, and picked up the program. "Anything but rubber chicken," he said. "You get a big group of people together like this and it starts to look *political,* you know?"

"When do they announce debutante of the year?" Alice's stepdaughter asked her. Alice drummed her fingers on the table and said, "Later." Just then, the master of ceremonies coughed into the microphone and the room got quiet. The girls lined up around the edge of the dance floor with their fathers. The mothers were stationed near them in chairs, so that they would be readily available for the father-mother waltz, which comes after the father-daughter waltz and after the special *quinceañera* waltz—a complex piece of choreography, in which the girls spin around their escorts and then weave through their arms, form little circles and then big circles and finally waltz in time around the dance floor. After all these waltzes, the mariachi band was going to play—although I had heard that for the sake of the teenagers, who appreciated their heritage but who were, after all, American kids with tastes of their own, the Mexican music was going to be alternated throughout the evening with current selections of rock and roll.

The announcer cleared his throat again and said, *"Buenos noches, damas y caballeros."* He had a sonorous, rumbling voice that thundered through the ballroom. *"Buenos noches.* We present to you this year's Vesta Club debutantes."

Lounging

Portland, Oregon

Being in a lounge band means giving up your weekends. Lounge bands also have a way of going out of business. On account of these conditions, the profession of lounge-band musician attracts people who can adapt to an unusual schedule and have a taste for a changeful life. Mike Swan, Dan Banham, Jeff Little, Burell Palmer, and Mary Phillips—the five members of No Means Yes, a band that plies its trade in Portland, Oregon, where I spent a Saturday night not long after I left Phoenix—have had between them about eight free weekends in the last eleven years. Each of the members of No Means Yes has also experienced some of the volatility of the lounge-band business. Over the last decade, their various musical associations have included the Bop-A-Dips, Natural Reaction, Bullet, Rubicon, Meredith Brooks and the Angels of Mercy, Red Axe, Ziggy Coefield, Hot to Go, Wilshire Champs, Rainbow, Mister Nice Guy, Nuance, Shakedown, the Shakers, Room Service, Freeway, Pulse, Freefall, the Kix, Cellophane, Fair Warning, Red Tape, Video, the Results, Moving Parts, Drama, Future Fox, Idol Threat, Point A, the Goods, Kicker, and the Dick Fisher Tribute to the Stars. One or two of these bands were 1950s nostalgia acts, one was an Elvis impersonator group, one was a Mormon rock band, one was a Vegas band, and the rest were an assortment of Top Forty bands, funk bands, glitter bands, disco bands, disco-funk bands, blues-revival bands, concept bands, folk-rock bands, and bands that played their own interesting musical concoctions to greater or occasionally lesser acclaim. Of these, the bands that would qualify under the rubric "lounge band" are the ones that play cover versions of songs someone else made popular, in places people go because they like the location or the wallpaper or the price of the drinks as much as because they happen to like the band. A lounge band is of just about the same consequence as a jukebox, and as it happens, the rise of the lounge and the lounge band corresponds almost exactly to the fall of the roadhouse and the jukebox—same social impulses, different forms.

The life of a lounge band, to an outsider, can seem a little less than rewarding: there are the long hours, the late nights, the working weekends, the elusiveness of success, the lack of respect in the musical fraternity, the constant smell of cigarette smoke in your clothes. The lounge-band life also includes the unlikelihood of wealth. In fact, a member of a bar band with a busy schedule will probably earn no more than he would working on, say, the silicon-chip assembly line at Tektronics, a large company in Portland to which many would-be or were-once musicians surrender when their personal debt takes on arresting proportions. Still, even musicians at the bottom end of the scale usually argue that, no matter what, playing music is a better life than any head-banger job with wages could ever be. Being in a lounge band, so the argument goes, at least affords you an unconventional life and the dream of someday being catapulted from playing Jimmy Buffet ballads at a Quality Inn lounge to performing your own music in front of a sellout crowd, dominating the Billboard charts, and being forced to investigate tax-shelter opportunities. Working on the assembly line at Tektronics, on the other hand, has health benefits.

Some lounge bands last a number of years. Others have a limited and even evanescent life. In each case, it is standard that at least one of the members believes that this band will be the one that will make it big and last forever. When I got to Portland, No Means Yes had been in existence for two months and twenty-five days.

No Means Yes, at the time, had a regular Saturday-night engagement at a Stuart Anderson Cattle Company lounge in Vancouver, Washington, a big mill town just across the state border from Portland. From the parking lot of the Cattle Company, you can see the Columbia River, a big bridge that crosses the Columbia, and the scooped-out top of volcanic Mount St. Helens, just a couple of dozen miles away. On a very clear day, part of Mount Rainier might show in the distance. Despite its dramatic scenery, Vancouver itself is not a popular destination. The recession of the early 1980s followed by the timber-industry slump followed by the growth of the suburbs and the subsequent enfeeblement of the downtown core have left the town in reduced circumstances. The new redwood-shingled condominium developments in the suburban areas east of the city look prosperous and crowded, but there is plenty of parking available around the clock downtown. In the center of Vancouver is a cluster of small, pretty nineteenth-century buildings with ornate cast-iron transoms and beveled windows and all the other architectural flourishes that signified prosperity and optimism on the part of the builder. Nowadays, as many of these buildings are empty as are not. The strip centers and shopping malls in the Portland-Vancouver metropolitan area have fewer interesting decorative embellishments but are busy all the time. Several years ago, when I was in Vancouver for other reasons, I dropped in at a store downtown that was going out of business. This was one of the biggest retail businesses in the city—an old-fashioned department store where you could buy pajamas and rugs and socks and mechanical pencils. I found out that the store had been closed since the owners had taken ill, and a trustee had finally decided to hold a sale to clear out the contents. The noteworthy part of this story is that the owners had taken ill in the first half of Eisenhower's first term, and this clearance sale was being held in the 1980s. Apparently, the balance of demand and supply for retail space in Vancouver is heavy on supply. The things that now seem to generate the most activity downtown are the poker rooms off Main Street, but from the looks of it, their patronage is drawn from a small and exclusive clique of elderly gentlemen with chewing-tobacco habits and antisocial attitudes. I will admit that before looking around downtown Vancouver I was one of the many people in this world who make lounge bands feel unappreciated. But after driving around and looking at the empty streets and storefronts downtown one Saturday night, I began to understand how places like the lounges at the Stuart Anderson Cattle Company have become centers of social life in towns like Vancouver where local social life has otherwise melted away.

Mary, the lead singer of No Means Yes, mentioned to me right after I got to Portland that it was ideal that I was in town during their Stuart Anderson gig, since the band had recently turned the professional corner and was playing better than ever, and that a Saturday-night engagement at a Stuart Anderson was a better-than-average opportunity. The Stuart Anderson Cattle Company is a steak-restaurant chain in the Pacific Northwest that uses an aesthetically discordant mix of barn siding, stained-glass lamps, tapestry chairs, and oversize menus to create atmosphere and attract flush and fun-loving customers. Well-modulated self-promotion is another one of the Stuart Anderson characteristics; a favorite corporate slogan is "Our Appetizers Can Be Described in Four Words: Good Wholesome American Cooking." Good wholesome Americans can be found at the restaurants most days of the week.

All of the Cattle Company branches have bars; some of them have big bars with extruding stage-and-dance-floor pods where bands perform. It has never been a policy at the Cattle Companies to cultivate a reputation as an enterprising musical venue. The policy appears to have been very effective. Musicians hired to play at the Cattle Company understand that they have not been hired to apply their interpretative powers to songs or to communicate the burning yearning they feel when they pick up a guitar. Their task is to entertain customers who are waiting to be seated. Their other task is to entertain the many people who come to drink and dance but are planning to do without the steak. On weekends, it is especially important that the band keep the lounge lively, since the Cattle Company bars are popular destinations for a great number of people in the area who are out on Saturday night. This is not to suggest that the Cattle Company doesn't appreciate what a band can do for ambience, but the official philosophy runs more toward the position that many elements are necessary to making sure customers enjoy themselves; in this equation, well-mixed drinks, attractive waitresses, and bands are given equal weight. As Andy Gilbert, the Portland talent agent who handles No Means Yes, once explained to me, "In an original-music situation, it's the band that draws. In a Top Forty situation, it's the club that draws. The Stuart Andersons are a Top Forty situation, and people go there because they're familiar with it and with what the situation offers."

Andy Gilbert also told me he had started booking acts at the bars when he noticed what he likes to describe as "a pretty hot B-band situation developing at the Stuart Andersons," which translated into non-talent–agent vernacular means that moderately experienced bands and Cattle Company bars appeared to have a potentially profit-bearing mutual relationship. Lounge bands rely on their booking agents to have a precise sense of these things. An A band would expect to be booked into the right A-band situation—which would be a bigger, posher lounge at someplace like a Holiday Inn. A C-band situation would be in a small town or in a more downscale restaurant than Stuart Anderson or someplace near a midsize airport. A D-band situation would most likely be something like what I saw in the Satellite Room, a bar in a part of Portland that time has apparently forgotten, where a guy with a microphone hooked around his chin, a keyboard hanging on a strap around his neck, and a drum set wired to his foot, was singlehandedly—literally—working the crowd into an entertainment frenzy. Aging doo-wop bands, folk singers with one decade-old rock-and-roll hit, relatives of better-known performers, reunited 1960s girl groups, and blues musicians getting over widely publicized substance abuse or serving the last few months of parole can play an A- , B- , or even C-band situation, depending. There are no E bands or E situations, as far as I know.

Mike: "The Cattle Company is a pretty good gig. It's middle America. You don't get rich playing in a place like this, but you also don't go to work every day thinking, 'Only five more years until retirement!' Sometimes I look at the people out there while we're playing and I think, Whatever life they've got, that's just not *it*."

Jeff: "We play five forty-five-minute sets—about four hours every Saturday night. We have to stick to real familiar, real medium stuff. People thrive on familiarity. It doesn't seem like we have to think about what we're doing up there, but if we're going to make it work, we have to put in a lot of thought. For instance, people aren't natural dancers. There's an *art* to teasing people into dancing. That's our job. Then for the people waiting for their tables in the lounge—it's up to us to help them make the lounge-to-dinner transition."

Burell: "Being in a band, we have to work every weekend, because if you're a band and you're *not* working on weekends, then something's wrong. Like you're not making any money. It's pretty lucrative to play a bona fide dinner set. I gag when I say 'dinner set.' I plan to play my own music someday, but in the meantime this pays the rent. We give up all our weekends, but that's the musician's life. My motto is 'Why Get Bored?' which is why I don't give up music and go get a straight job somewhere. My other motto is 'Why Starve?' which is why I'm willing to play in a Top Forty band, a lounge-type band, rather than trying to play just my own music and make zero bucks. We're into doing it right when we play. We know that if people in the lounge think they're having fun, they have fun, so it's up to us to make sure they think they're having fun. Sometimes we're just doing dog songs that everyone knows by heart, and we're just kind of slurping through the set, but as far as I'm concerned, we're still playing music and performing, and that's the real high."

Dan: "Before getting into a band, and in between bands, I've had a lot of other jobs—I drove a forklift, washed dishes, worked in a packing plant. Playing music is what I really want to do. Top Forty has its problems. For a Top Forty musician, the most important thing is to avoid getting bored. The stereotype is that musicians are always having a party up there, but it's not like that—it's work. Naturally, it's high-visibility work, it appeals to your vanity, and I would say we're all pretty vain. On the other hand, I personally do not know a single Top Forty musician who isn't terminally stoned who doesn't want desperately to get out of it and play their own stuff."

Mary: "I could hold a straight job, but to me, being involved in music is a dream. I've hung in there even when it's been hard. Top

Forty isn't glamorous, but it does pay the bills. At this point, though, I'd love to be playing our own music. There's a risk in playing your own music, because some people come to a place like Stuart Anderson thinking, 'Hey, man, I came here to hear some *Madonna*, not something I've never heard before that you wrote yourself!' Some places won't let you play more than one or two of your own songs. They've got their own worries. They have to keep the customers coming in. Top Forty clubs are really taking a nosedive these days— it's just harder to get customers. A lot of the clubs are going to prerecorded music and deejays. It costs them a lot less. So we've got to really work hard and appeal to the audience, which means playing those same old tunes. There are always some tunes that people really want to hear again and again that I'd love to put on the back burner and then leave the burner on high until they're charcoal."

The Thursday after I arrived in Portland, the members of No Means Yes were rehearsing in the basement of Jeff's apartment in southeast Portland, a crowded neighborhood of wooden bungalows with steeply peaked roofs and small front yards. Jeff's basement had an overabundant look. Besides a number of guitars, amplifiers, records, unidentifiable pieces of musical and electronic equipment, microphones, microphone stands, and parts of drum kits, there were several mismatched chairs that at one point long ago might have been new. It was four in the afternoon. The band members had just finished having breakfast. Among the other characteristics of lounge-band life is having a lot of breakfasts, since when the band is done working— around three in the morning, if you allow for the time it takes to dismantle equipment and drag it out of the club—the only restaurants open are twenty-four-hour diners serving pancakes and eggs. Mary mentioned to me once that she felt she'd eaten half her meals in the last decade at the Original Pancake House, a tepee-shaped place in southeast Portland that has the lock on after-hours dining.

Burell, who met me at the basement door, is the de facto president and senior statesman of No Means Yes. While all the members of the band have legions of experience, Burell is the only one ever to have belonged to a band that "went national" (Mister Nice Guy) and had a song on the charts ("We Deliver"). This has given him a stature similar to that which minor-league ball clubs confer on their one team member who played one inning in the big leagues a decade ago. Burell wears his eminence well. He is lanky and has adventurously styled fuzzy brown hair, a wide mouth, and the kind of husky laugh that segues into a smoker's cough. Like the other band members, he is in his mid-thirties. He plays bass, sings, and writes songs. Once, for a year and a half, he stopped performing and instead worked as an engineer for other bands. This was shortly after he and his fellow bandmates at the time experienced a tragic but common bar-band accident: all their equipment was burned up when their band van caught on fire, leaving them in a fairly bad situation. Burell got uninvolved in the situation by taking some engineering jobs and then quit those when he was offered a chance to play with a successful Top Forty band called the Shakedown, later renamed the Shakers. "The Shakers made *tons* of money," Burell says now of the experience. "The problem is they spent it on frivolous things like houses and cars when they should have been buying recording equipment." The other problem was that after making tons of money, the Shakers followed the customary route and broke up. Burell then got in touch with Jeff, whom he knew well enough to know that he wasn't happy with the band he was in at the time, and the two of them founded No Means Yes.

As the rehearsal began, Burell and Jeff were discussing a few new songs they had been hearing on the radio, and after a few minutes agreed on the ones they thought would be requested at the Cattle Company this weekend. Rather then buying sheet music, they decided to listen to a tape of the songs and figure out the music and words themselves.

"Listen to this," Jeff said, putting a cassette into a battered-looking tape deck and winding it forward to a mid-tempo rock song by Simple Minds. "I can't really understand the words. He really slurs them, right at the chorus. What is that second sentence?"

"It doesn't matter," Burell said. "I can just say something that sounds like the right words. How about 'Don't you look back/At the one fur head'?"

He started tapping a rhythm on a table and sang the line in a light, raspy voice, and then said to Jeff, "Does that sound right? Or

—

how about something like, 'Don't you take back/That one burr, Fred.' Or maybe 'Don't you look back/On the fun that's dead.' I think any of them sound fine. Look, Jeff, no one is going to care if the words are exactly right as long as they *sound* right."

"I'd stick with 'Don't you look back/At the one fur head.' That sounds better. I just wish Simple Minds would do us a favor and start enunciating more."

Burell nodded and hummed the line again. Then he said, "Jeff, man, the only problem is, do you think I can keep a straight face and sing the words 'fur head'?"

"It sounds the best, Burell. Seriously. Just stick with that."

"All right, all right," Burell groaned. "Hey, really, do you think this is any way to make a living?"

Jeff stretched and stood up. "It's up to you, man. You want a job at the electric company? I'm sure there's one waiting for you."

"I said all right, didn't I?" Burell said. He started to cough. "Hey, you guys," he said, after he had caught his breath. "I really want us to start thinking about a logo and buying some good lights pretty soon." Mike and Dan glanced up at him. "I mean it," Burell went on. "I think we've got to get a product going. Work on our own songs a little more. We don't want to play Stuart Anderson forever, do we?"

"By the way, Burell," Dan said. "What's our schedule now?"

"We're booked through November," Burell answered. "Pretty good, huh? First we're at beautiful Stuey Anderson's, and then we're at Branigan's in Beaverton for two weeks, and then at the Lone Star in Eugene for the next two."

"Branigan's?" Mike said, suddenly interested. "Big pickup spot. Friends of mine say that Branigan's is where all the Tektronics geeks go to pick up girls."

"Great," Burell said, rubbing his forehead. He looked pained and amused at the same time. He suddenly stood up and yelled, "I want you all to know that I am now living my lifelong dream. I am the social director of the Love Barge."

If observing the life of the lounge band took some of the romance out of music for me, I can still safely say that music itself has never faltered in its romance with Saturday night. Since at least the beginning of this century and the birth of contemporary popular music, the words "Saturday night" have been used in dozens of lyrics, as a kind of shorthand for a romantic abstraction that encompasses romance, absence of romance, rebellion, freedom, the outlaw life, and sex. "Saturday night" is more idiomatically utilitarian than just about any lyric, with the exception of "love," "moon," "my baby," and maybe "June."

In 1916, a man named George Meyer wrote a song for Al Jolson called "Where Did Robinson Crusoe Go With Friday Saturday Night?" Its chorus began "Every Saturday night they would start to roam/And on Sunday morning they'd come staggering home." It was one of the earliest popular lyrics to use "Saturday night" for connotation (even on a desert island, Saturday night was when you cast off your inhibitions), as well as the silliness and word acrobatics it allowed. Featured in a Jolson show called *Robinson Crusoe Junior*, the song was a hit. A lot of other Saturday-night songs followed, including "Saturday Night in the City," ". . . in Central Park," ". . . in the Log Cabin," ". . . at the Store," ". . . at the Corner Cafe," ". . . at Walhalla Hall," ". . . at Sea," and ". . . in Utah Valley." "Saturday Night at the Rose and Crown," by Noël Coward, celebrated a tavern where on Saturday night "everything would come right," as did an obscure song called "What'll We Do on a Saturday Night When the Town Goes Dry?" "Saturday Night," with words and music by P. G. Wodehouse and Jerome Kern, described the decline of a young woman's morals through the week, culminating with their bottoming out on Saturday night. Sammy Cahn's "Saturday Night Is the Loneliest Night in the Week" was made into a moody anthem by Frank Sinatra in 1944, just two years after the Glenn Miller Orchestra had a hit with "Juke Box Saturday Night." Other Saturday nights were celebrated in "Saturday" by Harry Brooks and Sidney Mitchell; "Saturday Date," played by Kay Kyser and his orchestra; "Saturday Night Fish Fry," a 1949 hit for Louis Jordan and the Tympany Five; and Duke Ellington's "Saturday Night Function."

The era of these songs was bracketed by world wars and characterized by simple romantic equations. It seems that the "Saturday night" of the time suggested something wistful (this is the night when lonely lovers pined) or escapist (this is the night when you left the troubled world behind you) or naughty (this is the night when men drank and caroused to excess and even dignified women let fly). Sam Cooke's "Another Saturday Night" ("Another Saturday night/When I ain't got nobody"), released in 1963, had some of the same goofy, melancholy sweetness and rambunctious horniness of the wartime songs, and a lot of contemporary-soul Saturday-night music still does, too—the Drifters' "Saturday Night at the Movies"; Earth Wind and Fire's "Saturday Night" ("Saturday nite/Shining down/Saturday nite's your curtain call/You found your place/After all"); a duet by James Harris and Terry Lewis called "Saturday Love" that begins "Never on Sunday, Monday's too soon/Tuesday and Wednesday, just won't do/Thursday and Friday, the weekend begins/But our Saturday love will never end"; Thelma Houston's mildly salacious post-disco hit "Saturday Night, Sunday Morning"; T-Connection's "Saturday Night" ("Saturday night in the magic city is such a trip/I couldn't feel better even if I was riding on the mother ship"); and "Saturday Night" by Herman Brood ("Chicks dressed to kill/Surrounded by boys like bees on the honey/Some do, some don't, some never will/I just can't wait/Saturday night/Saturday night/Saturday night").

When rock and roll appropriated the catchphrase for itself, the implications changed. Saturday night may be sweet and romantic, but in modern terms it is more importantly a time to ditch parents, shoot people, fight, drink, rebel, play music, be free of your boss, escape your teachers, ignore social convention, wear weird clothes, be with other kids, make a lot of noise—in other words, the temporal equivalent of rock and roll itself. My favorite Saturday night rock-and-roll song is still "Saturday Night" by the otherwise pretty awful Bay City Rollers; the song begins with a tuneless chant of the letters of the title, which sounds like a football cheer or a martial anthem, or like the whoops of someone recently liberated from bondage. The rest of the song's lyrics consist of a lot of stuttering and yelling about "heart and soul" and "the good ol' rock-and-roll road show" and about how the singer is going to dance with his baby all

—

night long. These are given something less than full lyrical development and, as a result, sound slightly banal. That still doesn't ruin the effect, because the song is really about nothing more than the exuberance of the yell "S-A-T-U-R-D-A-Y Night," treating it as if it were Morse code spelling out the message that rock and roll equals freedom.

Other songs about Saturday night: "Saturday Night Special" by Lynryd Skynyrd; "Saturday Night's Alright (For Fightin')" by Elton John ("So don't give us none of your aggravation/We've had it with your discipline/Oh, Saturday night's alright for fightin'/Get a little action in"); "The Heart of Saturday Night " by Tom Waits; "Saturday Night in Oak Grove, Louisiana" by Tony Joe White. Dozens of other rock-and-roll songs set their scenes on Saturday night—for instance, Bruce Springsteen begins "Tougher than the Rest" with the words "It's Saturday night" and Edgar Winter's "Easy Street" starts "Saturday night at the corner cafe/Had me some drinks and I'm feeling my way."

"Saturday night is the one free night, the night to go out and just do it," Burell once said, echoing a long line of pop philosophers including Noël Coward, Sam Cooke, and the Bay City Rollers. "It's all about cars and girls and fighting and drinking. It's one of those symbolic phrases that we songwriters are always looking for. Of course, as a musician, for me, every night is Saturday night, because I love what I do, and what I do is all about freedom, being what you are, and expressing yourself. The way I see it, if you're in some kind of lousy job where you have to wait until Saturday night to feel like a human being, then, hey, *quit your job.*"

Burell likes to begin the Saturday-night set by leaning into the microphone and saying, "Ladies and gentlemen, fasten your seat belts." This sometimes gets a rise out of the crowd and sometimes doesn't. He hates to begin and then immediately see the red light in the beam above the bandstand begin to flash. At Stuart Anderson's, this means someone's table is ready, and the band has to pause so that the hostess in the restaurant can call over the PA something like, "Burrows, party of four; Keiner, party of two; Cummings, party of seven." Announcements of this sort tend to interrupt the

SATURDAY NIGHT

musical flow. "That's just one of the little problems with playing at Stuart's," Burell says. "You just gotta go with it and hope they don't get you right in the middle of a good song."

You could be seated right next to the members of No Means Yes at the Original Pancake House someday and not realize you were sitting next to musicians, but on stage, they look the part. Makeup is liberally applied on performance nights, and when I saw them perform at Stuart Anderson's that Saturday night, each of them was wearing something that didn't look exactly like walking-around clothes. Jeff, the guitarist, who is tall and lean and has a rockabilly-inflected hairstyle, was wearing skintight black jeans, a sleeveless white shirt, eyeliner, and some cowboy accessories. Dan, the keyboard player, is stout and sleepy-looking, and had on an unconstructed paisley blazer, a tight jersey shirt with a scoop neckline, and long earrings. Mike was sitting behind the drum kit in shorts and a red T-shirt. Mary, the vocalist, has a large head, abundant dark hair, a long, thin neck, and a slender body; she was wearing a shiny black spandex bodysuit, fingerless lace gloves, and a shirt arranged so it fell off one of her shoulders—the Dickensian urchin look. Burell was wearing an Edwardian tunic with shoulder pads shaped like Alpine headwalls, fitted gray pants, and brown boots with stacked heels. The fifteen or so people in the bar when I arrived were wearing lightweight pastel leisure clothes. It was a mild, summery night, which meant that most people would probably stay outside late and not start their evening at the Cattle Company until ten or eleven.

At nine o'clock, Burell, bending over the microphone, said, "Ladies and gentlemen, fasten your seat belts. We're No Means Yes, and we are here to keep you happy." His manner was intimate and friendly. He winked at someone in the audience. A waitress taking drink orders began to roam around the lounge, which had eight stools at the bar and fifteen or twenty low-backed thickly upholstered barrel chairs arranged around small wooden tables with center stems, placed in a semicircle around the dance floor. The stage, the size of a desktop, was set in a tight corner of the room. After offering his greeting, Burell swung around on his heel and signaled to the band to begin, then glanced up at the flashing red light, signaled the band to stop, and took a deep, audible breath as the hostess read the names of a few parties.

"Let's try that again," he said, after the hostess finished. With that, the band broke into a mid-tempo song that I had heard twice on the radio that day. A man and woman, both of whom looked about forty and were wearing polo shirts and khaki slacks, walked over to the dance floor and began frugging. Earlier in the day, Burell had explained to me what he calls "The Burell Palmer Lemming Theory of Life," namely, that if you can coax one couple to dance, or get really lucky and have in your audience that one dance-happy couple who will move to anything—a drum solo, the hostess announcements, your original songs—you are bound to have a great evening. When the couple in polo shirts stood up and moved over to the dance floor, I saw a knowing and satisfied look cross Burell's face. A moment later, an elderly couple wearing square-dance outfits stepped onto the floor and began to touch-dance to the song. The rest of the people in the bar were engaged in conversation and seemed oblivious of the music. The song ended, another began and ended, the red light flashed, more people were called into the dining room. Another song began. The band's musical selections would have surprised no one who had been around a radio in the last three years. The execution would have surprised no one who has ever been to a moderately expensive wedding. Between songs, Burell and Jeff bantered, and then Mary would take the microphone, shade her eyes with one hand and say, "How're y'all doing out there tonight?" Mostly, no one answered; a few times, a man in a tan blazer who was sitting alone near the dance floor called out, "Fine, babydoll! Just fine!"

After several songs, Burell steadied the microphone with his left hand and said, "Now, we're going to play a little song by a young lady known as Madonna." One handclap exploded out of the far corner of the bar. "All we have to do is play one Madonna song, and the room breaks into total hysteria," Burell went on. "I've seen it happen. It's not a pretty sight. I'm going to gird my loins." Several people laughed. Burell smiled appreciatively. Four couples stood up and started to dance as soon as Mary began singing the first line. I noticed that it was already past ten o'clock; the number of parties being called to the dining room was dwindling, and more of the people coming in the front door were coming straight to the bar. When they finished with Madonna, Burell announced, "Now our dinner set is over, and it's time to rock and roll!" It was getting crowded in the lounge, but there was still an atmosphere of disconnectedness, as if each person or couple were alone in the room. Mary and Burell were leaping and thrusting with as much performance-style zeal as the tiny stage allowed but their energy seemed to emanate and then drop off at the end of the stage, as if it had bounced into an invisible shield. A few people danced to almost every song, but there was plenty of room on the little dance floor. No one was getting boisterous or impolite. In between songs, there was only the sound of couples murmuring to each other, and at one point, the voice of a waitress shimmying past me with a tray of drinks, calling out, "Mr. Long Island iced tea, where are you?"

During the break, Jeff said to me, "Vegetables. This is a crowd of vegetables."

"Quaaluded slugdom types here tonight," Mike said, with feeling. "God, I hate this kind of crowd."

The management likes the band to fraternize with the audience. It's good for business. As Andy Gilbert had told me, in a Top Forty type of situation, people are drawn to the club, but it doesn't hurt to nurture some cult of personality around the band. There are some B-band situations where a following can develop—say, in a small town with limited social opportunities, where it can become a big deal to be able to say you know someone in the band that plays at The Copper Kettle on Route 46. This is more of a neighborly feeling than one that results in hordes of women taking numbers for the attentions of the band members. Still, if you happen to be in a band that is mainly lounge decoration, even just a neighborly feeling is something.

As soon as the band takes a break at Stuart Anderson, a screen lowers from the ceiling into the middle of the dance floor, a logo saying "STUART ANDERSON MUSIC NETWORK: WE ENTERTAIN AMERICA" is flashed on, and then music videos are played until the band comes back. The rationale is that dead air in a lounge is unprofitable air.

People leave when it's too quiet. The bands hate the intermission videos. Mike was telling me that he found it all too ironic, since it's music videos that are putting so many Top Forty bands out of business. "People figure, why go hear No Means Yes play a Pet Shop Boys song when you can go to some other club that just shows videos and see the Pet Shop Boys play a Pet Shop Boys song? I don't like the fact that they play them when we're on break."

As the videos were rolling, Mary went over to talk to some people she had recognized, but then joined the other four band members, who were gathered at the end of the bar looking blue. Mary told them she'd been reading lips all night and had seen some curious exchanges taking place. "There's one guy," she said, and then interrupted herself and said, "Oh, never mind. I'd rather not say. But you know, people think the band is behind some kind of curtain or something, and they don't realize that we see every move they make. We know who's a good dancer and who looks ridiculous and who's putting the moves on who. It's like watching a soap opera. On a night like this, it helps to have something to watch, too."

"You know what we need? We need someone loud and obnoxious to break the ice out there," Burell said to her, scanning the room. He then cupped his hands around his mouth and said in a stage whisper, "Hey! Why don't one of you out there get loud and obnoxious? Please? Pretty please? The band you save may be your own!" He looked at his watch. "Nearly the critical hour here. At twelve-thirty, people usually decide if they're going to stick it out and really party or just give it up and go home."

Mary laughed and ruffled her hair. "I've got to go put on more makeup," she said. "Boy, this feels like it's going to be a long night."

Mike nodded and said, "After a night like this, when it doesn't go that well, I feel like I've just run twenty miles."

After a few minutes, the five of them got back on stage. There were now about twenty people in the bar—a few single men nursing amber-colored liquors, a group of five chunky women who were making themselves laugh, some couples in private clinches. The waitresses had taken to hanging beside the bar and examining their nails for minute imperfections. I took a walk around and saw that the restaurant was mostly empty. The parking lot was still partially full. The sign in the lobby that said "IN OUR LOUNGE: NO MEANS YES" had a few of its letters at a cockeyed slant, so that it looked like a title from a cartoon show. The band hadn't had a chance to get its promotional photograph taken yet, so the space where the band-of-the-week usually hung its picture was blank. I came back into the lounge as the band was finishing its first song, "Addicted to Love," by Robert Palmer. A woman sitting near me was telling her date, "I started with blended drinks. Then I switched to mixed drinks. I had shots later on, and now I'm on coffee drinks."

"Our next song is called 'I Wanna Be a Cowboy,' " Burell said when "Addicted to Love" ended.

"That's a dumb song!" a man at the bar hollered. Several people turned to look at him. He stirred his drink and then winked at the bartender.

Burell scratched his head. "Well, of *course* it's dumb," he said, sounding game. "Life is dumb! People are dumb!" Jeff started to laugh. He was hugging his guitar tightly under his arm. "So here's a dumb song for you," Burell said. A couple got up to dance, made it through the first two choruses, and then wandered out of the lounge. When the song was finished, Burell announced that the band was going to play one of its own songs. He and Mary looked at each other steadily for a moment, and then the band began a mild rock song that sounded inspired by Genesis, Simple Minds, and INXS. No one danced, but there was light applause. Burell then glanced around the room. He was starting to look tired, and his voice, always husky, had taken on a harsh rasp.

"Let me ask you something, okay? What do you guys really care about?" he said to the audience. He took the microphone with both hands, letting his bass guitar swing on its strap behind him. Mike and Dan gave each other bewildered looks; Mike put his hand on his cymbals to keep them from jittering around. Mary had her head bent down. "Honestly, what do you guys really care about?" Burell said. No one answered. "Okay, what's the most important thing you can think of? The most important—how about you there, in the stripes?" He pointed to a woman with curly blond hair who was wearing a rugby shirt. She was sitting at a table with a man with a mustache, who immediately put his arm across her shoulders. She giggled and mouthed something at Burell.

"*Nothing's* important?" he said, cupping his ear toward her. "What? It's obscene? Oh . . . it's obscene and important?" He shook his head. I thought he might laugh, but he just kept shaking his head. "All right, never mind," he said. "I don't want to know."

"Last call," the bartender announced. Someone booed. "It's one-twenty," the bartender said. "*Last* call."

"This is it!" Burell said in a quiet voice. "Let's get all you women on the dance floor."

Sometime after I left Portland, I spoke to Burell again. I was wondering what had become of No Means Yes. Burell told me that a little while after I had spent Saturday night watching them at the Cattle Company, Mary and Dan had gotten involved romantically and then had become born-again Christians and then felt that playing in bars was unsuited to their new convictions and they would have to bail out of the band. They announced this right after someone had designed a logo for the band, and right after No Means Yes had had a promotional picture taken and had lined up lounge bookings for a few months. There wasn't much warning, Burell said. He just woke up one afternoon to discover that he no longer had a band. Since then, he and Mike had set up a landscaping business to make money, and they had formed another band just for fun. The band is called the Jammies. They mostly play 1950s music, fun stuff, no pressure and not a lot of gigs. He now pays his bills with the landscaping.

We talked for a little while more. He mentioned that Dan was now playing with a Christian band, and that Mary had eased up a little and was starting to write some music with him again. Then I asked him to figure out something for me. After a couple of minutes he calculated that No Means Yes had been together about nine months and thirteen days.

Polka Dancing

Jessup, Maryland

Like most fashionable people, Cecelia Kostler knows when to dress down. Cecelia is an opinionated woman of eighty-two from Bethesda, Maryland, who takes fashion quite seriously. Her rule of thumb is to keep it simple except on the Saturday nights she spends at Blob's Polka Park, a dancing and beer-hoisting establishment in Jessup, Maryland. Cecelia has spent the last twenty-nine years' worth of Saturday nights at Blob's, so she has been able to maintain her own strict standards and still have quite a few occasions for dressing up.

At last count, Cecelia had three hundred and thirty-five outfits suitable for a night at Blob's. Her enthusiasm for wearing clothes is equaled only by her enthusiasm for acquiring them, so the collection is growing all the time. Some of the three hundred and thirty-five are traditional polka dresses—big, ambitious affairs with embroidery and puffed sleeves and shirring. The Saturday night I spent with her, she was feeling more original than traditional, so she had decided to wear an outfit of her own invention. This consisted of a ruffled white blouse, black bell-bottomed stretch pants, a silver vinyl belt with a large square buckle, silver spike-heeled sandals, a gold chain with walnut-sized links, and, as the most eye-catching addition, a side-vented, back-belted, zipper-fronted vest made of red Chinese satin and black-and-white artificial pony fur. "One of the best things ever," Cecelia says of the vest. "It is so nice to dress up on Saturday night. I think if you want to look nice, this is a very nice thing to wear."

Blob's Park was founded by a man named Max Blob, who emigrated from Germany to the United States in the late 1920s and settled on a farm in Maryland's rolling, grassy Anne Arundel County. The county was then mostly rural. It is now bisected by a six-lane freeway and is home to light industry, military installations, and a number of small orchards. After a few years in America, Blob built a small frame building beside his house to use as a gathering place for friends who had also immigrated to Maryland from Germany. His suggestive name notwithstanding, Blob was especially fond of polka and wanted a place to dance with his friends. The party room was so popular that in 1933, Blob named it Max Blob's Park and opened it to the public as a German beer garden and polka hall. The hall was rebuilt in 1958 after a fire, and in 1976 it was expanded to nearly twice its original size, but otherwise Blob's has been essentially the same place and has had the same purpose since Max Blob first opened it.

The current Blob's Park is closed every night except Friday and Saturday. If you were to walk by Blob's during the week, you would see a large, featureless, corrugated-metal building—maybe a warehouse or a small factory or a place where machinery was stored—set on farm fields that have lately become a lawn. If you came by on Saturday night, you would see hundreds of cars in the parking lot, and you would hear occasional blaring blasts of polka music, and you would see dozens of people strolling nearby outfitted in polka dresses or lederhosen, and if it were crowded enough and you stood on the lawn outside the hall, you would feel a thud every time the polka called for everyone to stamp their feet. At times like this, the building seems to be alive.

Katherine Eggerl, who took over Blob's Park after her uncle Max retired, once told me that she considers it a Saturday-night place. She said that a lot of people come on Fridays, but they've been at work late and they're tired. "On Saturdays, well, that's when it really comes alive," she said. "I just think Saturday is just more suited for this sort of thing." The sort of thing that "this sort of thing" seems to be includes the ingestion of knockwurst and brat-wurst, the expenditure of much energy on the dance floor, and the wearing of something special, as in, perhaps, a fake pony-fur vest. Mrs. Eggerl believes that the combination of knockwurst, footwork, and fancy clothes is too much to expect of anyone after a day of work.

Blob's has a high ceiling and it is so echoey that when I first went inside it struck me as having the cozy ambience of an airplane hangar, but the persistent, oily smell of sausage and the boisterous-ness of the crowd give it a much more homey party-in-the-high-school-gym sort of atmosphere. The room had dozens of metal tables arranged in rows around the dance floor and the bandstand. The chairs were the kind that are standard at political rallies and blood drives—that is, the kind of chairs that manage to stay cold in all circumstances. If you have the misfortune to be wearing a short skirt and sit down too suddenly on one of these chairs, you will probably be involuntarily sprung from your seat. Many beers at Blob's meet their end this way. One wall of the building was given over to the bar, a structure of dark shiny wood that was one of the biggest and widest bars I've ever seen. Above it, running the whole length of the room, was a wooden shelf filled with Max Blob's favorite things: ornate German beer steins and a hundred or so Elvis Presley artifacts.

When I arrived, Cecelia was standing with a group of people who were referring to her outfit in complimentary terms. This happens to her often. Even at Blob's, where unusual outfits make appearances fairly often, Cecelia is considered exceptional. "She comes here ev-ery single week," another regular once told me, sounding full of awe. "And every single week she's here, she's got something in-credible on." Cecelia usually receives the compliments with tolerant nods and smiles, in the manner of the Queen of England receiving subjects when she is in her box at the Royal Opera. This particular evening, Cecelia also had a pinched look on her face, and every few seconds she ran her finger around the collar of her blouse. After a moment, she stopped smiling and said, "This is a problem. Everyone likes my vest? Fine. It's very beautiful, I know. The problem with it is that it's too damn *hot*."

No one said anything. Then a short, dark-haired woman standing at Cecelia's elbow cleared her throat and said, "Cecelia, if you're so hot, why don't you just sit out a dance?"

"Oh, no I won't," she said. "Next week, I'll leave off the vest. I can't wait to come back next week. I'm going to wear something glittery."

Just then, another woman walked over and said, "Cecelia, it's so nice to see you tonight. You look wonderful, as usual. What a pretty vest!"

Cecelia bobbed her head. Suddenly, she unzipped the vest and took it off. "Here," she said, thrusting it at the woman. "You can have it."

The woman looked shocked. "I can't take your clothes!" she said.

"Take it! Take it! I have more things to wear."

"Cecelia, I *can't* take your clothes!"

"No, take it! Don't say no. Just take it. Just take it!" The woman hesitated, and then stuck out her hand and took the vest, holding it at arm's length, as if it might unexpectedly come to life. She gave Cecelia a weak smile.

"Oh, Cecelia, I don't know about you," she said. "I'll tell you, my husband will never understand how I got a hold of *this*."

Cecelia, who says that she has never missed a Saturday night at Blob's in her twenty-nine years of patronage, has straight white hair, a thrusting chin, small hands and feet, and a voice that can compete, volume-wise, with an accordion solo. It is a voice of enough assertion to confound the impression that she is a frail little old lady. She moved to the United States from Germany in 1953. Her husband had been a bookkeeper. She had lived alone in Germany for many years after he had died, but eventually she decided that she wanted to be near her daughter, Ingeborg, who lives in Rockville, Maryland, a suburb of Washington, D.C. After Cecelia arrived, Ingeborg installed her in a one-bedroom apartment in Bethesda, a suburb next to Rockville. Besides visiting with her daughter, Cecelia's social life was unexceptional. Then one Saturday night, a few months after she arrived, friends from Germany who lived nearby took her to Blob's Polka Park, an hour's drive from Bethesda. There is no simple way to sum up how she felt about that night. She now will dismiss the whole question by saying she has come to Blob's every single Saturday night since then.

We sat down and talked for a while about Saturday night at Blob's, about Maryland, and about polka. At one point, we were interrupted by a waitress who stopped beside us and rapped her knuckles on the table like a judge calling a courtroom to order.

"Anything from the kitchen?" she said.

Cecelia waved her away. The waitress, looking disappointed, shrugged and stomped to another table. Just then, the house band, Heinrich and the Rhinelanders, came up to the stage and dove into a polka. About fifty people got up and danced into the middle of the room, and most of the people at the tables started clapping. The band's accordionist moved his arms back and forth as if he were working with pruning shears, looking up between gestures and beaming at the crowd. The big room pulsed with the sound.

When the song ended, Cecelia and I started up our conversation again and began talking about clothes. We both professed to be ardent about them, although I suspected on the basis of her Chinese satin vest alone that her ardor might be more unbridled than my own. I asked what she liked to wear in particular.

"Hmm," she said, squinting in thought. "Oh, I love to wear clothes." Even though her apartment in Bethesda was small, she said, it had five closets. "That is good for me," she went on. "You know, all of my closets are full. I have so many clothes it's unbelievable. That's why I don't care about one vest, the vest I gave away. One vest, when you have so many clothes, is really nothing at all." Two of her closets, she explained, were just for ordinary clothes like dusters, housecoats, cotton housedresses, and pajamas—in other words, things that someone who favors Chinese satin vests might find a little pedestrian. She described these to me in that kind of offhanded way a grocer who's serious about French cheeses might use to tell you when you ask what he's got by way of canned tomatoes. On the other hand, she brightened when I brought up the question of what the other three closets contained.

"Clothes for polka!" she exclaimed. "Those are the good ones. Three closets of polka clothes. I have three hundred outfits at least."

"Three hundred?"

"You don't believe me? You want to know what I have in there?" Cecelia demanded, leaning across the table. "I've got beaded belts— do you know bugle beads? I've got bugle-beaded belts. I've got a dress that's blue—no, really it's more a purple color. It's trimmed in braid. Not braid. Maybe braid. It looks like gold. I have a gown made of, oh, what's it made of? Satin?" She craned her neck around and saw a drowsy-looking blonde woman in a tight blue sweater slouched at the table behind ours.

"Helen, what is that gown of mine?" Cecelia called to her. "What is that gown?"

Helen shrugged and rolled her eyes. "Satin?" Cecelia asked her. "Okay, you don't know? Okay, I don't know either. But it is a wonderful gown. It has got the sequins. Not all over. It has sequins on the edges. Beautiful. I have many polka dresses from Germany. Polka dresses, those dirndl dresses. I have many pantsuits. I have pantsuits in orange and one in blue and one bright red. I love pantsuits. I love my pantsuits. Helen, you've seen my pantsuits?"

Helen shrugged again. Cecelia raised her eyebrows and gave me a look. Done with the look, she went back to her list. "Okay, I have pantsuits. And I have, I have, oh, what do I have? Embroidered sweaters. I have beaded sweaters. Those are different from the embroidered. I have a paisley blouse. I have some capes. I don't know why I have the capes. It's hard to dance in the capes. I have some pleated skirts. I don't even remember all my skirts." She chuckled. "Oh, my god, I don't even remember, I have so many skirts! And I have many things in gold. I mean, gold material. Many things of gold material. And you saw my fur vest. I have *wonderful* clothes. I have a silver pantsuit that's especially good. I like when people dress up here. It makes the atmosphere better."

She stopped. Maybe she had emptied her closets. She clasped her hands together and smiled at me. A moment later, she unclasped her hands and began adjusting the waistband of her pants.

—
73

"Do you like to dress up for polka?'" she finally said.

"I dress up whenever I can."

She winked again and then took a photograph out of her purse and passed it to me. It was a picture of her in a purple satin three-quarter-length dress, white bloomers, and silver slippers. In the picture she was standing with her arm around an Arnold Schwarzenegger look-alike who appeared to be about twice her height and a quarter her age.

"My favorite dancing partner," she said, tapping the picture. She gazed at it for another second and puckered her lips. "Don't I look good in that dress? I think that's a really good dress."

We sat admiring it for another minute while Heinrich and the Rhinelanders finished another song. The crowd on the dance floor had swollen and begun to spill toward the tables. Cecelia grabbed my hand and whispered, "I want you to know something else. This is a true story about me that I'm going to tell you now." She gave a dramatic pause.

"Here at Blob's," she said, "they call me Liberace's grandmother."

Cecelia went off to check herself in the mirror in the ladies' room, so I took a turn around the room, stopping at a table of middle-aged women who had been dancing most of the evening. In repose, they made unlikely dancers. They were broad-hipped and fleshy and their hair was done up in identical stiff-looking cone-shaped hairdos. They were all wearing polka dresses.

"This is the only way to polka," one of them said to me, fluffing her skirt.

"Don't let anyone tell you different," another one said. "I love to wear a polka dress. It drives my husband crazy that I'm always buying new ones." She gestured behind her at a man who was working a toothpick with concentrated effort.

The first one stopped laughing. "My husband, too," she said. "Oh, I sneak the bag into the house when I buy a new dress! He thinks I'm nuts."

"Nuts?" her friend said. "I'll tell you who is nuts. He's nuts. You look so nice whenever you're at Blob's, and he always looks like a slob."

Cecelia, who by day usually wears a duster or a housedress, and who would never come out on a Saturday night in anything less than, say, a silver-lamé bell-bottom pantsuit or a chartreuse satin cape-and-skirt set, had returned from the ladies' room when I came back. She looked happy now that she had unloaded the vest, and was doing as much of the polka as one could perform in a seated position.

"You talked to the ladies in the pretty dresses, didn't you?" she asked. "Don't they look nice?" She glanced around the room. "I tell you, though, there are certain people whose names I don't want to say who I think could dress up a little better. I can't understand how people could come to Blob's in sloppy clothes." I realized that for someone who put so much thought and attention into her clothing, a night out in which she would encounter pairs of torn jeans, dirty Reeboks, and T-shirts with stupid sayings on them might provide endless irritation. She pointed to some soldiers who early in the evening had told me they were on furlough from nearby Fort Meade. "See that? Such tight pants! I don't like that," she said. "I like the boys, they're very polite, but the pants are not so nice."

A woman, probably a Johns Hopkins coed, in a miniskirt: "I don't believe in that. I don't believe in the short skirts."

A man in a leisure suit: "I know him. He comes here all the time, that man. He looks nice, but his hair is too greasy."

A couple in German polka costumes: "Beautiful. That is so beautiful."

A man in jeans; his date in a Mickey Mouse sweatshirt: "*Aaach!*" She gestured as if she were brushing the offenders off of her table. "*Aaach!* I don't know why they even come. Dressing up for the Blob's Saturday night is the most wonderful thing. I love to even think about it. I love to buy my clothes and love to pick my clothes for Blob's. I love to dress up for the polka hall and get ready to go to Blob's every week."

By then there were a few hundred people in the hall. Most were middle-aged and beyond. About half of them were dancing and the other half were not—they just talked, wandered around, waved to one another, ate sausages, hollered across the room, wandered more, formed and unformed little conversational groups. A man I know who has come to Blob's now and again over the years once told me that many people come here with friends, and that many regular customers have gotten to know each other just because they see one another here so often. He said that he himself had many Blob's friends—that is, people he'd come to know by seeing them here every weekend for years—but that he thought that he wouldn't recognize them on a street wearing something other than their polka clothes. At any rate, a lot of Blob's customers only see each other once a week, and only at Blob's, so all night throughout the big room, there were little reunions: the mechanic from Fallston spotting his favorite dance partner, who is a hairdresser from Baltimore, and the plumber from Bethesda running into the housewife from Joppa he had shared a sausage with the week before. People roamed around and bumped into one another and looked excited to see one another all night long, moving in time to the fidgety rhythms of the polka band. The room had that pleasant feeling of contained but constant movement I associate with beehives.

I had not really come to Blob's expecting to make lists of clothes—I had actually come to watch people dance, since that is something people have always liked to do on Saturday night. I knew that this was not the perfect time to investigate dancing, since even though ballroom, swing, and square dancing were the currency of Saturday nights in the past, they have declined enough these days to be categorized as relics, and where they still exist they are marketed as athletic or aesthetic pastimes rather than social ones. The most recent nationwide dance craze was disco, which peaked a decade ago. Many discos that were regularly packed back then are now holding aerobics classes on slow nights. When dancing was still a national fascination, new clubs—especially in New York—so immediately engendered a culture, attitude, behavior, and mobs of habitués upon opening that they instantly canceled out any notion of what life might have been like before they existed. Their social weight was so palpable and called up such an instant and full-blown life of their own that it was always hard to believe that the warehouse or factory or abandoned subway tunnel they were in had supported some previous use. Clubs were so culturally important to those people who were drawn to them that they were like galaxies filling black holes. But since then, many new night spots have been designed for sitting, not dancing, and the premium put on being energetic is now applied to looking good on a couch.

According to its partisans, folk dancing has suffered less in this downside dance economy because it had not been part of the boom, and so it is not really a part of the bust. In what will certainly come to be viewed as a glitch in the social continuum, there was a brief moment in this decade when certain artistic young people became enamored of polka and its weird phlegmatic rhythms and naive, delightful charm, as if they had come upon a giant piece of found art. Polka was trendy once before that, too. This was around 1830 or so, when it emerged from Bohemia as an antidote to the waltz, which was dominating Europe. Polka's invention is usually described with this apocryphal tale: a peasant girl in a Czechoslovakian town is seen dancing in the town square by Bohemian composer Josef Neruda, who finds her rambunctious invention fetching and inspirational. Neruda then composes music for the girl's dance and takes it to the Paris stage. When first introduced, polka was considered a vulgar dance full of ecstatic, primitive energy that contrasted nicely to the foppish precision of the waltz. It soon became the craze in Paris; in Central Europe it became a sort of emblem of nationalism and a native treasure.

Since being transported to America, polka halls have been to German and Slavic immigrant culture what dim-sum houses are to the Chinese; the fickle interests in them from the outside that have swept each into vogue and out again have never really changed them for the people for whom they had served as de facto community centers. Even now, with popular dance somewhat on the slide and the artistic and punk pursuit of exoticism diverted to whatever this week's newfound cultural shard might be, polka is back in the hands of its genuine devotees, wherever there's someone with an accordion and sausages, and a German or Slavic community still able to muster the necessary number for some of polka's more ambitious line maneuvers.

Even at Blob's, where since 1933 polka has been king, the dance floor has also served not just as a dance floor but as a display area for clothes. This is true of dance in general. The important element of disco, for instance, was not the steps to the Disco Duck but rather the strange things that people wore, and knowing the way you were supposed to flap your arms and turn left (or was it turn right?) was insignificant compared to the delight you felt when you finally found just the right tiny disco purse and spandex body stocking. Dancing in any form is as good an excuse as Saturday night for dressing up. When I say "dressing up," I don't mean putting on something with a lot of starch and buttons—I mean wearing something that is different from what you have to wear when you're not following your impulse to have fun. This rule does not always hold true—there are certain varieties of investment bankers, for instance, who don't seem to leave the house without a yellow foulard-print tie in place on any day of the week—but on average, I would say that most people find that Saturday night cries out for a change of scenery, personal apparel and otherwise.

This was on my mind when I came across something written by a sociologist named Marshall Sahlins suggesting that there is a well-upholstered theory about the Saturday night/clothing equation. Sahlins wrote, "We substantialize in clothing the basic cultural valuations of time"—that is, clothing can define situations and distinguish one event from another better than almost anything else, which is why it has always been a critical part of every ceremony from pre-Christian ritual lamb slaughters to white-tie weddings. Sahlins went on to say that time itself can't be made "different," but the experience of certain times can be made to feel different, and clothing is what can make distinctions in time seem and look real. Eventually, certain clothes become symbolic of specific times—for example, cocktail dresses, morning coats, wedding dresses, business suits, and that fashion category known as "weekend wear." In England, there is even something called a Friday suit, worn by proper gentlemen only on Fridays to signal the beginning of the weekend and the upcoming exodus to the country. The only people who fail to understand the association between the right clothes and the right occasion are those who are severely disassociated from reality. It occurred to me that if Sahlins is right, Cecelia is the sanest person I've met in a long time.

—

Someone who has spent a great deal of time considering the twin issues of clothing and time is a professor I know named Eviatar Zerubavel, who has written a few books about the origin of the seven-day week. Not long before I visited Blob's, I went to see Professor Zerubavel at his home on Long Island, where he lives most days of most weeks. Professor Zerubavel told me that his research had also supported the idea that clothing and the week were interwoven. He also mentioned that he had never been to a polka parlor and couldn't address any of his comments to polka in particular. He then said that the earliest formal proposals for specific weekend wear were in the Talmud, where stringent directions for the proper observance of the Sabbath are spelled out. Anyone who wants to honor the Sabbath properly is told to maintain two separate sets of clothing: one for everyday use, and the other to be saved for the Sabbath. Women are advised to even keep Sabbath-only jewelry. Anyone who can't afford two separate wardrobes is advised to at least do something *different* with what they have on the Sabbath—in the language of the Talmud, to at least drape his cloak in a special way.

"The purpose of Sabbath clothing and the later Christian tradition of Sunday best is the same as the modern-day ceremony of dressing up for Saturday night," Zerubavel said. "If you put on special clothes, you can make concrete the theoretical notion that one day of the week is somehow different from another, and that there is such a thing as 'ordinary time' and 'extraordinary time.' Clothes become the tangible evidence of what are just abstract ideas about the distinction between one twenty-four-hour period and another."

I asked him if there wasn't a simpler explanation—namely, that people dress up on Saturday night because they're trying to attract a mate. I reminded him of a popular store in New York called Saturday Night Lingerie, which has taken this concept to its extreme, selling garters decorated with toy guns as well as a full inventory of the kind of lingerie (crotchless panties, leopard-print teddies, black bras, day-of-the-week underwear) that some people consider romantic. Zerubavel shook his head.

"I don't know anything about the store, but I understand the concept—calling it 'Saturday Night' is probably a way to indicate to the consumer that this is a store that specializes in special sexy underwear. And that is certainly part of why people dress up on Saturday night. But there is another, more basic reason. People have an innate need to be able to mark off units of time, and they need a way to treat different days differently. Changing into special clothing is a very satisfying way of making one night seem special. Look at married people. Look at elderly people. They still make clothing an important marker, and they are presumably not looking for a mate." Zerubavel then directed me to a book of etiquette written in 1924, which proposed that the progression of thought that has led to wearing the right clothes is the story of human civilization itself: "In the world of good society, dress plays an important part in the expression of culture. There is proper dress for afternoon wear, and another for evening functions. There are certain costumes for the wedding and others for the garden fete. The gentleman wears one suit to business, and another to dinner." The treatise ends by suggesting that there is a critical connection between man's development and proper apparel. "Where civilization has reached its highest point," it says, "there has dress and fashion reached its finest and most exquisite development." That is the point where I began to picture civilization at this moment in time: Saturday night as a sort of secular Sabbath, and Saturday-night clothing finely and exquisitely developed, including, but not limited to, silver sandals, gold chains, black bell-bottoms, and red-satin-and-pony-fur vests.

I often think about this when I recall what a nudist told me a few years ago. I asked him whether there are any circumstances under which even a committed nudist will give in and put something on. He thought about it for a moment, and then said, "I'd say we serious nudists would go without clothes all the time, unless we're in a dangerous situation, like when we're cooking bacon." Later, he said that nudists do in fact give special consideration to Saturday night. This particular nudist happened to live in and manage a nudist enclave near Tampa, Florida, called Paradise Lakes—a full-service colony with hundreds of condos, rental apartments, and recreational facilities for nude residents, including a Paradise Lakes theater group. (At the time he and I talked, the Paradise Lakes theater group was presenting *Barefoot in the Park*.)

"Like people who wear clothes, some of the residents here do like to do something special on Saturday night," he said. "On Saturday, I've noticed that many of the guests who come to our nude disco will be wearing body jewelry. They might wear something pretty like a tummy chain, for instance. Some of them also wear a very nice gold neckpiece with the Paradise Lakes emblem on it that we sell at the gift shop. It looks very striking displayed on skin.

"I would say that when people *really* want to dress up for the weekend, though, they will draw on themselves with felt-tip markers, and some of them might wear funny hats."

Given her twenty-nine years of Saturday nights at Blob's, Cecelia's table has acquired the permanence you would associate less with a table than with an address, and people dropped by to visit with her all night. It is in a perfect spot, on the lip of the dance floor with a clear view of the Rhinelanders and within inches of the kitchen. Waitresses with trays loaded with bratwurst crossed back and forth behind us all night, and anyone venturing onto the dance floor would walk directly in front of the table and then teeter on the edge, as if negotiating entrance into a swimming pool. Cecelia, against her earlier protestations, had decided to sit out a few dances so she could talk to me, but she kept her feet tapping and would slap the table in time to the music every now and again. At one point, Cecelia spotted a young woman wearing a black-and-turquoise polka dress who was walking past the table.

"Hello, Eva," Cecelia yelled to her. "Go dance, go dance!"

"Omi!" she said. "Hello, Omi! I'll sit with you." She lowered herself onto a chair.

"Eva is here every weekend," Cecelia said to me.

"Not like you, Omi," Eva said. "I miss some." We talked for a moment, and she told me that she had been in a serious accident three years earlier and couldn't work any longer. She said she had come to Maryland from Czechoslovakia about ten years ago, and

—
81

that coming to Blob's was like a trip home. After a few minutes, her boyfriend, a barrel-chested man with black hair and a nervous smile, stopped by the table.

"This is my boyfriend. He's Greek," Eva said, taking his hand. "We can almost not talk to each other."

"Who needs to talk?" Cecelia said. "Just dance."

"I don't dance," Eva said to Cecelia. "Taki don't dance." She smiled and took his hand.

"Come on and dance, Eva," Cecelia said. "You're dressed up to dance."

"I like to dress up," she said. "I have ten polka dresses. Taki gets mad if he knows I buy another dress. But I love to buy new polka dresses."

Cecelia drummed her hands on the table. "I buy whatever polka dresses I want," she said. "No one is going to say to me ever that I have enough clothes for Blob's."

Eva pressed her hands against her forehead. "The week for me feels very long. I like to go to have my hair done on Saturday afternoon, and then Taki picks me up and we come to Blob's. I love that." She stood up slowly. "Bye-bye, Omi. Now Taki and I go back to our table and try to talk a little."

A lot of people come to Blob's in couples, and during the evening they dance together and then they break up and dance with different pairs. Cecelia told me that she usually alternated among several partners. Her favorite, the hulking young man in the photograph she had shown me, hadn't made it to Blob's this evening, which annoyed her no end. She had plenty of other partners, but he was her favorite. Cecelia made it clear, though, that all these men were strictly dance partners—in the twenty-nine years since she'd been coming to Blob's, no man had touched her except in those mano-a-mano maneuvers essential to a few polka moves.

"I take a nap every Saturday afternoon to get ready," she said. "I dance with the men here. Then I go home alone at the end of the night."

The band announced that they were taking a short break, and the people on the dance floor broke into applause and then wandered off to their tables. Cecelia began checking her clothes. She tightened her sandal straps and rebuttoned her blouse. She buttoned and then unbuttoned her cuffs. I didn't realize it then, but she was getting ready for the moment that she waits for every Saturday night—the moment that makes every one of those three hundred polka outfits worthwhile, the way that a fisherman might consider thousands of dollars in equipment justified by one good strike. After a few minutes, the band came back onto the little stage, and the accordionist motioned to Cecelia.

"I'll be back," she said to me. "Watch me." She stood up, smoothed her blouse once more, and marched onto the dance floor. At that point, about fifty people moved to the center of the room and formed a circle around her. She steadied herself and then waved at the accordionist. He began to play, and Cecelia began to dance. The entire hall was still, except for Cecelia.

This dance, like Cecelia's incredible outfits, has become a kind of tradition here. Every Saturday night after the band takes its break, she walks onto the dance floor and takes a solo turn. People who come regularly talk about it the way anthropologists talk about certain Samoan rituals—something that has emerged without formal introduction and insinuated itself into the collective sense of normal life. The dance is more expressionist than formalist—a flurry of kicks and hops and a lot of spinning around, finished off with a full complement of Rockette-style high kicks. Her face alternated between a wide smile and studied concentration. Her bell-bottoms flapped and the chunky gold chain around her neck banged up and down, just missing her chin on each swing. She danced for several minutes and then stopped, raising her hands at the end like a triumphant boxer. The crowd broke into applause and whistling. Cecelia bowed several times and then marched back to the table.

"I looked pretty good, don't you think?" she asked me.

I said she looked wonderful, and I meant it.

"Now you understand why someone like me needs so many clothes," she said. "You see, I'm in the public eye."

Blob's is a plain old barn of a place, and it's so close to a busy whizzing state road and an active Mobil gas station that anyone with a decent throwing arm could lob a knockwurst from its front porch onto the Super Unleaded tanks. But when you drive down the long winding driveway and walk in the door on a Saturday night, it feels as if it's miles from anyplace else. Some of its regulars observe that Blob's has this odd effect—once you've put on your polka clothes, and driven up Max Blob Road to the hall, you feel transported in some indescribable way. They say that without really thinking about it, they're in the door, dancing the Silver Slipper to Heinrich and the Rhinelanders, wearing something made maybe even out of Chinese satin, and feeling in the thrall of something remarkable. Most importantly, they say, when you're in Blob's, you know that it's Saturday and anything but another average night.

Scene Making

Los Angeles, California

Except for Cecelia, who will probably retire the title of Saturday-night clothing champion, my favorite contenders were two well-heeled and well-dressed Los Angeles high-school students I got to know shortly after my trip to Blob's. A trip to Los Angeles had struck me as the obvious next step after Blob's, since Blob's had gotten me so interested in Saturday-night clothing, and Los Angeles is the American city that is most dressed up. Considering that Saturday night is the night that most people in most places are most dressed up, a Los Angeles Saturday night was a concept squared.

Naturally, Hollywood has made dressing up a professional thing in California, but the attention to style there has transcended the industry, and these days Los Angeles has become a place where everything and everyone looks art-directed and executive-produced. I am waiting for the inevitable moment when someone I know decides to leave Los Angeles because they can't afford the right clothes. It is not even easy to shop in Los Angeles. It is full of scary stores that have one or two pieces of merchandise, lots of Italian metal shelving, and a handful of salesgirls who are always dressed in something ferocious-looking, like asymmetrical leather tunics that look like leftover costumes from *Dune,* and who are usually too busy to wait on you because they're doing something like giving themselves French manicures in preparation for their roles in the next Butthole Surfers video. Clothing in Los Angeles is not for amateurs. There is a whole local aesthetic addressing the issue of sunglasses alone.

My trip was actually prompted by a letter from one of the high-school students, a young woman named Cristina Clapp. In her letter, she described to me the complex strata of Saturday night Los Angeles social life and suggested that I would be remiss to miss it. Her taxonomy was so precise and intriguing that I immediately arranged to meet her and her friend Chris Liu for a night in the city. She had warned me that I shouldn't mistake them for run-of-the-mill teenyboppers: Los Angeles kids, she said, were heavily into sophistication. "It's hip to be an adult now," she had written. "We're not into kid-type stuff. It's not hip to say 'hip,' though. We say 'in vogue.' It's in vogue to be sophisticated, which is what we're into. For instance, Chris and I were the youngest people to be at Ma Maison the night before it closed for renovation."

Cristina and Chris grew up in the California canyons in two of those nice rambling houses that always seem to come with in-ground swimming pools and parents with credit cards. They told me they had met in a high-school freshman French class and soon realized they were kindred souls, and had spent virtually all their weekend nights together from that point on. In fact, they make a nice-looking pair. Cristina has a blonde bob, a small, sharp nose, and an athletic build. She likes French films. She is seventeen years old but can for sustained periods affect the weary, irritable vocal manner of a forty-year-old marketing executive in a sales meeting. Chris is tall and skinny, half-Chinese and half-French—an ethnic combination that in edible form happened to be the current favorite with Los Angeles's fickle restaurant crowd just when I got to town.

"That's *chinoise,*" Chris had explained to me when we first met. "*Chinoise* is very hot right now. I guess that makes me hot, too."

"*C'est vrai,*" Cristina had added. "Chris is utterly cool."

According to a schedule Cristina had drawn up, we would meet early on Saturday evening so we could tool around the Beverly

Center—a glitzy mall in Beverly Hills that was a requisite Saturday-night sortie for any self-respecting young Angelino—and still have enough time to hit a couple of clubs. I was instructed to wear something simple and to say, if asked, that I was from out of town and had lost my luggage. Cristina and Chris, on the other hand, said that they would be bringing along a few changes of clothing. "We have a different outfit for each place we go," Cristina said. "We believe that we should have the right outfits for each place in order to enjoy the night totally."

When the two of them arrived to pick me up, Chris was blinking rapidly and tilting his head back so that he could look forward without opening his eyes too far. It made him look both haughty and pained. Just as I was wondering if it were a new teenage affect, he mentioned that his contact lenses were bothering him. "These aren't actually corrective lenses," he said. "They change your eye color. My eyes are this awful brown, really. In reality. With these, my eyes look blue. They're illegal in this country. I bought them in a shop on Melrose Avenue. Four hundred dollars under the table to the guy who owns the shop. I know it's a lot of money, but I'm quite happy with the effect." He said he only wore the lenses on weekend nights. Both his parents and Cristina's thought the two of them spent too much money on clothes and too much time at clubs, and he said they probably would not be especially enthusiastic about his buying blue eyes. I asked how he had gotten around the problem, and he smiled and said, "I just use a little strategy. I just put them in after I leave the house, at the gas station where Cristina and I often change in the course of the evening. And I try to remember to take them out before I get home." So far, the system had worked. The only problem was extraparental and interocular: the contacts abraded his corneas.

"Cristina, I've got to take these out," Chris whispered, as we pulled onto Melrose. "They're killing me."

Cristina, who was painting on eyeliner as we were talking, stopped in mid-eyelid and gave him a harsh look. "Oh, Chris, leave them in! I cannot *believe* you! You look truly great! You look like the guy David Bowie played in *The Man Who Fell to Earth!*"

Chris squeezed his eyes shut. "Cristina, they're *killing* me."

"Come on, Chris. I'm telling you, you look *so cool.*" He sighed and shut his eyes.

As Cristina had promised, the backseat of Chris's Volkswagen Bug was jammed full of alternate outfits for the two of them to choose from as they went from place to place. "See, if we're going to several places, we need several changes," she said. "Tonight, for example, we're going to start at the Bev Cen, which is what I would call suburban-trendy."

Chris nodded and said, "Very suburban. I wouldn't necessarily even call it trendy."

"Well, it's trendy, too. Maybe not trendy of-the-moment exactly trendy, but it's a trend place. It is. I mean, it's probably going to be out pretty soon. But for the moment, it's a trend place. Then if we want we could go on to the Electric Circus, which is Anglo-Hollywood hip. It's very mod. The influence is the early Who. If we go there, it will mean we'll change out of our Bev Cen clothes, which is what I'm wearing now." She twisted around in the front seat to give me a better look at her outfit: a red V-neck pullover, an ivory blouse, baggy plaid pants, and patent-leather saddle shoes. After a moment, she said, in a low voice, "You're sitting on my mod outfit, by the way." I pulled a black-and-white miniskirt out from underneath me. We turned onto La Brea and ahead of us I could see the Beverly Center, a dark monolith that covers eight acres, is eight stories high, and has fifty-two functioning oil wells in the basement.

I said that in my experience, most teenagers' Saturday-night choices extended no further than deciding on which stretch of sidewalk they were going to exercise their freedom of assembly.

"Not in L.A.," Cristina said. "Here, there is a wealth of resources and we like to partake of them. Maybe that's pretentious. But we're certainly not *boors.* We don't spend money on our cars and stuff ourselves with pizza every chance we get. We have refined and fairly eclectic taste. That's why we like going to a few places on Saturday night. It's rather boring to just go to one place. Chris and I are creatures of many different scenes, right?" Chris nodded in agreement. "For instance, we go to the Bev Cen, but we're not really Bev Cen types. That's too boring. Of course, we're not decadent-bored. We're just looking-for-culture-bored."

We drove along listening to the radio and slowing down in front of restaurants Cristina wanted me to see. They all had dark, glassy facades and valet parking. "Valet parking is definitely hip," she said. Then she interrupted herself and turned to Chris. "You're not going to wear that to Mod Nite, are you?" she said. It sounded like a command rather than an inquiry. At the time, Chris was wearing a black turtleneck jersey and gray pants.

"Oh, sure," he said, rolling his eyes at her. "Cristina, what do you think I am, a real fool? I brought my houndstooth suit."

Cristina smiled at him and then turned back to me. "Maybe some other Saturday night we'd start at Dirtbox, which is kind of brainy-artsy. That would mean we'd change into something like, oh, maybe black jersey and a miniskirt and big earrings. I don't think I've got those in here tonight." She reached over the seat and rummaged through some of the clothes. She then said that they sometimes go to Carlos Guitarlos cowpunk concerts (wearing cowhide, Tony Lama boots, silver accessories), and sometimes they start the evening in Santa Monica, which is beach-freak territory (jams, gauze shirts, sunburns), and end up in Westwood, which meant they would have to change into something jock-but-chic (cotton tops, plaid shorts, Vuarnet sunglasses). On the matter of clothing, they seemed as rigid as Stalinists. Chris said they occasionally turned down invitations offered to them along the way if they didn't have the right thing to wear. Bear in mind that this does not parallel anything else in their lives. The Los Angeles school dress code, for instance, is so mild that it barely manages to advise students to leave explosives at home. By contrast to the laissez-faire of their dress for school, the exactness of their clothes for Saturday night was breathtaking.

"We embrace style, but of course, our favorite thing is fine din-ing," Chris said. Cristina had told me earlier that he occasionally made reservations for dinner under the name "Calandre." Chris added, "We really appreciate French food. We also like good wine. This year we ate regularly at Ma Maison. We love nouvelle cuisine. We're really disappointed that it's been closed for renovation, be-cause we really enjoy it. You know it has an unlisted phone num-ber, don't you?"

—

. . .

We parked, took the elevator to the mall, walked down the long corridor, stopped in a toy store, left without buying anything, walked past the huge crowd waiting to get into the Beverly Cineplex, looked at and rejected menus at a few restaurants, and finally sat down at a cappuccino stand. Chris complained that he forgot his pipe. We spent a few minutes talking about teenagers in Los Angeles in general, and youth gangs in particular. Cristina said that the skinhead movement had spawned a lot of gangs. In England, the movement is strongly associated with neo-Nazi politics. In Los Angeles, it is more strongly associated with the fashion statement of Dr. Marten shoes and shaved heads.

"I hate to tell you," she said, twisting a piece of hair. "I think skinhead is going to be the next big thing. Ugh."

"Did you know that five hundred teenagers arrive in Los Angeles each day without anything?" Chris said. "They come here with nothing. They're just hoping to get involved."

Cristina let out a long sigh. "The main thing is that at the time you're in a scene you make a real commitment to it," she said to me.

We sipped our cappuccinos. Dozens of teenagers walked by and lined up in front of the movie theater. Chris pointed to someone wearing a nice leather coat and looked wistful.

"Maybe it's good that Ma Maison is closed for a while," he said to Cristina. "We were spending an awful lot. We always bought a fine wine with dinner." When I looked surprised he said, "Oh, they knew we were underage, but they understood we were not your average teenager looking to get drunk. This is not Ripple we're discussing. We really appreciate a fine wine."

"We both look forward to dressing up and going out somewhere elegant," Cristina said. "School, in my opinion, is simply dull. I like Friday, but it's not as big a night for us as Saturday. Sometimes on Fridays I actually baby-sit. Saturday night is when we really like to go out. If we go out, we always take the trouble to dress."

"Clothing is extremely important to the Los Angeles teenager," Chris said. He rustled around in his pocket, pulled out an herbal cigarette, lit it, and then leaned back in his chair. He held the cigarette in that upside-down way perfected by French actors. Then he said that upper-class Latin and Asian teenagers in the city had taken clothing to new extremes. Even the rich kids from the canyons couldn't compete. The new wave was called "The Fashion Crowd" and gathered at clubs to show off their clothes to each other. The best-dressed girls were called "vogues" and the boys were "GQs."

"In this city, maybe during the week you're just a regular kid, but on the weekend, you are what you drive and what you wear," Chris said. "During the week, you just wear your school clothes, but on the weekend, you want to express yourself. You spend everything you have to do it. You want to be in Versace or Armani or Chanel, and maybe Valentino and YSL. Leather is very important. Sunglasses are very, very important."

"Watches are important, too," Cristina said, and turned to Chris. "Don't you think watches are important?"

"Cartier," he said. "Anything from Fred."

Cristina interrupted him and pointed to a short man walking by. "Chris, look, there's that guy! I know he's somebody."

Chris looked at him and then said, "I don't recognize him, Cristina. Maybe he's in a commercial or something." He shuddered and said he thought the worst thing in the world would be to be a character actor in a commercial.

Cristina said, "Can you imagine? You'd go around and people would say, 'Oh my gosh, it's the Pepto Bismol man!' *Très, très* terrible. The coolest thing, on the other hand, I think, is to do a cool art film or be on the cover of *Interview*."

"Or to have guest-spotted on 'Miami Vice' when it was still good," Chris said. He puffed once on his cigarette and then stubbed it out. "Listen," he said. "Let's go, okay? We're about to have to pay for another hour of parking."

"See what I told you about skinheads?" Cristina said, as we bought our Mod Nite tickets. Behind us in line were four large, pink-headed kids wearing white shirts and big black shoes. She and Chris exchanged knowing looks. Mod Nite is a dance party held every other weekend in a gay Latino disco called the Electric Circus, which is next door to a rockabilly dance hall and across the street from a hard-core heavy-metal place, an Asian social club, and a punk after-hours club. It was a fairly diverse neighborhood. Apparently, when the Electric Circus is leased for Mod Nite use, the Latino regulars stay away in droves. Teenagers from around the city, who like Motown music and tidy, early 1960s British style, flock in. The night we were there, Mod Nite had attracted about seventy-five teenagers, a few of whom had shaved heads and the neo-Aryan attire typical of skinheads. The rest of the kids looked as well fed and snappily dressed as Cristina and Chris, who had stopped at an Exxon station near the Electric Circus and changed into their mod clothes after we left the Bev Cen. Chris was now wearing a black turtleneck and black-and-white houndstooth suit with pegged pants. He had a handkerchief square in his coat pocket, and it drooped over the edge of the pocket. Cristina was wearing the skirt I had been sitting on, a black top, black tights, and black-and-white shoes.

Not long ago, the mod ethic had been described to me by the young woman who supplied the records for the Mod Nite parties. "Mod is a way of living clean under rough circumstances," she had said. "It's really just punks who look cleaner and have ideas like that the government really sucks." I had run this definition past Chris and Cristina, who looked unimpressed. "That doesn't really explain it at all," Chris had said. "It doesn't explain that mod is a sophisticated style."

"Mod attracts smart kids who are cosmopolitan," Cristina said. "A lot of our friends are interested in mod. They're not mods, and we aren't mods, but we appreciate what mod *is*." I asked them what skinheads were. "Tougher," Cristina said. "Valley kids. I don't know, maybe more small-town kids. Mods are totally different."

After we bought juice at the bar and looked around the room, Chris and Cristina started dancing. It would not be entirely accurate to say they were dancing together, because, like most of the kids at the club, they were positioned in front of a mirror that covered one entire wall of the Electric Circus, and as much as they could have been said to be dancing with anyone, they were dancing with their reflections in the mirror. Having spent the night before this one at a private Hollywood nightclub where I watched Harry Dean Stanton dancing with three Asian girls while he talked on a cordless telephone, I had come to believe that there was a whole landscape of dancing in Los Angeles that was yet to be explored. After about ten minutes, Cristina took a break and came over to talk to me. "I'm mortified," she said, catching her breath. "My little sister is here, and she looks pretty unenlightened." She started laughing and then said, "What I mean is, I told her not to wear what she's wearing. She just doesn't quite have it."

Chris joined us and we all went downstairs to the parking lot for fresh air. There were about twenty kids striking a variety of practiced, languid poses on and around the cars in the lot. "Listen, Cristina," Chris said, when we found the Bug and leaned up against it. "You're not going to believe this, but Lisa shaved her head." Cristina gasped. Chris told me that Lisa was a friend of theirs who had been a mod—or, rather, a mod appreciator—and recently she had gotten friendly with some skinheads and had mentioned that she might actually shave her head. "No one really thought she would do it," Chris said. "Skinhead is just, oh, I don't know. I mean, it's not the same as style. It's . . . I can't explain it." He stood there for a moment, looking perplexed. We leaned against the car for a few minutes, breathing the night air. Just before we left to go back upstairs, a stocky girl walked up to the Bug. Her head was entirely bald. She had the aspect of a cute, pinkish light bulb.

"Hi, Cristina," she said in a low voice.

"Hi, Lisa," Cristina said. She looked down, and then looked away, and then down again. In all the time I'd spent with her, this was the longest she'd been quiet. After a minute, Cristina said, in a brisk voice, "Okay, listen, we really better go. We're going to see if that new after-hours club is open yet."

On the ride home, we stopped at the Exxon station again and waited while Chris took his contacts out. The guy working the pumps gave us a dirty look when we pulled in. It was the third time that evening we'd used his bathrooms and we had yet to buy any gas. While Chris was in the bathroom, Cristina and I sat in the car and talked. She was still marveling over Lisa's newly bald head. I asked her whether this meant that she would have to add skinhead to her repertoire of styles. "I don't really think so. See, that's what I said about skinheads," she said. Chris walked out of the bathroom rubbing his eyes and got back into the car. "There used to be three or four skinheads in all of L.A.," Cristina went on. "Now there are three or four *hundred. C'est vrai.* God, I don't want to shave my head."

"So, don't," Chris said. "It'll pass. Hey, let's go to a gallery next weekend." He looked into the rearview mirror at me and said, "You know, in Los Angeles, there are at least fifty or sixty performance art galleries. There's also Film-X, the film exposition. Cristina, when is Film-X? Film-X is very cool."

Cristina, who was staring out of the window, said, "Being mod is cool."

Chris made some light coughing noises. "Come, come, now. This should all be amusing, Cristina. We are the embracers of style, *n'est-ce pas?* By the way, did you know that someone opened a club just for transvestites?"

Cristina put her chin in her hand and struck a contemplative pose. "Now what would you wear to that?" she said. Then she started to giggle. "Forget it, Chris," she said. "We definitely do not have the right clothes."

I was sort of sorry to hear, some months later, that Cristina had decided to go to college at a small semiprecious liberal arts school on the Eastern Seaboard, where I knew the standard outfit to be something plaid and preppy—sort of a street version of a field hockey uniform—and weekend wear is just the same, plus earrings. It seemed that someone with such a knack for fashion would be wasting herself in knee socks and glen plaids, with or without earrings. From what I hear, though, she made the transition in style.

Killing

Pembroke, North Carolina

For reasons that are likely to remain unknown forever, Charles Roscoe Brooks decided sometime on or around Saturday, November 8, 1986, that he no longer wanted to date Joan Locklear Jacobs. At the time, Charles was fifty-four years old, divorced, and painting houses for a living in Pembroke, a small town in North Carolina's hilly Robeson County. According to some people, Charles was the sort of man who enjoyed the company of women but also the sort of man used to making his own breakfast. His relationship to Joan had been a famously unquiet affair. They had courted for a while, then lived together for a while, and then, at Charles's suggestion, went back to keeping separate homes. Around the time they moved apart, Charles abandoned a steady drinking habit and seemed determined to change a lot of things in his life. He kept seeing Joan after they moved apart, and she still talked hopefully about getting back together, but people in Pembroke now say that by that time, Charles's attitude had changed and it was clear that the relationship wasn't long for this world.

On Saturday night, November 8, Charles invited Joan to come over and asked her to bring the gun she'd borrowed from him.

95

When Joan arrived at his home on Chapel Road, Charles was sitting at the kitchen table, sipping a cup of coffee. He looked grim. There were none of the customary familiarities couples usually exchange on a Saturday night. Joan said hello and told him she had brought back his gun. After a moment, she put the gun on the table and poured herself a cup of coffee and sat down. Charles got up and started to leave the room; on his way out, he told Joan to read the letter that was sitting on the table. It was a note he had written telling her that he didn't want to see her anymore.

According to the Chapel Hill coroner's report, Charles and Joan then started a "discussion/argument." Joan later told the police that Charles "had broken up with me and told me he did not want to see me anymore." The report continues: [Joan] states she then got a gun and told him she did not want to live without him and was going to kill herself. Charles insisted that she was not going to kill herself in his house." In fact, Joan did not kill herself in Charles's house. She stood at the door with the gun pointed at her chest. She yelled at him, said she wanted to die, and cocked the trigger. The gun clicked once. Charles grabbed it. It clicked again, discharging two bullets into Charles's right axilla—the chest—directly over the heart. For a moment, he stood upright. By the time the police arrived, Charles Brooks was dead.

Some time ago, I started gathering reports of Saturday-night homicides from coroners around the country, and the account of Charles Brooks's death was among them. At the time, I had been collecting anything I came across that had to do with Saturday night. At first, I expected the coroner-report collection to remain a modest one. Then it began to grow faster than the lists of song titles and newspaper stories about towns holding their first Saturday-night dance in fifty years, and controversies about cruising and incidents of snake sacking and cow toppling, and all those other things I usually thought of as part of Saturday-night culture. This, of course, is no accident. As American Saturday-night traditions go, crime—and particularly the lovers' quarrel punctuated by a fatal gunshot wound—is more of a standard than, say, bowling. This is not to say that most people end their Saturday nights with an act of violence, and it is unlikely that there will ever be more people murdering one another on weekends than going to the movies. But Saturday night is the high time for almost every kind of violence. Everything that makes Saturday night distinctive for pleasant reasons also makes it the night that mayhem is likely to take place.

Death certificates make peculiar reading. Many of the ones I collected sounded like synopses of better-than-average prime-time television crime shows. Some of them were far more sensational than the murder of Charles Brooks. A report I received from the coroner's office in Cleveland described an incident in which a man was stabbed to death at his own surprise birthday party. A terse, handwritten form from Portland, Oregon, recorded the murder of a "transient-type" woman, who, after a long night of drinking, was picked up by someone in a van and was tossed out, dead, a few blocks later. The strangest came, as did Charles Brooks's, from North Carolina. It described a murder that took place at a card game in a college dorm in Durham. According to the report, the card game was interrupted late Saturday night by a knock on the card-room door. One of the players answered it and found a nervous-looking student standing in the doorway. A strange man was standing behind him, demanding to know the whereabouts of someone named Darryl. The students at the card game later told the police that they couldn't figure out what was going on—among other things, they didn't know anyone named Darryl—so they shrugged the whole thing off as a drunken prank and returned to their cards. A few seconds later, the stranger shot the nervous student to death and fled.

It happens that there have been more remarkable murders in Robeson County, North Carolina, in recent memory than the murder of Charles Brooks. Julian Pierce, a Lumbee Indian attorney who was bidding to become the first Indian judge in this largely black and Indian county, was killed in his home by three blasts from a shotgun a few months ago. A year before Charles Brooks was killed, a supervisor at a local textile plant was kidnapped, raped, stabbed, and left to die in a weedy field outside of town. Some months after that, three Indians who had gone fishing in a local river were found shot to death. The county sheriff's son shot a man—rumored to be

---

an unarmed drug dealer—for swinging a bucket at him, a few days after Charles Brooks died. The first woman executed in the United States in decades was Thelma Barfield, a Robeson County grandmother who was found guilty a few years ago of killing a half dozen of her relatives and husbands with ant poison. A Thelma Barfield copycat, a man who had lived in Robeson County his whole life, was convicted last year of having poisoned his wife with homemade turnip-arsenic soup.

As a matter of fact, Robeson County is full of murders. Nearly everyone in the county carries a gun. The county murder rate is the highest in North Carolina and 100 percent higher than the national average. Gunplay is not out of the ordinary in this sort of place. Racial tension and economic hardship make for short tempers. Such a context makes an argument over ending a relationship—or over a few dollars or over a perceived insult or over the question of when Person A was going to start respecting Person B and the A-B relationship—less than memorable, even if the resolution is fatal. Such a context makes the death of a local man who fell into an unsatisfactory negotiation with his girlfriend and his gun somewhat run-of-the-mill. This happens to be exactly what interested me about the murder of Charles Brooks. It is the most commonplace sort of violence—domestic murders, five-dollar muggings—that take place on Saturday night, for reasons that have a lot to do with everything else that is true about Saturday night. Such unnatural events turn out to be a natural part of the tradition.

When do crimes take place? Until a few years ago, there were only educated guesses and hands-on experience to answer that question. Everyone had the feeling that Saturday was rather wild and woolly, but no documentation existed. Then, a few years ago, sociologists at Northeastern University in Boston traced numbers and types of calls the Boston police received and then showed their hourly, daily, and weekly distribution. They wanted to show that weekly crime patterns reveal more about social habits, and would be more useful in police staffing and crime prevention, than studies that just chart the quantity of crime rising and falling throughout a year.

The report covered the years 1977 to 1982, and in the end

showed that all the educated guesses had been right. Crime has a specific and predictable weekly pattern. The report showed that 20 percent of all criminal homicide calls to the police came on Saturdays. Fridays were second (17 percent), and the rest of the week was far behind. Rape and assaults were much higher on Saturdays than any other day of the week. Nineteen percent of the weekly family-trouble calls came on Saturdays. Sunday accounted for another 16 percent of the week's total calls. A third of the entire week's noisy-party complaints were made about Saturday night parties that had lasted into Sunday morning. (The calls clustered between 12:01 a.m. and 1:59 a.m. Sunday morning.) Money crimes (robbery, larceny, and burglary) were highest on Friday—payday— and second highest on Saturday. Gang disturbances, vandalism, and the catchall category of "drunks/disturbances" were highest on Saturday, as were car accidents and complaints about cars blocking driveways.

The study concluded that every type of police service but one was in highest or second-highest demand on Saturday night. The only exception was reports of abandoned cars, which was at its weekly low on Saturday night. I asked one of the researchers what he attributed this to. He said he thought a car got abandoned for one of only two reasons: It might have been stolen and had to be gotten rid of, or it was a junker being dumped for insurance money. He said that he thought that in either case, you might be inclined to keep the car until you were done using it for the weekend.

The Boston report didn't cover high-profile crimes such as terrorism. "Never on Saturdays," says Charles Bahn, a terrorism expert who teaches at John Jay College of Criminal Justice. "News coverage of Saturday events is too erratic, which terrorists don't like, since they rely on coverage to make their actions significant. Also, it's harder to plan a terrorist attack for a Saturday because the movement of people, air traffic, buses, trains, and so forth is so different from the rest of the week." Sometimes, of course, the erratic news coverage of Saturday events works exactly to the benefit of the criminal. Anyone who wants to commit in private a crime or an act that would ordinarily draw a lot of attention would be best to commit it on Saturday night. It seems quite likely that the phenomenology of Saturday night is exactly what Richard Nixon had in mind at the time of the Saturday Night Massacre.

Murder and family fights are the most characteristic violence of Saturday night. People are with one another for longer stretches and in closer quarters on weekend nights, and these extended times together—what family psychologists call "increased time at risk"—mean more opportunity for them to drive each other crazy. There is also more sexual tension on Saturday nights. Couples on regular working schedules are together the most on weekends. Saturday is the only night that neither follows nor precedes a day of work, so you can sleep in Sunday after a late Saturday. Saturday becomes the night when sex seems most possible and likely.

Over half the homicides in the United States are committed by friends or relatives of the victim. Of those, fully half are a case of a spouse killing a spouse. These are exactly the people who are going to be together on a Saturday night, rather than strangers. A study of homicides in Chicago recently concluded that except in very rare cases, homicides are committed for these reasons in this order: general domestic disagreements, money, liquor, sex, love triangle. Take away the word "disagreements" and "triangle" and you have the standard ingredients of a typical enjoyable Saturday night. In 60 percent of all murders, the murderer or victim or both have been drinking. The majority of people who drink do the majority of their drinking on Friday and Saturday nights. Saturday night is usually the more drunken of the two nights, because most people don't have to work at all and can start drinking earlier in the day. There is even a condition doctors call "Saturday-night paralysis"—nerve damage caused by sleeping too long in a strange position, which usually only happens to someone who is falling-down drunk. Most murders occur on Saturday night and very early Sunday morning, between 8 p.m. and 2 a.m., at which point anyone who has been drinking steadily will be fully drunk.

Occasionally, drinking excessively and homicide and Saturday night combine in an extraordinary way. A police officer I know told me that one Saturday night she was sent to investigate a murder in a bar. She didn't rush to get to the bar because the dispatcher had said that the victim had been shot right between the eyes, and no

KILLING

amount of speed on the officer's part appeared likely to change the course of his personal history. While she was writing up the homicide report, the supposedly dead man sat up, stared at her, and groaned. It turns out that he was so drunk that he had passed out more from surprise and inebriation than from injury and hadn't even felt the bullet, which, through some miracle, had merely lodged under his scalp. While the officer leaped away in shock, the man reached up and touched his forehead delicately, and said, "My God, do *I* have a *headache*."

There is a very good chance that the man with the headache had been shot with a handgun. Most people are. Light, easily concealed, small-caliber handguns have been known by a number of curious brand names and nicknames. The Protector, the Little All-Right, Little Giant, Tramps Terror, Banker's Pal, Little Joker, and the Pocket Positive were all brands of handguns manufactured in the 1850s. The Four-Barrel Sweetie, also made at that time, was advertised as "smaller than the female hand." The Wesson Escort ad campaign proclaimed the gun "Small Enough to Fit in a Uniform, Yet Packs Enough Fire Power to Pull You Through When the Going Gets Rough!" The nicknames are a lot more to the point. Before it was called the Saturday Night Special, the small handgun was called Murder Special, Suicide Special, 7–11, Bellygun, or the Manstopper. The most popular nickname, of course, is Saturday Night Special.

Different sources claim to have come up with the name, but credit is generally given to the residents of Detroit, who supposedly coined it in the late 1950s or early 1960s. It is fitting that a gun would be christened in Detroit. One story about labor leader Sidney Hillman maintains that on a tour of the city years ago, he exclaimed, in frustration, "Guns! Always guns! Why is it there are always guns in Detroit?"

In the 1950s and 1960s, it wasn't as easy to come by a gun in Detroit on short notice—say, on a Saturday night—as some people in Detroit apparently would have liked it to be, whereas an hour away, in Toledo, Ohio, there were loose gun laws and firearms for sale in most convenience stores and markets. A Saturday-night cruise out of the Motor City, topped off by the purchase of a Man-

101

stopper .22 in Toledo, became a Detroit-style date of some popularity. It was a cheap date, too, since some of these guns sold for as little as three dollars. It was around this time that people in Detroit started calling the guns "Saturday Night Specials," since Saturday was a popular time to go to Toledo to buy one, and because the guns were so often bought to settle something that had seemed particularly annoying—a debt, a cheating spouse—on Saturday night.

In their heyday, small handguns were made by fifty different companies in a dozen different countries including the United States, Italy, Spain, and Germany. They were bought with enthusiasm by Americans. In the first twenty years after their introduction in 1850, 150,000 handguns were sold in the United States. In 1968, U.S. Tariff Commission records show that $450,000 worth of guns valued between four and eight dollars each were imported into this country. It is not likely that they were admired for being finely tooled machines. In fact, like the murders they figure in, Saturday Night Specials are known for being fast, short, unpredictable, unreliable, and full of unexpected drama. They will sometimes fire accidentally when dropped from as little as six inches. They are notorious for backfiring, and upon occasion one will discharge so erratically that it will end up killing the person firing, rather than the person being fired upon. In 1968, noting delicately that these small guns "far too often mar the urban weekend," Congress passed the Gun Control Act banning the import of Saturday Night Specials. The term Saturday Night Special gained a legal definition: any gun with a barrel length of less than three inches.

The law was soon discovered to have a manufacturer-friendly loophole. The Gun Control Act banned guns but not the import of gun parts, so the American Saturday Night Special market simply converted into a two-step business. Brazilian, German, Italian, and Taiwanese handgun manufacturers shipped parts, rather than the finished product, to brand-new American assembly plants. Miami, where residents now have the same ardor for firearms that Detroit's citizens had been known for in the past, became one of the most popular locations for assembly plants. In 1985, 1.5 million handguns were put together in this country. That same year, RG Industries—the American assembly branch of the German gun manufacturer Roehm Gesellschaft—went out of business, complaining that the cost of liability insurance had gotten too high. The decision followed several lawsuits against the company alleging that the guns had blown up, fallen apart, fired backward, or killed innocent people.

The name Saturday Night Special has outlived the names Manstopper and 7–11 and Bellygun and Murder Delux. It has also outlived, in connotation, the limits of its legal definition. Almost anytime there's a dispute resolved by gunfire or any murder involving a firearm, the weapon will be described as a Saturday Night Special, whether the gun involved is a five-dollar, five-ounce, Asian-made two-inch-barreled Little Joker or an $85 Charter Arms Undercover tempered-steel sixteen-ounce collector's-item pistol. A Saturday Night Special is understood to be any weapon bought in a hurry and used in a pinch—an instrument of an act of passion that seems most characteristic of Saturday night.

Saturday night is also a big time for criminal business. By this I don't mean the Joan Jacobses of this world, those sad cases who will be, once and probably once only, so bummed out by their boyfriends or girlfriends that they pop them with the closest pistol or poke them through the heart with a kitchen knife and spend the rest of their lives sorry and in jail. I mean the crime professionals who regularly and purposely break the law. For most of them, Saturday is the biggest night of the week because of money.

Saturday figures into the economy in an unusual way. In an industrialized society, weekdays are for production and weekends are for consumption, and Saturday is the biggest consumption day of all. Most Americans buy most of everything they buy, including clothes, cars, jewelry, and groceries, on Saturdays. On Saturday night, people spend like crazy, too: it's the biggest night in restaurants, movies, theater, bars, dance clubs, skating rinks, bowling alleys, and video-rental shops. Money is more important and more on our minds than usual on Saturdays. Most people spend it more, carry more of it, and need it more than at any other time of the week.

At the same time, Saturday, the big-money day, is the one business day of the week when banks are closed. This has given rise to a special breed of businessman—a sort of vampire businessman, who does most of his business on Saturday night. Thanks to vampire businessmen, the crimes of commerce flourish on Saturday night. It is quite logical: people carry more money, so they're better targets for robbers; they need more money, so they're more likely to borrow it in unorthodox places, such as the neighborhood loan shark; they spend it more in cash-only transactions, such as drug deals and gambling.

Arthur Kill State Correctional Facility, a medium-security prison on the far side of Staten Island, is known among prison regulars as Artie's by the Sea. It is thought of, by people who have made prison life an area of personal expertise, as relaxed and pleasant. It is surrounded by flower beds and the salty smell of the nearby ocean. Artie's is full of vampire businessmen—drug dealers, loan sharks, small-time hoods, muggers—because many of them fit the requirement of requiring only medium-level security and having a fairly short length of stay.

Not long ago, I went to Arthur Kill to talk to some former vampire businessmen. After walking past beds of marigolds and daisies and being frisked by a sour-looking guard, I was taken to the empty office of a prison functionary who had stickered most surfaces in his office with Garfield the Cat paraphernalia. The office's small window opened onto a little garden that led to a walk that led to double security doors that led to the rest of the world. Artie's is the largest general-confinement facility in the New York City area, and most of its inmates, like most of the inmates in the entire New York State prison population, come from the New York City area. Since Artie's also caters to inmates at the tail end of their sentences, it is also full of people who are just a few months from leaving, and just a few miles from home.

The inmates who were going to talk to me were assembled amid the Garfield-stickered furniture. Their personal histories were various. David was slight and studious-looking, and wore the kind of wire-rimmed glasses that are standard issue for English professors, which is what he intends to be as soon as he gets done in jail. He told me he used to be an armed robber. Chris was barrel-chested and thick-thighed—body by steroids—and had spiky blond hair; he said he had been a drug dealer, loan shark, and an occasional car thief before coming to Artie's. Gus, Chris's best friend, who said he was in for murder, was also thick and muscled but his hair was shiny and black, and he had a barking voice and the sort of alarmingly loud laugh that makes you wonder what you just said that's so funny. The other man, Thomas, used to drive a bakery truck and said he had done a little extralegal appropriations-and-removal work on the side.

I asked the men what Saturday night had meant to them in their previous situations.

"I liked Saturday nights really well," David said. "They were a great time for me. Man, I loved Saturday nights! I mostly ripped off drug dealers when I was outside, so it was great. They'd be doing a lot of business and have a lot of cash on Saturday night, and I was doing a lot of my business, and ended up with a lot of cash, too. I guess you'd call it a cycle. They had cash, and that way, I got more cash. I did some jobs on other days of the week, but Saturday was really the best, because there was so much more money around."

"I loved Saturdays, too," Gus said. "I loved them because I'd have these guys come to me who were absolutely frantic for a little cash for their dates. They'd come to me, like, 'Hey, man, I really need to impress this chick, I got to get some money.' I mean, where are you going to get money at that time of night? I don't mean from the bank machine, either. I mean, these were loans for some guy who wanted to impress his date. I made loans all week long, but on a good Saturday night, I could do $5,000 of loans."

"I had a group of friends who would rob the same goddamn Lafayette Radio store every Saturday they needed cash," Chris recalled. "It was like the bank for them. It got to be sort of funny."

"I remember those guys!" Gus said. "Every weekend?"

"Really. Every weekend. The store owner must have been going out of his mind."

"Whew," Gus said, sounding impressed. "If I was him, I would have invested in a security system."

We talked for a while, and the men agreed among themselves that it wasn't just the atmosphere (freewheeling, careless, devil-may-care), but the access to customers (people on their way to having fun, wanting drugs or money) and inventory (people, on their way to having fun, not paying attention to the drugs and money they were carrying) that made Saturday night special. "I used to say that there's more opportunity for Murphy's Law on Saturday nights," Gus added. "See, on Saturday, there's more going on and there's more money. People carry more cash, so they're going to get ripped off, and they need more cash, so they're going to look for ways to get it. There's just more going on, so there's just more ways for things to go wrong."

The rest of the men nodded their heads at him and smiled. The conversation struck me as being exactly what I would have expected to hear from a group of retired pharmacists fondly recalling flu season.

"The only thing is that it wasn't all great," Gus said. "It really wasn't. I can tell you that things could get a little crazy on Saturday night. I also believe that the cops are out to make your life especially miserable on Saturday night. That's the night I got popped."

I asked him what happened. "Well, I'll tell you," he said, his voice dropping into a deep register. "I was just doing my usual hanging out, and things were going on, and eventually, there was a *disagreement* about some bullshit."

"What exactly was it about?"

"Money I'd say," he said, shrugging. "And consequently a murder occurred."

Thomas looked up. "Mine was murder, too," he said. "Hey, Gus, what night did your incident occur?"

Gus said, "It was, oh, gee, now let's see. I'd say it actually *was* a Saturday night."

"So was mine!" Thomas said, leaning far forward in his chair. "Maybe there's something to this! My incident was on a Saturday night, too!"

Time and again, when I've asked people what they most wanted to know about Saturday night in America, they would say they wondered what it was like to be in prison on Saturday night. Rarely did the people who mentioned this seem to have a particular interest in the penal system. I finally decided that this recurrent curiosity came about because many people wonder what Saturday night would be like in a place where you are cut off from everything Saturday night embodies—freedom, extravagance, romance, socializing. Prison is such a place. Even time itself has a different quality in prison, since you are "doing time" and see it as a distance to be traveled, rather than a condition of being alive.

The men at Arthur Kill Prison told me that in prison Saturday night was still different from the rest of the week. The warden at the prison agrees. "I like to keep the week different from the weekend," he said to me. "Life inside here should be as much like life outside as possible. You know what would really scare me? A prison full of guys so out of it that they didn't care about Saturday night any more." On Saturday night at Arthur Kill, curfew is later; there are visiting hours; there are extended hours for use of the telephone; there are no classes or normal work schedules. Movies are shown at nine and eleven on Friday and Saturday nights. Often prisoners "date" other prisoners—that is, arrange to spend the night together, without its necessarily having any sexual connotation. Gus recalled that when he was in a much more restrictive prison, some of the men would hold small mirrors outside their cell bars so they could talk to the men in the next cell and see their faces. "Maybe we did it every night, I don't know," he said. "I just remember it as a weekend thing."

After having gone to Arthur Kill, I wanted to talk to a crime professional who was still in the business, so I called a drug dealer who specialized in providing young white-collar people in the New York–New Jersey–Connecticut metropolitan area with drugs for home recreational use. He said his competitive advantage in a crowded field was that he would deliver to your door, or to the men's room of a restaurant of your choice. He also said he was happy for me to accompany him on a Saturday night of business, but then his beeper started beeping and he had to get off the phone. The next time we spoke, we set a time and date to meet, but when it rolled around, he never showed up. I called his beeper and he called me back and said, "Sorry, I got an emergency call from a birthday party in North Bergen County and I had to go. Let's try another time." The next time he stood me up, he said he had gotten busy working a big weekend bash on Fire Island, and the time after that, he told me he had been tied up bringing drugs to a few suburban couples having a quiet Saturday night at home in southern Connecticut.

Finally, I admitted to him that I was getting frustrated, and he complained that it was just impossible for him to schedule anything on any Saturday night, because it was his highest-volume night of the week. He said he would be happy to make it Tuesday, or Thursday, or some afternoon, but Saturday night was too critical. "Look," he told me the last time we spoke. "If I don't keep up with demand on Saturday night, I'm as good as out of the game." The business cycle, for the vampire-business world, peaks on Saturday night, and a drug dealer busy escorting a reporter that night is the commercial underworld equivalent of an eggnog factory closed for repairs during December. He was blunt about it. "You know, I tried to help out," he said to me, in a consoling but grave tone. "I would really still love to help you out, but you've got to understand that this is business. I've got a job to do, too."

The other people with a job to do, of course, are the police. Because of the high rate of crime on Saturday night, it might seem that police would be reluctant to take a Saturday midnight shift. This isn't just speculative fear: more police officers have been killed in the line of duty on Saturdays than any other day of the week. But just about every police officer I talked to said he or she still preferred working Saturday night to the rest of the week.

"I love it because Saturday is when all the interesting stuff happens," a police sergeant in Cleveland named Emily Broder explained to me. "All the things you don't want to have happen, happen. It's really jumping. Other nights can get incredibly boring, but Saturday never is. You can set your watch by the first drunk-driving accidents on Saturday night. You've got guaranteed fatals between two and four a.m. You go downtown, and you'll see all the civilians out trying to have fun, and you feel like a spectator, completely apart from it, but you are the one who's in charge. We see all the people lined up to go into bars or restaurants, begging to get in, and you feel really different from the people in the line. Saturday is when

everything weird and interesting happens. The night goes by fast."
She said that Saturday night makes cops really feel their *cop*-ness:
their braveness, their separateness from civilians, and their willing-
ness to face a job that includes the possibility of death.

The night that Joan Jacobs shot Charles Brooks had been a manageable Saturday night for the Pembroke police. As it is, Pembroke
is a manageable town. It has just over three thousand residents, one
big employer (a trailer factory), one big trade (Sheetrocking), and
one big street, which leads from Pembroke, where on Saturday
night nothing much ever happens, to the bigger town of Lumberton,
where one or two things usually do. There are nine police officers
on the Pembroke force, and 33 percent of them are named Strickland. The three Stricklands are not related. As someone in Pembroke once told me, some things just happen that way.

Officer Mickey Strickland was working the midnight shift the
night of the murder. He says the night was chilly and clear and
quiet. He says he had little to do, in fact, until he got a call on his
radio saying there was shooting on Chapel Road. He knew by the
address that the shooting was at Charles Brooks's house. He had
known Charles Brooks "by face," as he puts it, and had known
Charles's two children ("Fine children," he recalls), and he had
known Joan Jacobs well enough to think of her as a nice local girl.
This wasn't Officer Strickland's first dead body. Still, when he
walked in the door of Charles's three-bedroom house, it took him a
minute to collect himself. As Officer Strickland puts it, in spite of
how common they are, it comes as a fresh surprise each time you
come across a couple—a seemingly average couple, whom you
might just as easily have run into on a date at the local spaghetti
joint—in that particular and irreversible condition of one being dead
and one having done it. At the time, Officer Strickland had been a
Pembroke police officer for five years, most of which he'd spent on
the night shift.

"We have a lot of these, what you call 'family beefs,' " Officer
Strickland said to me not long ago. "We usually referee these things.
We usually get to the house and let them talk it out, unless it comes
to push and shove. It's not something anyone enjoys, but it makes
the shift go faster. You know how it is. We have two or three

murders here in a year. Most of them are arguments, I would say, such as arguments over a woman, or over a man, or about some money. They all seem to happen on Fridays or Saturdays. Sunday I suppose everyone tries to mellow out for Mondays, and anyway, most people are away at church. A neighbor of Charles's had called the police station when she heard the arguing at his house. I was out on another call in the area, so I went over there. I was on the shift that goes from eleven p.m. to seven a.m., which I suppose seems to be when everything happens. But I don't mind, as I said, because it makes the shift go faster.

"The night of this call was actually a very quiet night. Here in Pembroke, our biggest problem seems to be traffic on Main Street, because everyone gets in their cars on Saturday nights and goes over to Lumberton. We don't have any entertainment here in town, in Pembroke. We don't have a bowling alley, and we don't have a theater. But Lumberton is only twelve miles away, and they have everything there, and they have a little old park there in Lumberton where people sit and talk.

"Sometimes Saturday shifts can be like Mondays, just quiet, but normally they are real busy. If I were to count, I'd say three out of four Saturdays in a month something or other will happen. I'd say usually it's just a fight, like someone says something about someone's girlfriend, and then someone will get a stick or bottle. Everyone here has guns, of course, because it's a farm area, but I'd say it's unusual to have a weapon in one of these fights. Although, actually, now that I think about it, last year there was a shootout in town. There were these two men who were fighting about a woman, and they run across each other in town one night and started firing. It was a Western-type deal. They both got killed."

I asked him whether he knew Charles very well. "Charles was real well liked in town," he said. "I knew him, but didn't really *know* him, if you understand. For instance, I didn't know he was seeing Joan until I was there that night. From what I'm told, though, they were on what people might call a better-than-first-name basis. She, that is, Joan, was real upset when I arrived. She's been married and divorced, and she has children. She lives on the edge of town,

110

on her father's farm. It is a strange thing. It was Charles's own gun that killed him."

There was a long silence, which Officer Strickland broke by saying, "I would like to say one thing, that no one should get the wrong idea about Pembroke from this. Pembroke is not what you'd call a very violent town, or even an *action* town. What we have going on here most of the time, when it comes to any problems, is usually something folks call boyfriend-girlfriend difficulties, or somebody-with-a-grudge difficulties. What I mean is that what we've got going on in Pembroke is just typical Saturday-night stuff."

Dining

Saugus, Massachusetts

One of the things I have found out about Saturday night in America is that it is the night when many people like to go out for dinner. I have also found out that many of those people like to be going to the Hilltop Steak House on Route 1 in Saugus, a blue-collar town about ten miles north of Boston. The Hilltop, which is a light brown Western-style building with a twelve-acre parking lot, a sixty-eight-foot-tall neon sign in the shape of a cactus, chairs and tables for fifteen hundred, and a herd of ten life-size fiberglass Herefords and two life-size Black Anguses on the front lawn, is the busiest restaurant in the United States of America. Statements of this kind understandably inspire many people to demand statistics. Fortunately, statistics about the Hilltop Steak House do not disappoint. Last year, the Hilltop grossed forty-seven million dollars and served food to two and a half million people. This represents more food sold and more people served than at any other single restaurant in the country. On a typical Saturday night, the average wait for dinner is seventy-five to ninety minutes. If the circus happens to be in town, the wait is usually a few minutes shorter; evidently, the kind of people who like the Hilltop like the circus a lot, too. In an ordinary week, the Hilltop makes use of two hundred and forty thousand pieces of china, ten thousand dinner rolls, thirty-five hundred pounds of butter, two hundred cases of French fries, four thousand pounds of poultry, four tons of seafood, six hundred gallons of the house salad dressing, forty-five thousand pounds of beef, and one Heimlich maneuver.

Gigantic versions of things can sometimes become distorted, so as I headed off to watch the restaurant in action one wintry Saturday night when the circus was not in town, I wondered whether the Hilltop's hugeness might mean that it had lost the characteristics of an ordinary restaurant and now had more in common with other things also notable for their enormity—say, the Hoover Dam or Asian elephants—and whether my interest in the American tradition of dining out on Saturday nights would be better served by watching an evening unfold somewhere more demure—at Tad's Chicken 'n Dumplings in Troutdale, Oregon, perhaps. Everyone at the Hilltop assured me that this wasn't the case. "We're still just a restaurant here," Steve Nelson, the dining-room manager, likes to say. "Okay, definitely a big restaurant. You know, very big. Huge, even. But when you get down to brass tacks, we serve food to people, just like any regular restaurant you can think of. We just serve more of it."

Amazingly enough, the Hilltop does manage to be the sort of place where its thousands of regular patrons perceive themselves as having an individual and even intimate relationship with Frank Giuffrida, the Italian meat cutter who founded the restaurant in 1961. Some of the people who feel this closeness with Mr. Giuffrida have probably never even met him. Pervasive would be one way of describing Mr. Giuffrida's influence on the Hilltop, and that would account for the familiarity his millions of patrons feel toward him. His signature running in neon across the middle of the neon cactus greets customers who are driving up Route 1 to the restaurant. Most of the two and a half million customers of the Hilltop probably take the encomiastic phrase-making in the free four-color Hilltop photo brochure—such as the description of the Hilltop's kitchen as "the SHINING HUB of the STEAK LOVER'S KINGDOM"—to be Mr. Giuffrida's very own. The reason a Western-style steak house with dining rooms named Dodge City, Sioux City, Kansas City, Carson City, Virginia City, and Santa Fe is in a blue-collar suburb of Boston, where the Wild West would follow every county in Ireland and most provinces of Italy on the list of places that have local cultural impact, is simply that Mr. Giuffrida, who lives in a neighboring blue-collar Irish-Italian suburb and likes steak, is a Western buff. The imposition of Frank Giuffrida's fancies on what you might have thought, given its colossal success, was a monument of corporate marketing calculation could explain the busiest restaurant in the United States of America's congenial and even capricious personality.

"People always wonder how we got to be so successful," Mrs. Giuffrida said to me one morning. This was a few days before the Saturday night I was planning to spend at the Hilltop, and I had stopped by to look around and get familiar with the spread. At the time, the Giuffridas and I were sitting in a glassed-in office overlooking the Hilltop Butcher Shop, an appendage to the Hilltop Steak House which, as Mr. Giuffrida had been pointing out with understandable pride, is the largest refrigerated store in the world. The meat in the butcher shop sits out on ordinary shelves rather than in cooling cases because the store is one giant refrigerator. People button their coat collars fast when they step into the Hilltop Butcher Shop. Because the shop sells every item used in the Hilltop dining rooms, there are also rolls of aluminum foil, salt, pepper, potatoes, salad dressing, and doggie bags sitting on the refrigerated shelves.

Mr. and Mrs. Giuffrida, who now spend some time at their condominium in Florida and some time checking in at the Hilltop, had come by that morning to look at a few sirloins. In the early days of the restaurant, they did everything from cutting the steaks to refilling the pepper shakers, but in the last decade their role has evolved into something of a benign stewardship of the Hilltop tradition. They no longer have any hands-on association with the meat, except for that which their own curiosity compels. It was early and a weekday at the time of our meeting, so the Hilltop complex was uncommonly quiet. There were only a few dozen cars in the parking lot ("Carefree parking is the byword at HILLTOP STEAK HOUSE," according to Mr. Giuffrida's brochure). Mr. Giuffrida was sitting with his back to the window, facing a wall which was layered with photographs of the Giuffrida children and grandchildren, and he spun around at regular intervals to see what was going on in the butcher shop. Frank Giuffrida is short and broad, like a welterweight boxer, and has a friendly face with wide features, architecturally complex hair, and the punctuating hand gestures and comic timing of a Borscht Belt regular. Irene Giuffrida, who was sitting across from him, has a medium build, a pile of blonde waves, long and extravagantly curled eyelashes, and a husky, engaging laugh.

"For example, people always wonder why we went Western—well, we went Western for just one reason," Mrs. Giuffrida said. She pointed a finger at Mr. Giuffrida, who raised one eyebrow at her. "He loves Westerns. John Wayne is his absolute favorite. With him, everything is always John Wayne, John Wayne, John Wayne, John Wayne. And at the time, there were no Western-style buildings in the area, and we also thought it would be something different for the area. So we went Western. Everything at the Hilltop is just the way Mr. Giuffrida likes it." She grinned at Mr. Giuffrida. He grinned back, and then asked a chef who was passing by to bring us a steak.

"We also don't serve sour cream," Mrs. Giuffrida added. "We don't serve sour cream because Mr. G. doesn't *like* sour cream. Anyone who wants sour cream, they can bring their own sour cream. And they do, I'm telling you. You see them lined up outside with their little paper bags with their containers of sour cream, right, Frank? We don't call people to their tables by name, because Mr. Giuffrida doesn't like to cater to a particular clientele and for everyone to hear over the loudspeaker, 'Doctor This, table for two' or 'Judge That, your table is ready.' He doesn't go for that. That's why we use numbers in the line. We get plenty of celebrities, but no one gets preference here. That's not Mr. G.'s style. David Niven came here one night, I remember, and was that ever the ruination of a Saturday night! That's when we decided we didn't like celebrities, right, Frank? If you come to the Hilltop, you get what Mr. Giuffrida likes. What does he like? He likes steak, lots of butter on his potato, and a big salad with Italian dressing on it. That's what we serve, and apparently people like it. You know, business is pretty good. But if you want anything else, you can go somewhere else."

—

Mr. Giuffrida slapped his hand to his forehead, as if something had just dawned on him. "You know, I just thought of something, Irene," he said. "Maybe we should hire a manager to tell us how to run things here, because maybe we don't know what we're doing."

Mrs. Giuffrida gave him a look of mock exasperation, rapped her polished fingernails against the table, looked back at me, rolled her eyes, and said, "Oh, look what an *actor* he is."

Carson City is one of Hilltop's upstairs dining rooms; dark, with low ceilings and a somewhat more subdued decor than the other five dining rooms, it is one of the first to be closed down at night when the crowds begin to thin. Carson City also happens to be where the waitresses gather for coffee and cigarettes before the dinner shift, and on the Saturday night right after I met the Giuffridas I sat down in Carson City with a group of waitresses who were going to be sharing a station that night in Sioux City, the big dining room downstairs. This turned out to be the last night the waitresses would be allowed to wear white pants—the new dress code would be white shirts with black pants or skirts—so much of the conversation debated the pros and cons of the change and included reminiscences of previous Hilltop dress codes. A low cloud of Winston smoke and a flutter of anticipation hung in the room. It reminded me of a ready room at a B-1 bomber base, where pilots stand by before they're called up. Someone sitting at the table mentioned that the weather report looked promising, which by Hilltop standards means rain. For some reason, the worse the weather is, the bigger the turnout at the restaurant.

On average, more breakfasts, lunches, dinners, and snacks are served on Saturdays in the restaurants of America than on any other day of the week. Restaurants have 18 to 20 percent more business on Saturday night than on any other night. There are usually about seven thousand dinners served at the Hilltop on Saturday night, which is, of course, the busiest night at the restaurant. All transactions at the Hilltop are cash. No one at the restaurant, most particularly the off-duty Saugus policemen hired by the restaurant to fortify the inaccessibility of this information, will say exactly how many times the registers are emptied and their contents removed by armored truck during the course of the night, but it is probably a lot of times.

There are eighty-five Hilltop waitresses on duty on Saturday night, compared to around seventy on other nights. There are also fourteen hostesses; seven bartenders; six bar hosts; six bar backs; three cashiers; thirty-three cooks and dishwashers; and one person calling out the numbers of the people waiting in line. A Saturday night at the Hilltop Steak House is considered a juicy assignment. Quite a few of the waitresses only work on Saturday nights and go home on most of them with stuffed pockets. Hundreds and hundreds of people living in the Saugus area work at the Hilltop, have worked at the Hilltop, or someday will work at the Hilltop. Dynasties have developed. There are mother-daughter waitress teams, in-law teams, husband-wife teams, brother-sister teams, and sister-sister teams. I found out that of the three waitresses I tagged along with in Sioux City that Saturday night, one of them had two sisters at the restaurant, another had a sister and a sister-in-law, and one had her daughter waiting tables upstairs that night in Virginia City. For a brief period some years ago, a manager put the kibosh on hiring related people, creating a ripple throughout the economy of Saugus, Massachusetts. That rule now seems as repressive as Prohibition.

Saugus is a no-nonsense town of old but not especially charming clapboard houses and small, square commercial buildings. The New England it relates to is the one of sooty mills and dank shoe factories rather than the one of cobblestone streets and whaling museums and bookstore-cafés. Route 1 runs through the town like a big zipper. It began as an extension of the Pequot Path, which was an Indian trace; then it became a stagecoach road, then the Old Post Road, then a turnpike, then a highway. In 1925, when the federal government began its uniform highway numbering system, the road, which runs from Calais, Maine, to Key West, Florida, was officially named U.S. Route 1. By 1938, it was described in a guide written by the Federal Writers' Project as "depressingly ugly, being characterized by hideous shacks, enormous signs, dumps, and raw cuts." The northern sections of Interstates 95 and 93, both limited-access, six-lane, divided high-speed highways parallel to Route 1, were opened in the early 1960s and immediately rendered the old road obsolete. Those Route 1 businesses such as motels and gas stations that had relied on the traveling trade closed up. Land along the road got cheap. After a while, businesses like muffler shops and discount warehouses that weren't welcome right in the centers of towns and that didn't need to be on the modern highway but needed to be accessible by some kind of big road settled along Route 1. So did businesses that would profit by having enormous amounts of cheap land, such as high-volume restaurants needing gigantic parking lots.

What often strikes people driving down Route 1 these days is the wackiness of the man-made landscape. Coming from Boston to Saugus, you would drive across the Mystic River, cut through the last of the flat, swampy fells, climb a hill where snaggly granite chunks stick through the grass, and then round the last corner a mile south of the Hilltop and immediately come upon a huge orange dinosaur (part of a miniature-golf course), a Polynesian treehouse with totem poles (the Kowloon, a Thai–Chinese–South Seas restaurant), a red schooner (The Ship, a family seafood restaurant), a reproduction of the Leaning Tower of Pisa (a pizza restaurant), and the neon cactus and fiberglass steer of the Hilltop. Personally, I think if I had nearly unlimited land, no fussy zoning laws to contend with, the need to catch the attention of people driving by at fifty or sixty miles an hour, and a fertile and perhaps fervid imagination, I might also build a restaurant on Route 1 in the shape of something spectacular and easy to remember, like the Lost City of Atlantis or a giant poodle. In other words, the iconographic architecture of Route 1 makes a great deal of sense to me. What strikes me as more extraordinary and strange about the road is the way every single place on it is complete and unto itself—a closed-Polynesian-hut universe beside a closed-waterbed-warehouse universe beside Frank Giuffrida's complete-Western-village universe. There is no way to walk across the road from one place to another (a barrier runs the length of the Saugus section of Route 1) and only a fool would dare walk along the shoulder; for that matter, the businesses on Route 1 are spread far enough apart and separated enough by uninviting expanses of parking lots or empty, trashy, grassy spaces that you can barely see or have any sense of what store or restaurant is next to or across from the one you're in. When you drive to the Hilltop Steak House, you arrive directly, exist there for a few hours, and depart directly. It is as if you swallow the experience whole.

The other major industries in Saugus are boat yards, sheet-metal plants, machine shops, and the Kowloon Restaurant, a twelve-hundred-seat restaurant one-half mile down the road from the Hilltop. The Kowloon is the fourth largest Oriental restaurant in the country. If you were to travel somewhere like the iron region of Michigan and were told that the country's two largest iron smelters were located in a small town in the region, you would probably not be surprised. To find two restaurants on the scale of the Hilltop and the Kowloon—both of which have menus that have nothing to do with any foodstuff raised, caught, or cultivated nearby—within a half mile of each other in a city with no discernible natural characteristics that would seem to promote huge-restaurant husbandry is really something.

Many theories have been run up and subsequently shot down about the Route 1 big-restaurant phenomenon. In the last five years, dining out has generally become the mainstay of American leisure time, displacing music appreciation and parties as the most popular weekend activity for affluent people entering their thirties and forties. Maybe this is because dining out is less strenuous and more reliably gratifying than either of those activities, or maybe it is just the logical end point of a continuum that began with the hippie fascination with the politics of food and health, which was followed by the enthusiasm for cooking in general, which was then refined into an interest in eating and most particularly into an interest in eating food that someone else has prepared. Restaurant industry associations are gratified by the fact that in the last decade the two-career household has replaced the one-career/one-cook household, and by the fact that nutrition and the exploration of exotic and arcane cuisines have become the hobbies of the moment. Restaurants are called for in both cases. There are now more restaurant guides, hotlines, reviews, trends, and reservation logjams than at any other time in recorded history. Restaurant sales are higher than ever—$202,000,000,000 in 1989—and have grown steadily, even discounting inflation, for the last nine years. A recent Roper survey concluded that most Americans have tried and liked American, Italian, Chinese, southern, Mexican, German, French, New England, Japanese, Spanish, Jewish, Greek, Middle Eastern, and Indian cuisine. Just a few years earlier, before the restaurant boom began, another survey revealed that more people had painted their nails an unusual color than had ever tried sushi.

The Hilltop and the Kowloon have probably benefited some from the current robustness of the restaurant industry, but they also seem to have an implosive prosperity all their own. My own theory is that the Hilltop and the Kowloon offer moderately priced good food in an area where there are a great number of people who have just enough money to go out regularly for a pretty nice meal, but not quite enough to go to fancier restaurants or to more elaborate recreation like theater or nightclubs. This accounts for some major growth. The availability of land for expansion (the Hilltop has added thousands of square dining-room and parking-lot feet since opening in 1961) makes for more growth. Then both the Hilltop and the Kowloon got so big, and a weekend dinner at each became such a production, that they themselves have become a full evening's entertainment. So legendary has the Hilltop become that it attracts people from sixty and seventy miles away, from New Hampshire and Maine and Rhode Island as well as all over Massachusetts, which means those outlanders put up with an hour or so of travel time in addition to their hour or so of waiting time before dinner. Anyone coming to the restaurant on a weekend night knows they are in for a wait, and they seem to take to it cheerily. After all, if there's one thing that I have found to be consistently true about Saturday night it is that it breeds a sense of conviviality in almost everyone. Even people who want to be alone—that is, couples on dates—usually do it in crowded places, like restaurants. Busy places feel awash with pleasant social lubricants. The busiest restaurant in America might be more awash than some people would care for, but most people going out on Saturday do share the desire to find themselves somewhere where there are a lot of other people. The Hilltop's customers suffer the wait and the crowds not just gladly but ingeniously. People waiting for dinner at the Hilltop on Satur-

day nights have been known to knit, have drinks, play backgam-
mon, play whist, play checkers, meet new people, read, converse,
and do crossword puzzles. The waiting area is a long, narrow pas-
sageway that calls to mind a cattle chute, and it has a small bar,
some benches, and a lively atmosphere most nights. Parties break
out spontaneously in the chute. The whist-playing/spontaneous
party/waiting period takes up an hour or two; then you eat; then
the night is effectively through. An average dinner at the Hilltop
costs thirteen dollars. The predinner entertainment is free.

Patti Nardone, Betty Dillge, and Jeannie Suprenant are often three
of the eighty-five waitresses on duty at the Hilltop Steak House on
Saturday nights. Betty and Jeannie work a few other lunch and
dinner shifts during the week, but Patti is a Saturday-only. The
work at the Hilltop is good enough to sustain long careers. Starting
in 1961, when the restaurant first opened, all waitresses were assigned payroll numbers in consecutive order. Waitress number one,
Mary Comer, and waitress number five, Sally Varjabdian, are still
working tables. Betty Dillge has been at the Hilltop for three years.
Jeannie has worked twenty-three. Patti has worked nine.

When I got to Carson City, I found Patti and sat with her as she
prepared for the dinner shift. As I was sitting down, I noticed that
she was painting bright pink polish onto her fingernails. At twenty-
nine, Patti is younger than many of the Hilltop waitresses. She has
spiky blond hair, bright blue eyes, a nice smile that time-shares her
mouth with cigarettes and Juicy Fruit, and the high spirits of someone who probably got to know her way around detention hall in
high school. She grew up in Lynn, an unglamorous town near
Saugus that is well within the sphere of Hilltop influence. Many
people Patti knew growing up now work at the Hilltop. She used to
wait tables in a nearby pancake house, fell in love with a guy who
was bartending at the restaurant next door, married him, and soon
thereafter got a job at the Hilltop. She now spends most of the week
at home with her two young sons, works Saturday nights at the
restaurant, and picks up another shift or two during the week as her
schedule allows.

"What's the weather like?" Patti asked Jeannie Suprenant, who was sitting across from her at the table. She flapped her hands to dry the nails on her left hand and then started polishing her right thumb.

"Rain, I hope," Jeannie said, sighing. Jeannie has a low, gentle voice that verges on a tremble every few sentences, round blue eyes, and a puff of pale brown hair. She faintly resembles Shirley Booth in her middle years, but she has a steadily worried look in her eye. She goes by the nickname Jeannie Mack because there are several other Jeannies at the Hilltop. "I hope it rains so we really get a crowd," she added. A few people nodded. Jeannie stood up, bade everyone a good night, and left to set up the waitress station downstairs in Sioux City. Many of the other waitresses had begun to clear away their coffee cups and leave for their stations. As soon as Patti finished her last nail, she tied on her waitress apron and announced that she was ready to go.

"Another night in the trenches at the Hilltop," she said, gesturing toward the stairs. "I can tell you that six hours from now, it will all be over, no matter what. Thousands of dinners down the drain."

I asked her if she liked working Saturday nights.

"Oh, yeah," she said, picking some stray polish off her finger. "My husband can stay home with the kids, and I can make some good money. Besides, Saturday is the best night here, definitely. You make the most money, for one thing, and it's a real rush because it's so busy. I like it pretty much. I'm used to it, anyway. Friday is busy, but it's a different kind of busy. A lot of people come in right after work, and there are always a lot of guys out for a night on the town. It's a different sort of customer. Friday is a little rowdier. Saturday, you get a lot of couples on dates, so sometimes that's a little different. I get a kick out of waiting on the couples. When they're here, you can tell they're thinking, like, 'Hey, are we gonna screw tonight or what?' I find that very interesting." We walked downstairs and I then saw something most of the two and a half million patrons of the Hilltop Steak House never see: the tables of Sioux City, Dodge City, and Kansas City completely empty. Seeing them empty gave me a moment to appreciate what the restaurant looks like. Whenever I'd been at the Hilltop in the past, the sensation of constant activity, of noisiness, of the wave of diners waiting to crash past the door, of hundreds of pounds of beef and potatoes being shuttled at top speed throughout the restaurant—the sensation of fullness of every sort—was so overpowering that I had never noticed the inside of the place. Each of the dining rooms is slightly different. Sioux City, where I planned to spend most of the night, is in the front of the building on the ground floor. It seats 324, or as Mr. Giuffrida prefers to describe it, Sioux City has a population of 324. It has red-checkered carpeting, brown beams running across the ceiling, saloon chandeliers, wooden booths, wood-grain linoleum tables, and a carved wooden Indian locked in salute near the cashier. One is probably not going to be fooled into thinking that prairie dogs and tumbleweeds are piled up in the parking lot and that the plains are unfolding just outside the door, but if Annie Oakley had run a steak house it might have had a few stylistic elements in common with the Hilltop. Through the windows near the cashier, I could see a few people already lined up in the waiting area and some cars rushing by on Route 1. One of the off-duty Saugus policemen hired as Saturday-night security came by and said hello to Patti. A minute later, his wife, who was waiting tables that night in Sante Fe, joined us.

"How'ya doing there, Patti?" the policeman said.

"I'm so happy, Herbie," Patti said, poking him in the gut. "I'm so happy that I can't find enough words to tell you about how happy I am. Hiya, Claire, where are you tonight?"

"Santa Fe."

"Ooooh, I'm in Sioux, with Jeannie Mack and Betty. Hey, Claire, did you put your dollar into the pool yet?" The pool is a Saturday-night-only Hilltop tradition: all the waitresses and the kitchen workers and bartenders each throw a dollar into a bucket, and midway through the night, a name is drawn. The winner can walk out with close to three hundred dollars. Patti plays the pool every Saturday and she has never won it. Claire mentioned that she hadn't put her dollar in yet but that she figured she would, as usual. "I'm going to win tonight," Patti told her. "I know I've been saying that for nine years, but this time I mean it."

Patti's first customers were two beefy young men who were both wearing quilted baseball jackets and a few thin gold neck chains. As they were being seated, about fifty other parties were being led into the dining room and directed to seats. Within a few minutes, every table in Sioux City was full.

Patti, Betty, and Jeannie Mack were assigned to the waitress station in the left center of Sioux City. The two young men were seated at a booth directly in front of the station. One of them immediately waved Patti over. "I want a cheeseburger," he said.

"You really should have the tenderloin," Patti said, tapping her order pad with a pencil. "It's much more tender. It'll satisfy you more than a cheeseburger."

The two men gave each other a look and then each of them ordered a cheeseburger and a tenderloin. The more talkative of the two then asked Patti whether the restaurant had any potato skins.

"Do you think we'd have potato skins and not put them on the menu?" Patti replied.

"Hey, look, are you wise or what?" he said, thrusting out his jaw and looking annoyed.

This question astounded Patti, who scowled and then forced a smile. "No, I'm just logical, fellas. Let's be nice, now." She stepped around to the station, pulled Betty aside, lowered her voice and said, "Keep an eye on them for me, would ya? These guys are the perfect candidates to skip out on their check." Betty obligingly glared at the backs of their heads. Jeannie, who had just delivered a few steaks, stood beside the station wiping her hands on her apron. She gave Patti a sympathetic grimace and then began to say that so far she had gotten all parties of four, which she found objectionable.

"I tell you, I'd rather have deuces any day," she said.

"Me, too," Betty said.

"Me, too," Patti said.

"They're in and out," Jeannie added.

"In and out," Patti said, nodding.

"In and out," said Betty. She looked over her section, and turned back to Jeannie and Patti. "I think the people at my tables are never going to leave. Never. They're here for the night." She pulled her face into an exaggerated pout. Betty has a long, smooth, soft-looking face, short reddish hair, and an imperturbable air. When I asked her early in the evening whether I was pronouncing her last name correctly she said she was perfectly happy for me to pronounce it any way I wanted and that she wasn't even sure she had it right herself. A nearby Friendly's restaurant was her employer for a long while, but she finally decided three years ago to join her two sisters at the Hilltop. The pace continued to impress her, and she liked to keep Patti and Jeannie updated all night on the length of the wait. Throughout most evenings, she sidles over to one of the hostesses every few minutes, checks the progress of the line, and reports back with whatever data she has obtained. At half past six, she announced that the wait was estimated at forty-five minutes.

Over the years, the number-callers at the Hilltop have gotten so tired of anxious diners asking when they would be seated that they drew up length-of-wait information signs and hung them on the number-caller's desk. The signs go in increments of five minutes, from fifteen minutes to ninety. When the wait is longer than ninety minutes, they usually stop handing out numbers, and people coming for dinner have to wait in line to get a number to wait in line. I wandered out to the waiting area and noticed that a rope had been put up at the far end, and that about forty people were clumped behind it. The number-caller for the evening, a man named Jack, told me that the wait had shot up to ninety minutes and that the people behind the rope were waiting in line to get numbers. The rest of the waiting area was crowded. A lot of people were clustered around the waiting-area bar. Some of them looked dressed up, but most were wearing out-for-the-evening casual clothes—jeans with fancy seams, sweaters, a little jewelry. One young couple who looked Vietnamese were wearing dressy black clothes with lots of challenging angles and zippers. I walked through the crowd and talked to a few groups. There were dates, a few gatherings of friends, and lots of couples, some with other couples and some alone. Most of them were planning to eat dinner and go home. Everyone seemed excited and most everyone had been to the Hilltop before, and seemed surprised that I would even ask. I stood in line for a minute and listened to the clatter of voices in the waiting area, the rumble in the background of Route 1, and the rumble in the foreground of the restaurant. It seemed as though most of the population of the

—

area had convened here for the moment. No one seemed particularly restless, although when the rope came down and the people in line were allowed to come into the waiting chute and get numbers, they scrambled in as if someone had thrown down a pile of money. A voice came over the loudspeaker a moment later, calling, "Number four-oh-two, number three-fifty-five, number twenty-nine, Kansas City. Number two-thirty-three, number fifty-six, Sioux City. Four-oh-two, three-fifty-five, twenty-nine, Kansas City. Two-thirty-three, fifty-six, Sioux City." The chosen stepped out of line and into the restaurant. A couple in office clothes who were ahead of me in line but hadn't been called walked up to Jack clutching their number and looking anxious.

"Look, we're just wondering," the man said. "Do you think we'll get seated in time to get to a nine o'clock movie?"

Jack shook his head. "Most people don't come to the Hilltop with that attitude," he said. "You probably can't go anywhere else tonight."

I went back into Sioux City. The room was buzzing. All of Patti's tables had cleared and been refilled, and I saw her coming back from the kitchen with a round tray stacked with steaks balanced on her shoulder. She delivered the meals and then went to take another order from a table of two middle-aged couples. The two men ordered steaks black and blue—charred on the outside and cold in the middle—and beers. One of the women ordered a medium-well tenderloin. The other woman closed her menu and gave Patti a sheepish look. "I'd like a salad with no dressing," she said.

"No dressing?" Patti asked. "Well, okay." She scribbled something down.

"Okay," the woman went on. "Now, I have a slightly odd request. I'd like a cup of recently boiled water." The two men started to laugh. One of them grabbed Patti by the elbow and said, "Hey, we don't know this woman. Never seen her before in our lives. Honest."

"Cut it *out*, Al," the woman said, slapping him on the arm.

Patti had stopped writing and was standing still with one eye shut. She looked as if she were trying to do long division in her head. After a minute, she said to the woman, "Okay, let me get this straight. You're going to have a salad with no dressing and some recently boiled water? Would just plain *boiled* water be okay? And when you say recent, like exactly how recent do you mean?"

The woman put her face in her hands and started to groan. "I'm on a diet," she said. "I have my own special dressing in my purse, and I have some soup crystals with me, and I'm just going to have some salad with my dressing and some soup made from my crystals and then watch them eat their steaks."

"You're on a diet and you came to the Hilltop?" Patti asked, sounding genuinely impressed. "That's guts! You've got real guts! I mean, there's a lot of food around here to not be eating. Okay, I'm willing to try this. I just want to get it straight. I don't want to screw this up for you. Okay, recently boiled, and a plain salad." She walked over to the waitress station, where Betty was wiping up some spilled water.

"You're not going to believe this, Betty," Patti said. "Recently boiled water." She interrupted herself and said, "Hey, did they do the pool yet?"

Betty motioned across the room. "June Bell won again," she said.

"Again?" Patti said. "Oh, well, I'm happy for her. That's great. June Bell. What is that, her fortieth time or something?" She cracked a knuckle. "Well, I've got to go get some recently boiled water. I'll see you in a minute."

We walked through Sioux City to the back of the room, went through two swinging doors, and ended up in the kitchen. There were about twenty-five waitresses carrying salads and steak and Cokes and desserts, slapping potatoes onto plates, slopping dressing onto salads. A long line of cooks stood behind a plastic sneeze guard and in front of a huge grill. Most of them were holding long tongs and striking accidentally belligerent-looking poses. The statistic-defying June Bell hurried in, waved to Patti, got some steaks, and hurried out. Patti waved after her and said nothing. After she took four salads off of a rack that held probably two hundred salads, she started talking again. "You know, I got to work on my luck. What's happening to my luck? Geezus! Well, that's the breaks. You know, this is a *crazy* place. It's so huge. People come and line up for hours, and for godssake, I don't know if I'd be up to it. Me, I want to eat when I want to eat. People love it, though. Why? Because it's good food and it's cheap. You get a lot for your dollar here. They eat half their meal and take the rest home in a doggie bag. I'm serious. You get everyone here, every type in the world—goofballs, smart alecks, rich people, everything. I get a kick out of seeing people, which is why I like this job. It's like being an amateur shrink. I figure people out a little faster, though. Of course, there are plenty of people I could do without. I won't mention any names, okay?" She ladled dressing onto the salads, remembered that one was supposed to be plain, threw it out, picked up another salad, started to ladle dressing on it but stopped herself in time, put all of the salads on a tray, and then stood up. "Hey, Kenny," she yelled over the racket. "Let's see some steaks with my name on them already? What do ya say, pal?" She walked over to the grill and winked at one of the cooks. He had red hair, a red face, and a long-suffering manner.

"Oh, gee, I must have lost your order, Patti," he said. "I'll start some right now."

She put her hand on her hip and started tapping her foot. "Hey, Kenny," she said. "How about you get those to me while I'm still young? Huh? While I'm still good-looking and young?"

At the end of the night, I again saw the remarkable sight of the Hilltop Steak House, the busiest restaurant in America, mostly empty. The rain had never materialized, so the crowd, daunting by most standards, was only ordinary by the Hilltop's. There had been a line until ten-thirty, and after the last batch of people were seated, anyone coming in got a table right away. Patti looked at her waitress report and saw that she had served sixty-seven people, thirty dollars worth of hard liquor, nine dollars worth of beer, six dollars worth of wine, and twenty cups of coffee. She had also served one cup of recently boiled water. "That was a hot one," she remarked to Betty, recalling the water. "I've had some strange requests, but that's going to be one I'll remember." The bottom of her waitress report showed that her customers had spent an average of $11.72 each and her total receipts for the night were $785. "Maybe that doesn't sound like that much," she said to me, "but there are a hundred girls working, and they each probably served around that much." She made a note on the form, cleared off the last of her dirty tables, and then started asking around to see where everyone was going for their after-work drink. A lot of the waitresses and cooks at the Hilltop like to go out together after a busy Saturday night. The restaurant staff is so big that whatever bar becomes the current favorite enjoys a providential upturn in business. For some time now, a number of Hilltop people have been going to Augustine's, a fern bar a few miles north on Route 1, and others go to the VFW Hall a few miles south, which is also popular with Saugus policemen and firemen.

"Cheap drinks," Patti said of the VFW Hall. "Not a lot of what I would call atmosphere, but it's, you know, pretty nice and very friendly. A lot of us types who work on Saturday night end up there. Very friendly place." It was almost twelve-thirty. About fifteen of the Sioux City waitresses were already changed into their street clothes and were lingering in the back of the room conferring about their evening plans.

"Augustine's anyone?" Patti called out.

"Nah," someone said. "I've had it up to here with Augustine's." Some discussion continued. One of the women suggested that the night had already been very full and rewarding and that she wasn't sure she needed to continue it.

"Hey, are you wimping out?" Patti asked. "Betty? Jeannie? June? You guys? Hey, I'm ready to go out and I'm filling in for someone on a double shift tomorrow!" She lowered her voice and said to me, "Okay, it's a wimpy double—I'm working the takeout orders, which is no biggie, but it is *still* a double." Several people then said they were eager to go. A choice was made. We headed out of the Hilltop. It was a chilly and damp night with no stars at all and a faint salty smell in the air. We walked across the parking lot, got into our various cars, pulled out onto Route 1, and reconvened a few minutes later in the lounge at the Kowloon.

Dieting

Miami Beach, Florida

At the Pritikin Longevity Center in Miami Beach, I was worried that my recent visit to the Hilltop Steak House would make me a marked woman. The Pritikin Diet eschews fat, salt, and protein. Once you "become Pritikin," as the program's disciples like to say, things like fat-marbled twelve-ounce medium-rare sirloins, which combine the forbidden three into an intoxicating but toxic form, are looked upon as edible forms of the devil. For that matter, the entire world outside the three Pritikin centers—there are centers in Santa Monica and Downingtown, Pennsylvania, as well as the one in Miami—takes on a greasy, diabolical glow. When I stopped by one afternoon to arrange to spend a Saturday night at the center, a portly middle-aged man who was in confinement for cholesterol violations waved to me as I was leaving, and said, "Be careful out there!" Thinking he was referring to the racial violence going on at that time in downtown Miami, I smiled and said that I wasn't going anywhere near Liberty City. He gave me a blank look. "I don't know anything about this Liberty City," he said, sounding exasperated. "I just think you should watch out for all the food out there. Miami Beach is full of food!"

Enrollees in the Pritikin Longevity Center programs are usually overweight and often have accompanying heart problems. They come to the centers for thirteen or twenty-six days, during which they learn to eat and cook Pritikin-style and begin an exercise regimen. A few hard-core eaters stay beyond the twenty-six days. In any case, everyone stays over at least one Saturday night. Knowing that too much denial can make anyone cranky, the Pritikin people used to try to make Saturday-night supper at the center a little special. This did not mean the addition of any fat, salt, or protein to the menu, but the residents were treated to a Saturday-evening cocktail party, where drinks (light juices or tea) and hors d'oeuvres (slices of pita bread or lettuce leaves cut into attractive shapes) were served, and a musician strolled around the dining room and amused the partygoers with song.

The general consensus was that the party was very nice but that it didn't quite work—"work" being code for "distracting the residents from the particular food cravings that often reach their peak on Saturday night." The Pritikin administrators, knowing they were whipped, gave up on the strolling musician and the lettuce leaves and gave in to the natural course of things. As it stands now, enrollees who feel they need a break from the rigors of the program are encouraged to take it on Saturday nights. Armed with a list of restaurants near the center where Pritikin-appropriate foods can be had, they are dispatched into the night with the cry "Try not to cheat!" Given the proportion of approved restaurants to unapproved, and given Miami Beach's historical association with a cuisine that is sometimes nothing more than large portions of protein artfully intermingled with lavish amounts of fat and salt—Wolfie's corned beef on Twenty-third and Collins, and the late-night high-cholesterol snack called "Pork Midnight" that is served at Cuban restaurants all over town, come to mind—it is assumed that some cheating will inevitably occur. Perhaps a third of the Pritikin enrollees on any given Saturday night will have their evening meal somewhere besides the center; the rest gather around the Pritikin salad bar at six o'clock and dine out on the knowledge that they didn't give in.

The Saturday night I chose to spend at the Pritikin Center turned out to be especially brutal. As if the pickle buckets at Junior's and the *arroz con pollo* at Puerto Sagua—both just blocks from the center—weren't enough, it also happened to be the night before the Super Bowl, which was being held that year in Miami's Joe Robbie Stadium. Dinners, brunches, beer brawls, and buffets were breaking out across the city; there was, quite literally, food all over the place. A cocktail party hosted by National Football League Commissioner and big eater Pete Rozelle, billed as "The Commissioner's Pig-Out," was being held just a few miles from the Pritikin Center. In the week preceding the party, the Miami *Herald* had twice printed the menu: whole roasted pigs, stone crab, lobster, leg of lamb, barbecued duck, guava-banana shakes, key lime pie, fudge, and one ton of fried shrimp. The amount of fatty salted food expected to disappear during the Super Bowl was the topic on a number of local radio talk shows. Moreover, in order to capitalize on the prodigiousness of Super Bowl–related beverage consumption, a prominent beer company had anchored an inspirational twelve-story-high inflatable beer bottle in the city park right on Biscayne Bay—visible for miles across Miami's wide, watery vistas. Things like this are known to give the early-stage Pritikin student some amount of pain. Some will confront their discomfort by talking about forbidden foods aggressively—enemy management. Others consider verbal or visual representations of foods they shouldn't eat to be hexes that a sane person would avoid.

When I was first wandering around the Pritikin Center early that Saturday evening, I bumped into a conversation that addressed this point. I had just left the gym, where I had been watching a group of plump individuals strolling on treadmills in time to an easy-listening version of "Oklahoma!" and had walked into the lobby and joined a few people waiting for dinner. One of them, a stout man with neat silver hair, was talking about a walk he had taken earlier in the day. Walking is another part of the Pritikin credo, and participants are expected to put in many miles a day. Because the center is on the beach and also near a very strollable street, many people choose to do their mileage outdoors, but that puts one within striking distance of innumerable hot-dog stands, knish vendors, and lox outlets. Others choose to forgo the fresh air and Florida sun and food temptations and instead spend hours every day in the gym thudding along on the treadmills. The stout man was saying that he usually did his walking on the treadmills, but he had chosen that morning to partake of the splendid weather and do some of his miles outside. He mentioned that he was a pilot for United Airlines, a job that tested his fearlessness in the face of challenge and had whetted his taste for open space.

"I walked down the street," he said, motioning past the registration desk. "*Right here*. This street. I walked and walked and walked and kept my mind on my feet. Finally, I got to the end of my walk, and I just paused to rest a minute before I turned around and headed back here. Do you know where I was? I had stopped in front of a Hungarian restaurant. *Hungarian*. Oh, God. They had a sign posted out front, with photographs of the food. Dumplings and stews. Color photographs of them." He sighed and shook his head as someone in the group stifled a gasp. "I'll tell you," the pilot went on, "*that* was really scary."

Anyone who's bailing out of the center for dinner tends to leave by five-thirty on Saturday night. This is also when the people who are staying in for dinner gather in the lobby. A number of people who live in the Miami area have relearned living according to the Pritikin principles, and now come to the center for their meals rather than risk going to restaurants or being let loose alone in their own kitchens; they begin showing up in the center around the same time. This means that at five-thirty on Saturday night in the Pritikin Center lobby, there is a commingling of enrollees guiltily departing, the stoic staying put, and loyalists returning to the fold. This gives the place an anxious buzz. Otherwise, it is not a memorable lobby. It is decorated in pale, sandy colors and outfitted with that requisite wicker furniture which is probably brought by container ship from the Philippines directly to the hotels of Miami Beach. The wicker is arranged in several conversational groups; it seemed to me that most of the chairs had been rotated slightly so that they faced the dining room.

The center is in a renovated hotel on Collins Avenue, the main strip on Miami Beach; the hotels around it are tall and thin, whereas the center happens to be a short, squat building. This might strike people as a droll coincidence. The sign saying PRITIKIN LONGEVITY

CENTER out front might seem even droller. Miami Beach, even though it is now experiencing a little upheaval of popularity among younger people and European art directors, has for many years been mostly a monument to longevity. The preponderance of older residents has made for some curious effects—for instance, the vocabulary of Miami Beach contains a multitude of words to distinguish among types of old people, the way Eskimos use a slew of words to distinguish among various types of snow. Not long ago, I asked a rabbi in Miami Beach what the average age of his congregation was and he said, without missing a beat, "Deceased." This might suggest that Saturday night is not observed as enthusiastically here as it is in places that do not have an advanced median age and the naturally pacifying effect of relentlessly warm, humid weather, but that is not the case. Miami Beach visitors attack Saturday night with a purposefulness that I have rarely encountered anywhere else. Once, on an earlier visit, I spent some time at one of the little art-deco hotels on the far southern tip of the beach. Most of the hotel residents down at this end of Miami Beach are widows from the Northeast who seem to spend most of their days applying zinc oxide to their noses or complaining about the price of produce in local markets. I had expected Saturday night among them to be a complete bust; I was wrong. Vaudeville washouts who sing naughty songs and riff creakily through collector's-item jokes came to the hotels on Saturday nights to entertain in the lobbies. The ladies would have their hair done on Saturday afternoon and would dress in their best clothes for the event. When I expressed surprise about this to Sadie, a woman from Boston I met who had been wintering in Miami Beach for thirty-two years, she expressed some irritation. "What, I'm not going to dress up on Saturday night?" she had said. "I brought twenty-three suitcases down here for my trip. All right, maybe Saturday night isn't exactly the way it used to be. You used to be ashamed to go out in Miami Beach without a mink or a fox stole. Nowadays you don't have to be so dressy. But it's still Saturday night, isn't it?"

The last report I had heard on the Commissioner's Pig-Out before getting to the center that Saturday night was that the unusually warm weather was wreaking some havoc on the ice sculptures. This information had apparently not filtered into the center. Most of the people in the lobby waiting for the dinner bell appeared to be interested less in hearing news of the pig-out than in watching the parade of Pritikin enrollees who were leaving for outside restaurants. I was sitting with a gray-haired woman named Liz who had the lean arms and taut neck of someone who has sworn off all acquaintance with fat, salt, and protein. She paid no attention to my comments about the pig-out and instead was clucking under her breath each time someone walked out the door. "It's scary!" she whispered to me. "Who would want to go out? It's scary to go out to a restaurant!" She mentioned that she had been through the program ten years earlier, and had eaten lunch and dinner here every day since then. Conveniently, her apartment was three blocks from the center. As she was talking, she nodded in greeting to a young man with a number of chins, antic dark hair, and thick black-rimmed glasses who had slumped down on the couch across from us. "Don't you get spastic being here all the time?" he said to Liz. "I get spastic. By Saturday night, I'm spastic. Maybe you're just deconditioned. Maybe you don't need to go out anymore."

"You're Phil, aren't you?" she said. "Tell me, Phil, where are you from? Maybe that has something to do with it."

"I'm from Oklahoma City," he said, sliding farther down in the couch and sounding mournful. "We're big on chicken out there. We're not pigs about steaks, we're just big on chicken. But it's not a geographical thing. I just like to eat."

"It's worse on the weekends, I know," Liz said, clucking again. "But I'm not part of the younger set. I don't need to go out on Saturday night. You'll get over it, too."

Phil spread his fingers out across his belly and squinted his eyes. "Let me ask you something," he said to Liz. "Is there anything else I should know about getting old?"

Just then, someone signaled that the salad bar had opened, and everyone in the lobby stood up, stretched as if they were in no particular hurry, and then raced over to the dining room. On the way, Phil told me that he was a lawyer but he had stopped practicing a few years ago upon receiving an inheritance from his late father, and had since considered his time most profitably invested at the kitchen table. His life's scenario had been spreading out comfortably around him until a few months ago, when his best friend threatened to stop speaking to him unless he lost some weight. He was about to opt for losing the friend rather than the weight when his mother added a few digs of her own regarding his pants size. Thus compelled, he signed up for an unlimited stay at the center and was planning to stay at least thirty-nine days and maybe more. He said he would leave and go back to his condominium in Oklahoma City as soon as he felt he was ready to face without fear a world teeming with cheeseburgers. In the meantime, the whole experience at the center seemed to fill him with a nearly crushing nostalgia for his previous life-style. He told me the story of his journey to Pritikin in a wispy, irregular voice verging on the hysterical. Cumulatively, his voice and the rest of his physical presence were dissonant. One might have expected a man with Phil's critical mass to have cultivated a bellow, something that would have sounded authoritative whenever he hollered, "Waiter!" Instead, it tended to dribble off—an effect sometimes known as "swallowing your words"—giving him the air of someone who was shy unto mortification. In spite of this, though, he was able occasionally to sound pretty insistent. As we were getting up, he said, "I know someone who was caught sneaking sausages in here. I'm not kidding. Sausages! Climbed over the fence with them! Believe me!"

I believed him, and then we walked over to the stainless-steel salad cart, where various greens were arranged in bowls. The diners circled the cart and scrutinized its contents several times, as if they were making sure they weren't overlooking, say, a tub of fresh hot-fudge sauce. Then they would let out long, defeated-sounding sighs, stack some salad on a plate, and move into the dining room, where about thirty tables were set with linens and candles. I took some salad and then sat down at one of the tables with Phil, Liz, Arthur (the pilot who'd happened upon the Hungarian restaurant), a stately woman with a blonde ponytail who said her name was Alicia, and a couple named Jean and Mel.

Jean and Mel, like Liz, live in Miami and had been eating every meal at the center since going through the program. When friends asked them out for dinner, they accepted the invitation only if the friends agreed to have the dinner at the Pritikin Longevity Center. This meant that many Miamians who considered it their right and due to elevate their blood-sugar levels on weekend nights sometimes found themselves eating endive and beef broth after asking Jean and Mel out to dinner. Jean was one of the smallest women I've ever met. A mother of two and comfortably into middle age, she had still passed handily as Robin (of Batman and Robin) at a Halloween party a few months earlier. Her husband, Mel, a hospital vice president, had a round, bald head and a round, peachy face. He looked fit but ample, and every few minutes or so, he would smooth his polo shirt down over his torso and then stare in wonderment at the change in topography that took place around his waist. It wasn't quite alpine, but there was at least evidence of continental drift. The sight of his stomach exposed in this manner seemed to drive Jean into a snit.

"This is all jellybeans," Mel said, smoothing his shirt down before starting his salad. "Jellybeans or potato chips or something like that."

"Oh, Mel, come on, you're awful," Jean hissed. "Liz, tell him he's awful."

The table was silent for a minute. In fact, the entire dining room was silent. The seventy-odd people who were having dinner were fixated wordlessly on their plates. Waiters stood at the perimeter of the dining room, watching to see who was ready for their main course. The only noise besides the crunch of lettuce was the sound of cars rushing by now and then on Collins Avenue. There was another moment of silence, which was broken when Alicia mumbled, "I went out for dinner last Saturday."

No one said anything at first. Then Phil turned to her and said, "Well, did you feel guilty?"

She shrugged. "I tried not to be too bad. I had a few of those stone crab things." Her face lit up. "Have you had any of those? Mmmmm*mmmmm*. I could have had about two hundred." The waiters circled around us and began to take the salad plates away, replacing them with dinner plates. For dinner: a bean stew and three miniature squashes.

Phil, who was sitting next to me, started to chuckle. "Miniature food!" he said. "Oh, God, *miniature* food! It makes me crazy just to look at this. But you know what? Something snapped in me yesterday and now I'm completely happy. I even enjoy miniature food."

"Speaking of food," Mel said, from across the table, "have you ever eaten at Peter Luger's in New York?" A few of us nodded. "Talk about food, they had the best steaks. God, thick and perfect. They'd cook them perfectly. Very juicy." Jean started to glare at him. He poked at his miniature squashes. "There are great steaks in New York, but I really loved Peter Luger's the best."

Alicia said, "I used to go there every now and again. I also loved, oh, what was that place called? They had the best fried fish. It was—oh, you know, in Brooklyn."

"Lundy's," Jean said, looking embarrassed. "I think you're thinking about Lundy's. I loved Lundy's. I loved everything at Lundy's." She scooped up a little more bean stew and then rapped her fork against her plate. "Mel, what was that place, that huge deli we used to take your mother to in Baltimore? Oh, it was incredible. Incredible. Mel, what was it?" As Mel was thinking, I heard Arthur telling Phil that he was at the center because the Federal Aviation Administration wouldn't certify him to fly until his blood pressure dropped. Phil was grinning.

Mel finally said, "I can't remember what it was called. Oh my gosh, it was incredible. Liz, you would have loved this, it was, you know, a really incredible *real* deli. Everything you shouldn't eat. You'd go there for lunch and cholesterol would be coming out of your ears. The pickle bowl, the bread, the corned beef. Right, Jean?" She rolled her eyes.

"I'm seventy-five years old," Liz said to me. "My heart is as clear as a baby's. So I don't get to go out for a lavish Saturday-night dinner anymore. Who wants it? I live without fat and without salt."

"My guru," Mel said, looking at Liz with admiration. "Liz is my guru. You should see her arteries. My God. Anyway, what the heck was that deli called?" At this point, we were all nearly finished with the beans and squash. "Then there was that other incredible place in Baltimore. What's it called, Housner's?" Mel went on. "Oh, was that ever incredible. Ever heard of it? Housner's? Hey, Phil, do you get a lot of good steak in Oklahoma?"

Phil, who was using his last squash to squeegee the last of his bean stew off his plate, shook his head and said, "Chicken. We're not that big on steaks in Oklahoma. You must be thinking of Brooklyn."

"Oh, Brooklyn," Liz said suddenly, in a hushed voice. She looked down as the waiter took her dinner plate away and replaced it with a small bowl holding a baked apple. "Brooklyn, oh my, oh my. I grew up in Brooklyn. I still remember when we used to pack a picnic lunch with sandwiches and take two bottles of beer and spend the afternoon sitting on Sheepshead Bay." A dreamy look passed over her face. "I still remember that at Sheepshead Bay, the air smelled like *salt*."

"Maybe salt substitute," Arthur said, in a disgusted tone.

I'm not sure if every table devoted so much of dinner to discussing previous dinners—previous fatty, salty, high-protein dinners—but by the time we seven were done eating, we were fuller of food memories than of food. Liz even admitted at the end of dinner that she had been hungry for ten years. The meal was so quick—we were done by quarter to seven—that I guessed that the pig-out ice sculptures were probably still intact and that the guava-banana shakes and fudge were nowhere near being served yet, and that any of the good restaurants in Miami were just seating the first of their Saturday-night dinner reservations. It just doesn't take that long to eat miniature food. We had a long conversation about dining out, which ended with the consensus that Saturday had been, pre-Pritikin, the big night for eating, and that it would always feel that way. Phil then told me that before signing up at the center, he had thought that you were restricted in what you could eat but that you could have as much of it as you wanted. He said one of his worst days was when he had discovered that this was a misconception. He looked depressed when he told me this story.

All seven of us at the table were sipping coffee in a thought-induced gloom when Mel stood up, reached for his wallet, and said,

"Look at *this*." He passed around an invitation he and Jean had received to attend one of the many Super Bowl brunches that was being held the next day.

"Mel, put that away," Jean said. "We're not going. Or if we go—nope, we're not going." Then she shifted in her seat and said to me, "By the way, do you know that restaurant in New York, great pastas and bread, oh, let's see—Ernie's, I think. Do you know it? My son lives near there."

By this time, the dining room had mostly emptied. The Pritikin regimen begins at six o'clock every morning, so everyone is drained by nine at night. "What's there to stay up for anyway?" Arthur muttered, as we were walking out. "That's all the food you're going to get, so you might as well call it a day. These will go down in history as the most low-key weekends of my life."

Alicia, who was standing beside him, said, "If I were skinny, I would go over to the Fountainbleau right now and have a drink."

I noticed that a few people had gone to watch the movie *Ruthless People* playing in a lounge upstairs, and a small group had gone into the gym. I ended up on a couch in the lobby with Phil. On the other couches and chairs were about twenty people who had been at other dinner tables. Some of them had visitors who had come to check in on their progress. I heard the phrases "five pounds," "seven pounds," and "got my pulse down" several times. One man, who had long, saggy jowls and was wearing a safari suit, kept announcing in a loud voice, "I feel *great*. I really feel *great*."

"I'll bet he does," Phil said to me. "Everyone walks around saying they feel great. You know, I'll tell you a dark secret. The dark secret of this place is that Dr. Pritikin committed suicide. I think I'm about to start hating this place again." The front door opened and about ten people who had gone out for dinner walked in. One of them was carrying a paper doggie bag.

"Contraband!" Phil hooted. "Is that contraband? Because if it is you should get it out of here! We're not kidding. And if it's chocolate, you're in big trouble."

By nine, everyone, including the man who felt really great, looked wan and exhausted. Little by little, the visitors would leave, and the enrollees would wander off to the elevator and bed. Phil finally stood up and announced that he'd had it for the day. Then he narrowed his eyes and glowered at me. "Are you going to go somewhere now and eat? Something other than miniature food? Are you?" I shook my head and wished him well, walked out of the center, got into my car, drove directly to a restaurant I'm fond of on Washington and Twelfth, ordered dumplings and a beef dish and started to eat. The place was jammed. I ate everything I had ordered and then ordered and ate ice cream and on my way to my hotel I picked up the newspaper. It was too early for news of the pig-out, but there was a short article that said one-half of all Americans go on diets in the month of January, which makes weight loss the most popular New Year's resolution in America.

Hostessing

Park Avenue,
New York, New York

There are many people in the world for whom giving a party would be an unnerving prospect, but Mrs. Thomas Kempner of Manhattan is not among them. Mrs. Kempner, an attractive, well-bred woman who is known to her intimate friends and readers of certain gossip columns as Nan, is not one to worry about burning her roast or getting stood up or not having the table set on time. She is the sort of person who can wrestle a cumbersome guest list into a delightful salon. She knows seating arrangements and reminder cards and table settings cold. She gives dozens of dinner parties every year and none of them makes her so much as slightly nervous. Nan Kempner, in fact, is not just a skillful hostess but an ardent and confident one who has a hostess's temperament and poise and instincts, as well as all those other things that go along with being good at giving nice parties, such as a big apartment on Park Avenue, an investment-banker husband, a butler, a masseuse, a cook, and a horse.

Nan pays most of her hostessing attention to the few hundred Manhattan-based multinationals who are known in cultural shorthand as "society"—a crowd that might actually be blessed with an oversupply of poised hostesses. But even among them, the party-giving skills of Nan Kempner are well known.

"Nan gives a certain kind of party that is very, very alive and very gay. They are very good parties, extremely good parties," Pat Buckley, Nan's good friend and an admired hostess herself, likes to say.

"Her guest list is amusing and her food is very good," says society fixture and interior decorator Chessie Rayner. "She's never changed her living room around in all these years and it works terribly well for any number of guests. Nan was also the first one of us to make a big effort with her food. Then her fabulous cook left. Some people would have just withered on the vine, but Nan just picked herself up and found another fabulous cook and kept on."

Someone who often eats at Nan's says, "Other hostesses aren't as relaxed and welcoming as Nan is, but maybe they don't love it as much as she does. Her mix of guests is good, too. She often has Europeans, and that's fun."

Catie Marron, wife of Paine Webber chief executive Donald Marron, has said, "Nan has immense style. Her parties are wonderfully relaxed and easy. People don't race out ten minutes after dinner at Nan's. You sink into her parties and forget your cares. She's an exceptional hostess."

A society regular who has been invited to Nan's many times said recently, "Nan, in one word, is determined to be the best."

Not surprisingly, Nan Kempner does not traffic in speculative social ventures. She invests in blue-chip stocks such as the top-heavy guest list, the formal dinner for twenty, the crafty seating plan, and the air of upper-class precision. These efforts have not gone unrewarded. Not for nothing has she had Nancy Reagan at her table several times. It is also no surprise that blond Texan billionaire Sid Bass chose a party at Nan's to make his first public appearance with Mercedes Kellogg, the patrician beauty who reorganized his marriage. Nan has, and gives, entrée. These are the hallmarks of a power hostess, which Nan Kempner clearly is. There are many people who contend that Nan is the preeminent hostess in New York

City, which means that by most standards she would be considered one of the preeminent hostesses in the United States of America, and maybe even the world.

In spite of her preeminence, certain facts of Nan Kempner's host-essing style clash with generally held principles of home entertainment. For instance, most people would agree that the best night for parties is Saturday night. This is because a Saturday-night party allows a full day for the host to prepare and for the guest to work up enthusiasm, and everyone is comforted by knowing they have all of Sunday to clean up or recover. People giving Saturday-night parties also try harder to make their parties attractive because they know they're facing off so many other entertainment options that can distract potential guests.

While this is certainly true for most of America, this is not the case for Nan Kempner. Not only are Saturday-night parties in high society infrequent, they actually represent a breach of the basic tenets of upper-class behavior. Before the turn of the century, the typical society schedule was full almost every day of the week, Saturday night included. At the time, most American workers put in a six-day workweek. The new century ushered in the five-day week for most workers; for the first time, the two-day weekend became available to nearly everyone in the country. Saturday night was seized upon as the focus of working-class leisure. As soon as Saturday night became available to ordinary Americans, ignoring it became a primary indicator and diagnostic feature of the upper class. Some of the high-society types I know will admit that once in a while they have a few friends over on a Saturday night, but only if it's a discreet affair held somewhere unobtrusive, like their library or kitchen or country estate. As one widow richly left once explained to me, the trouble is that if you treat Saturday as a big deal, it gives the impression that you don't attend dinner parties and charity balls every other night of the week, and that you don't have an out-of-town weekend retreat, or that you might have needed Saturday afternoon to prepare because you actually work for a living. And that, she said, would be bad.

"I can hardly imagine giving a party on a Saturday night," Nan herself has said. "I'm always out in the country riding my horse and so forth on the weekends, and even if I weren't I can't imagine who would be around to *invite* for a *Saturday* party. I honestly can't imagine it."

A friend of Nan's, a woman who lives on Fifth Avenue, offered the same observation. "Saturday night is for amateurs," she declared. "We aren't amateurs. So naturally, our social lives don't revolve around Saturday night."

"*No one* would think of giving a party on a Saturday night," another New York sophisticate said. "It's absolutely hopeless. I never accept invitations for Saturday night. I never *make* invitations for Saturday nights. I have an ironclad rule about being out of the city by Friday at five. Have you ever heard the expression 'Saturday night is for amateurs'? It's absolutely true. You really should keep that in mind."

"I think people need to rest now and then, don't you?" says Suzy, the New York *Post* gossip columnist. "You go out every other night of the week, so you *must* take the weekend off from the party circuit. Otherwise you simply get too much of muchness and not enough fun."

Another hostess of some renown, who once hired a bagpiper to play at her dinner party for Prince Philip, and another time hired a Russian bear named Rosie to drink beer with her guests, says, "I certainly understand that Saturday night is an important night to many people. I'm sure it's very important to—how shall I say this?—Middle America." Then she shrugged her shoulders and added, "But to *us,* dear, it simply doesn't mean a thing."

Of course, there are a few circumstances under which a society hostess will break ranks and give a party on a Saturday night. Even Nan Kempner will confess to this. What might qualify would be a weekend visit from titled or recently deposed European royalty, or if Johnny Carson were in town on a weekend, or if one were asked to give a Saturday-night party by the kind of friend who really knows how to ask—Henry Kissinger, maybe. In other words, the circumstances would have to be pretty good. When I first met Nan Kempner, a very dear friend of hers from Paris, the Countess Isabel d'Ornano, had just announced her intention to zip in and out of New York for a few days. The countess was one of those people whose visits didn't come and go without notice, just the way a visit by a grizzly to a Yosemite campground would probably not go without notice. In the case of countesses, the standard notice given is a formal dinner party for sixteen or twenty. The prospect of such a party would have ordinarily delighted Nan, because, as she has told me, there is no better and no more wonderful party than one you give in honor of a special friend. The trouble with this occasion was that the countess's schedule was only open on Saturday night. No matter what her instincts told her, Nan was going to have to give a regulation-sized full-bore dinner party on a Saturday night.

Being something of a congenital optimist, Nan was still able to find a few things to be thankful for. For instance, she made note of the fact that the countess's visit would be after everyone—that is, that small universe of everyones who were potential guests at the affair—was back from the couture collections in Paris, and it would be just after the Aspen ski season, and it would fall just before everyone would have to leave for Nassau, the standard site of the society spring break. Considering that there might not have been anyone in town at all, let alone on a weekend, this was a little consolation for having to give a party on a Saturday night.

On the Thursday morning before the party, Nan was lounging in the library of her Park Avenue apartment while she worked the phone. She has a low, strong voice that has that oxymoronic quality of sounding simultaneously energetic and bored—a quality that is extremely rare except in people who don't like parties on Saturday nights. It is a voice that is both cultured and brash, like the ones you hear in those old MGM movies where everyone drinks a lot of neat-looking cocktails and has a lot of mildly irritating fights.

I'd never met Nan in person before this Thursday, but I'd spoken to her on the phone, and that voice had led me to expect an ample MGM-style gal. Actually, Nan is 100 percent ectomorph. She was perhaps the least overstuffed item in her library, a large square room paneled in old, burnished, dark brown wood and carpeted with a number of densely patterned Persian rugs, and otherwise filled with bulbous chintz-covered couches, chintz pillows, needlepoint and Bargello pillows, antique Bombay chests, life-size porcelain dogs, china fish, china birds, wooden apples and pears, narcissus in terra-cotta pots, exotic grasses in terra-cotta planters, bowlegged end tables, oil paintings in batches leaning against the wall, watercolor paintings in stacks, charcoal sketches, cigarette boxes, and ivory netsuke in the shapes of fishes, fishermen, dogs, and wild animals. One wall was entirely given over to books—among them, ones about Chinese painting, Antonio Gaudi, Cole Porter, orchids, Balthus, Botticelli, Degas, Africa, Japan, France, how to quit smoking, and Odilon Redon. Frankly, it was a little busy. From the library, some of the rest of the apartment was visible, but not much except a large, curving stairway with a dark, shiny banister that sprouted off of the formal entrance hall, and a few rooms that looked as if they might sprout other rooms and other stairways. The roominess of the place gave me the feeling that there might be whole industries being built and destroyed in various outlying parts of the apartment.

"Hello, darling! Did you get my message?" Nan was saying into the phone as I sat down. She waved at me distractedly as she listened into the receiver. After a minute, she covered the phone's mouthpiece with her hand, arched her eyebrows, and mouthed the words "my florist" to me.

"No? Yes? Good. Wonderful. Darling, I need flowers for Saturday night," she said into the phone.

". . . . ."

"Yes, yes. You've got all day. The party isn't until Saturday night."

". . . . ."

"Yes, *Saturday*. This Saturday. Darling, I want something *pretty*. Lilies, maybe. Lilies last. Darling, just make it something that will *last*. I've a luncheon here on Wednesday. It would be nice if they would stay nice until then."

". . . . ."

"Wonderful. Good, darling. Love you! Byyyeee!"

· She hung up the phone and then immediately lifted it again and dialed the intercom in her personal secretary's office.

"Barbara, did you hear from Peter Sharp yet? Is he coming? You sent him the reminder card?"

". . . . ."

"Are you certain? Call him and remind him, please."

". . . . ."

"Yes, I suppose. It's already Thursday."

She pressed a button on the phone and then dialed her chef.

"Margaret? Yes, hello, dear! How is everything?"

". . . . ."

"Yes, dear, I want the Apple Brown Betty. Oh, you know how much I do love dessert. I want this whole meal to be very American, you know. It will be a lovely thing for the countess. Oh, Margaret, you're going to make your crabmeat in aspic, aren't you, dear?"

". . . . ."

"Terrific! Good, darling. See you Saturday. Byyyeee!"

This time when she hung up, she pushed the phone aside, and leaned back into the couch cushions, which bulged up around her like dough. Nan is almost as well known for her wardrobe as her parties, and as a result, any mention of one of her gatherings usually includes a resume of her dress and its designer. The affection is returned, it seems, since Nan is welcomed at every designer's show-room; Bill Blass, for one, recently described her in an interview as "one of [his] gals." This morning, though, Nan was dressed plainly in a mint-green flannel bathrobe that was wrapped tightly around her and cinched to a chokehold with a matching belt. She has ashy blonde hair, which is parted in the middle and hangs just past her ears; small, shiny, round eyes; a wide, flat mouth; and a long neck. She moves her hands gracefully and often. She is renowned for her extreme thinness. In photographs, she gives the impression of bright, barely contained energy and hunger. In person, she has a strong-featured look of command.

"We're running late today, and I *hate* that," she said. "I've just finished my pedicure, and that was late, and I've got a luncheon at noon that I must go to, and I still have to make these calls. It might be a rather hectic day."

I asked if she was finding a Saturday-night party particularly hard to put together.

"Well, it's *certainly* not my favorite night for parties," she said, and then began a hoarse, robust laugh. "I definitely prefer the mid-dle of the week. I'll tell you what I love to do on a Saturday night—I love to rent a movie tape and sit in bed and watch it! To me, that's the perfect Saturday night. I absolutely *hate* to go out on Saturday night. I think that's when most people go out, though, isn't it? And Tommy, my husband, is a real Joe College type, you know, and he so hates to go out any night of the week. And on Saturday? Oh, my!" She slapped her knee. "I especially hate to give a *party* on a Saturday night, but we simply had to schedule this for a Saturday. A few people can't come because they're away for the weekend. I'm usually in the country every weekend, of course. But I imagine this will have to do. The countess is a great and dear and wonderful and charming friend of mine, and she's just the prettiest and most lovely person, and has just the greatest taste of anyone I know, really—or at least, she has taste that is as wonderful as anyone I know—and really, she's just so *pretty*, and such a dear person, and her family is so lovely. Her cousins have done so much for Deauville and that part of France, you know. She and her husband, Count Hubert d'Ornano, have this lovely company that makes natural perfumes and bath products that they sell at Bergdorf's that is the most wonderful stuff I've ever used. Have you ever tried it? It's wonderful. At any rate, when I saw Isabel in Paris in September, she told me that she would be coming and would like to see some of her friends. I love my apartment, you know, and one does love seeing one's friends in one's apartment. I'd much rather have people here than go out, absolutely."

The phone rang. "Helloooo?" Nan said.

". . . . ."

"Yes, oh, Glenn, darling!"

". . . . ."

"Yes, yes, Wednesday for lunch."

(Glenn is Glenn Bernbaum, a Manhattan restaurateur who serves in the unofficial but widely recognized position as the preeminent hostess's host and upper-crust confidante. His restaurant, Mortimer's, has for many years been to the wealthy people of the Upper East Side what the American embassy in Nepal is to trekkers from Pittsburgh. Mortimer's, to the untrained eye, is a nice but ordinary-looking café with checkered tablecloths and good chicken hash, but to society folk, it is a place where they know they will be recognized, seated well, and treated the right way. They know that Mortimer's is governed by the same exceptional social conditions as they are—for instance, even though Saturday night is by far the busiest night for restaurants around the country, Saturday nights at Mortimer's are pretty dead. They also know that at Mortimer's they will not bump into people from New Jersey looking for a rowdy good time. As a result, many hostesses give dinner parties and luncheons at Mortimer's on those occasions when they don't want to give them at home—when their household staff or florist is on vacation, for instance. Nan was planning to give a small lunch party there a few days after her Saturday-night affair.)

"Around one o'clock," Nan said to Glenn. "Three of us."

". . . . ."

"Noooo. Just three, darling. Oh, and Monday I'm giving a lunch, too. There will be eight on Monday."

". . . . ."

"Yes, darling, I am. Yes, Saturday night. Sixteen. Love you, darling. Byyyeee!"

Nan says that she can't remember how many parties she's given, but she still remembers her first one: London, 1952, roast beef. At that time, she was a recent bride who'd come to New York society by way of a wealthy, upright San Francisco upbringing. Her husband Tom's ancestors had exercised caution and daring at the respectively pertinent moments on Wall Street, and had thus provided their descendants with certain fungible advantages in life. Before Tom and Nan Kempner stepped into New York society, they spent the year in London that is standard with those people who want to polish their graces.

"It was the first year we were married," she said of her year in England. "Food was still rationed then. I used to have roast beef shipped in. Can you imagine? The first night I would have friends over and run the beef through the grinder and serve it as steak tartare, and the second night I would have other people over and serve it as regular roast beef, and the third night, I'd have a few more people over and serve it to them as roast-beef hash. We had to use ingenuity then, and it worked." Now Nan believes a party of real quality depends more on a mastery of details than on the ability to stretch beef. She is someone who maintains, as Ludwig Mies van der Rohe once said, that God is in the details. "Naturally, when one has a dinner in Manhattan, one buys one's basics at Butterfield Market," she said. "Fish we get at Leonard's, of course. And these Korean markets"—her voice suddenly rose—"well, my, they are marvelous, really. Do you ever go to them? They have absolutely everything, and they really have the most wonderful stuff, and they're open all the time, and if we find we're short a head of lettuce or a banana, we can just pop! over to the Korean market and grab it." She clasped her hands in her lap. "How do I actually put together my party? Of course, one calls with an invitation and I have Barbara send out reminder cards, and I just try to put together the most amusing and fascinating people I know."

She leaned farther back into the cushions, and then she stretched her long, thin feet out on the coffee table, pushing aside about a dozen priceless little things. Her legs looked about as wide as small-sized cardboard mailing tubes. Her toenails had a pearly polish. Just then, a housekeeper with a soft, grayish face padded into the library, set down a silver tea set, and padded out to a remote outpost north-northeast of the entrance hall. A car honked somewhere on Park Avenue.

"I like to pick out something special for the table first, of course. For this Saturday night, I have a very special embroidered cloth from Italy that some cousins gave us," Nan said, pointing toward the dining room. "That's what I've chosen for the table. I'm fortunate because I don't use a caterer—Margaret, my special chef, comes in for parties, and she and I have already arranged the menu. I love thinking about what we're going to eat. I also have some wonderful waiters, one of whom is my former butler, and they come in to help, and they make sure there are fresh cigarettes out in the cigarette holders and fresh candy in all the dishes, and we put a few flowers all around to make the place a bit more gala. On the table I put my collection of antique porcelain birds, and I move them around at whim until they look just right.

"I think the magic number for dinner is eight or ten, but I'm very, very bad, and once I get started I just can't stop. I can seat thirty at my dining-room table, and quite a lot more if I break it into several smaller tables, although I really like having a party seated at a single table. I love giving spaghetti parties on Sunday nights, and those are big, oh, informal things, where everyone takes a tray and they're just so much fun! Those Sunday spaghetti dinners are big crowds and they are absolutely so much fun. I'm having sixteen guests this Saturday. Of course, everyone has an assigned place at the table. I make up the seating plan ten minutes before they come, when I'm still in the bathtub, and then I'll just go to the closet and just pull out something to wear. That's exactly when I'll start preparing. On Saturday morning, I'm planning to go out to the country and play tennis and ride my horse, and then I'll have my daily massage in the late afternoon. I don't get nervous in the least when I'm giving a party. I've always felt the best parties are the ones that just happen, not the ones that are overly planned. I can give a party at the drop of a hat. That's why I don't give many black-tie dinners at home, except if it's absolutely necessary. I just think black-tie puts a thud-dull thing on a party, don't you?"

I once asked someone who attends a great number of New York society dinner parties how a person could go about achieving pre-eminence as a hostess, and she said, "Unless they're very rich or quite attractive, they should stay where they are. That's what I'd recommend. I'd say 'Please stay home, whoever you are!'" This is to say that hostessing, at least as it is practiced by Nan Kempner, is not a real growth industry, and whatever jobs it offers are mostly already taken by people who are born into the business. Lately, charity balls and galas, staged in public arenas like Lincoln Center and the Metropolitan Museum of Art, have started to overtake the fancy dinner party. Hostesses adept at booking rooms and managing thundering mobs are beginning to eclipse those like Nan, who relish entertaining at home and picking the perfect sixteen or twenty friends to spend an evening together. New York society has gone through this cycle before. In the 1800s, there was a rage for social clubs—The Friendly, Drone, Kraut, Turtle, Bread and Cheese, Union, Lotos, and Century Club, among others—and most clubs had big clubhouses where members hosted gigantic parties. Then at the end of the century, a prominent family built a new mansion on

Fifth Avenue with a ballroom on the first floor, causing ballroom envy to break out in high society and bringing back the fashion for parties at home. The private society soiree was then at its peak, piloted by those preeminent hostesses who have preceded Nan, such as Elsie De Wolfe, who was known fondly as "the monster of frivolity," and Elsa Maxwell, Noël Coward's "darling fat girl." Clubs shut down or shrank in importance.

Now, public spectacles are taking over again. This also happens to be true in Washington, D.C., the only other American city where hostesses ever reach the kind of social momentousness that they do on Park Avenue. Like their counterparts in New York, serious capital party givers also never schedule anything for Saturday night. Everyone blames the airlines for the ruination of the Washington weekend, because they made it a cinch for members of Congress to head back home every Friday night. As any Washington observer will tell you, a party without at least two congressmen is a flagrant waste of lamb chops. While a certain equation of ambassadors and cabinet members can sometimes reach parity with a congressman, most hostesses don't even bother trying and just schedule their important salons during the week. But these days, big parties given in restaurants and halls to celebrate the opening of an exhibition or to raise money for a popular cause have become the currency in Washington's haute social life just as they have in New York's.

Some people think the spectacular showiness of charity balls is perfectly suited to this era of conspicuous conspicuousness, and that the private party is just too discreet a life-form to survive. Others have said, and mean it seriously, that the shortage of good household help has made being a hostess in the grand tradition a hellish undertaking these days. The general agreement, though, is that Nan is becoming a rare breed. "The day of the top New York hostess is over," Suzy, the gossip columnist, who has written about many of Nan Kempner's parties, says. "The lovely, graceful days when there were wonderful hostesses who knew everything about food and manners are over. Now everything is a mob scene. It's an ego trip to have so many people and such large events. I never judge a good party by that. When I judge a party, I go by fun. I go by laughs. I go by amusing. That is not what you get in these huge public spectacles. It's so rare to have a little private party now that whenever there is one, everyone just shouts for glee."

When a table is set for a proper society party, it is a harmony of many elements. Nan's table, on the night of her party for Countess d'Ornano, had sixteen place settings arranged on a dark, heavy-legged dining table that had been draped with a white handkerchief-linen tablecloth embroidered with sprays of tiny wildflowers. Each place setting had three bubble-thin crystal goblets of graduated profiles; three forks; three knives; and two spoons. There was enough silver on the table to make your hands itch. The silver was placed precisely around a white porcelain plate edged in gold leaf. The white plate was just a marker. It would never have food on it. It would be lifted and replaced with a floral Royal Doulton plate on which the first course would be arranged and served, and that in turn would be replaced with a cream-colored piece of Spode for the main course. Dessert would be served on small plates of antique Chinese porcelain. Nan has more sets of china, which are piled in cupboards in the butler's pantry, but she had earlier that day decided this was the combination that would work tonight. Two large arrangements of flowers—some lilies—were set out on the sideboards. In the center of the table were cigarettes and four porcelain roosters set in a row.

As I was admiring the table, one of the waiters began to lift one of the roosters. Someone in the kitchen called out, "Just leave the roosters alone. Nan will do that." The waiter, one of four who had been setting the table, put the bird down and walked out of the dining room and back into the kitchen. The chef—a sturdy, dark-haired young woman named Margaret Hartnett, who left a job at a Manhattan restaurant to cook for Nan and several other hostesses—murmured something to him and then went back to defrosting frozen spinach.

"That's Nan's thing, the roosters," Margaret explained. "They're fine how they are. That's something she likes to do herself. All the hostesses have something they like to do themselves. We just leave them as they are and she'll fix them when she comes down." The intercom buzzed.

—

"Yes, Nan?" Margaret said into the receiver.

". . . . ."

"The ham looks fine. It looks great. It's twenty pounds. I'm sure it will be enough."

". . . . ."

"Everything's set. The waiters are already dressed."

As she was saying this, the waiters looked at her sheepishly, pulled their ties out of their pockets and put them on. Margaret hung up the intercom, looked at her watch, and said in a loud voice, "Seven-fifteen, guys," and then picked up a list and said, "Let's see, ham, okay, crabmeat in aspic, yep, lemon mayonnaise sauce, okay, yams, fine, spinach over there, corn muffins. Corn muffins! Damn!" She skipped over to the oven and took out a tray of pale muffins, poked them, and put them back in. Then she surveyed the kitchen, a huge, white, L-shaped room with a tall, old stove, glass-front cabinets that went all the way to the ceiling, and several worktables. Off the far end of the kitchen was a stairway that led to the servants' quarters.

"I'm usually in the country with Nan over the weekend, cooking out there," Margaret said. "Nan just got home from there at five. She's upstairs having a bath. Mr. Kempner's getting ready, too. Maybe I'm a little out of synch because I'm never here on the weekend. Okay, let's see, muffins, Apple Brown Betty. Fine. You think it's weird to use frozen spinach? Come on, *everyone* uses frozen spinach."

Earlier in the week, I had asked Nan if I could come to her dinner party. At the time, she looked baffled, as if I had said something in Chinese. After it sank in, she gave a hoarse laugh and said, "Oh, well, it would be lovely but, you know, everything is set for the guests already. It's not just a matter of adding someone in, just like that. These things involve a little planning." She agreed, then, that I should drop by before the party to at least see the last minutes before the event began. When I arrived, the apartment appeared to have been overtaken by a phalanx of waiters, cooks, housekeepers, and butlers. Nan's usual schedule allowed for her to come down a minute or two before the guests would arrive so she could sign off on the last details. The intercom helped with any intermediate concerns. The effect was not unlike Mission Control radioing commands to a space capsule. Otherwise, Margaret took charge.

"It's important to keep all of this going smoothly," Margaret said. "Hostessing is unforgiving work. I realize that the secretary does all the inviting, and the chef does the ordering and the cooking, and the butler and waiters do all the serving, but you just don't get to the top by screwing up. Nan's at the top. She's consummate. She is one of the great hostesses. She gives it a special touch. She comes down and arranges the birds. She brings people together. Nobody does this anymore. Nobody knows how important these things are to this kind of society. It's a very formal thing. People are introduced into high society this way. It's going to end someday, because nobody does it like this anymore. I feel like I'm cooking for the final march of the dinosaurs."

At seven forty-five, Bernardo, who is Nan's head waiter when she has parties and had been her butler before that for years, closed the heavy swinging door between the dining room and the kitchen. Margaret finished with the spinach and dumped the dirty pots and pans into the sink, checked her list again, and started to whistle. "This isn't a biggie," she said. "We're all under control. The guests are set to arrive in about three minutes. The waiters will get out there with the hors d'oeuvres, and then we'll wait a bit and serve supper. I'll be home by midnight. This isn't a late-night kind of crowd." The intercom buzzed again.

"Yes, Nan?" Margaret said.

". . . . ."

"Okay, Bernardo took out the wine."

". . . . ."

"All done."

A few days later—a few days and a couple of hours after I had been firmly escorted out of the apartment by the back door—I spoke to Nan about the party. She felt she had invited a group that was solid and important and had a nice amount of variety. Pat Kennedy Lawford was there; three Radziwills; Ambassador and Mrs. William Luers of the Metropolitan Museum of Art; Ambassador Julio Santo-Domingo, who was the most in-demand attaché in the city at the time; Lady Grace Dudley; and a few others less well known. Naturally, the guest of honor was the Countess Isabel d'Ornano, who for a brief, queer moment on Park Avenue had managed to make Saturday night into what it is everywhere else in the country. I asked Nan how she thought it had turned out. She said she found it very amusing. "Just a wonderful good time, with lots of conversation and laughs," she added. "This was, you see, just a marvelous group. It was really wonderful. It was a lot of great old pals." By her description, I guessed that it was a success by most measures, and one that would get some mention in the press, as Nan's parties ordinarily do. This time, though, it ended differently. There wasn't a word of it in the press. The party had taken place on a Saturday night, so naturally, none of the columnists who usually keep track of these things would have known there was anything of note going on. Most of them, anyway, were away for the weekend.

Recently, I read something about the nature of American party giving. The study, conducted by the University of Chicago, had been completed in 1960, just when middle-class values had become an end in themselves rather than being strictly imitative of upper-class style, and middle-class habits had finally overtaken upper-class habits as the important social index of the time. It said the formal, carefully arranged, detail-specific upper-class dinner party was a relic that no one wanted to imitate anymore. It said that the party in America was now dominated by "the mode of documentary realism." The distinction between the host and the guest, real-life behavior and party behavior, that had been the style of the upper-class dinner party, was now blurred or gone or just forgotten.

So when Nan Kempner orchestrates a guest list, and sends out reminder cards, and hires her waiters, and plans her menus, and chooses her tablecloth, and orders her flowers, and draws up her seating chart, and rearranges her porcelain birds, and shepherds every detail, as she does a few dozen times each year, she is bucking the doctrine of the documentarily realistic party. She is carefully maintaining the distance between the world where parties just happen, especially on Saturday nights, and her own world, where even now parties are still carefully plotted, blocked, and staged.

—

• • •

It happens that I have attended and hosted many parties myself, and I would say that for most Americans, documentarily realistic parties are still the dominant mode of social life. Some parties happen to be more documentarily realistic than others, such as a party I managed to attend not long ago in Atlanta, Georgia. I had been talking to a displaced southerner who mentioned to me that a real sub–Mason-Dixon Saturday night couldn't be considered complete without a post-college-football-game party. He explained that there are so few professional sports teams in the South relative to the number of people and, more specifically, to the number of sports fans, that college games in the region end up attracting a huge and impassioned audience from outside the student body. Because the games always take place on Saturday afternoons, they seem to segue into Saturday evening, in the form of either celebration bashes or consolation parties. In either case, he said, the parties are carried off with considerable enthusiasm. "That's my memory of my southern childhood," he said, sounding wistful. "College ball games and many kegs of beer."

Of the games scheduled for that weekend, I was advised that the one that had the most potential was a Georgia Tech–Auburn matchup at the Georgia Tech stadium in Atlanta, so I made my way to Atlanta early that day. Even if I had just arrived in town from, say, Alpha Centauri, I wouldn't have had too much difficulty finding the football game. By noon, hundreds of people dressed in orange-and-blue Auburn outfits and thousands in Georgia Tech yellow-and-black were already walking down North Avenue to the stadium. On the way, I passed the parking lot of an Episcopal church. Four or five station wagons, their tailgates flattened and laden with liquor bottles, were parked in the lot, serving as makeshift bars for a lively group of sports fans. A few of the fans near the station wagons were singing the theme song from *The Flintstones* while crushing beer cans in their fists.

My seat turned out to be near one of the goal lines and next to two Georgia Tech students—a heavyset blond young man who was wearing a slightly shredded T-shirt that said "I Love NY Subways," and his friend, who had dark hair and the beginnings of a beard, and who exuded the restive air of juvenile menace. The dark-haired one was carrying a handmade sign that said KICK 'EM IN THE BUTT and was wearing a white T-shirt that said "Sig Ep: No Regard for Life, Limb, or Date." He sat mute except for anytime the announcer spoke, at which point he would scream "Big fuckin' deal!!" and turn bright red in the face. He screamed especially loudly when the announcer intoned, between a first and second down, "Dr. Marvin Feldstein will deliver an address at seven a.m. tomorrow morning at the College of Management auditorium." The dark-haired guy kept up his screaming until the blond one finally slugged him really hard in the chest and told him to shut up. They livened up the game for me, and I thought they might know of some parties.

"Parties, yeah, of course, what do you think?" the blond— Chris—said to me. "Sure, there's going to be some parties tonight! You should come with us! My frat's having a Redneck Weekend celebration, and we're definitely going to have a great party tonight. We have a party after every home football game. We've had four home games so far this season, so it's been a little hard on the students, if you know what I mean. I'd guess that everyone here, even including the old people, are going to some party or another after the game. See, in the South, football is an all-day and all-night event. My frat's goal this year was ten parties in ten weeks. We're doing really well. We've already had ten parties and we still have six weeks to go." He went on to say that Saturday-night post-football parties were especially important at Tech because unlike some other colleges, they did not have nonstop parties. "We have a fairly high percentage of geeks. I'd say about sixty percent of the school is jocks and thirty percent I'd call geeks," he said. "At some places, like University of Georgia, they party constantly because they have fewer geeks. Here Saturday night is pretty important because it's football night, and that's the only night we can really get the whole place going."

After the game, Chris, Dan (the screamer), and I walked to the Varsity Drive-In, the restaurant on the very outskirts of the Georgia Tech campus that claims, among other things, to be the world's largest drive-in and a "cosmopolitan spot known to all." The Varsity also boasts of selling more than one ton of onions, two miles of hot dogs, and five thousand fried pies each day, and of selling no food more than twelve hours old. As the Varsity is the traditional post-game, pre-party stop for Georgia Tech fans, the place was mobbed. When we finally got to the front of the hot-dog line, one of the men working behind the counter was saying to someone, "I think the punks just come here on Saturday night because it takes them all day to do their hair." Chris, Dan, and I ate about a tenth of a mile of hot dogs and then walked back to the frat house, which was a gracious southern mansion with a huge porch surrounded by enormous, arching oak trees. It was already dark outside.

Beside the house, a band on a makeshift stage was playing a sludgy rock song. About eighty or a hundred people, all college age, milled around the stage; about half were dancing or moving fast enough to look as if they were. Most of the lawn had been churned up into a paste of mud, beer, and grass. Next door, music from some sort of sound system was exploding out of another gracious southern mansion and another hundred or so revelers stumbled around. Across the street, another party of about seventy-five was spilling off of the lawn, across the sidewalk, and into the street. In fact, down the entire block—a gently curving street lined with sumptuous old houses—parties were erupting like reports of gunfire across a battlefield. It seemed quite informal. Dan started to run toward a row of beer kegs sitting under a tree. "This is it!" he screamed. "This is a release from tension!"

Just then, a pickup truck drove by slowly, and a guy sitting in the bed of the truck hollered to no one in particular, "What's the world coming to?" The truck idled in front of one of the houses and then disappeared down the street.

"In case you were wondering, these days we've sort of moved out of drugs," Chris was saying to me as we walked toward the bandstand. "This is much more of a beer thing these days."

Within a minute or two, I was abandoned by Chris and Dan, who had commenced constructive engagement with the beer kegs, so I wandered aimlessly around the party. After a while, a "party van" full of middle-aged Georgia Tech alumni cruised up and down the street; a pimply kid in a rented limousine persuaded two girls to ride around with him, and a few minutes later they emerged from the car screaming and laughing; about ten students who said they'd been studying all night descended onto one of the parties and chugged beers; people rolled in the mud and sang; someone shot off a few small firecrackers; a few people threw up in the bushes; small groups broke off, headed to the Varsity for food, and came back just as another group broke off; the band quit playing and started drinking beer, but then someone turned on an oldies radio station and the dancing kept on; a Georgia Tech student pulled me aside and said that he thought that most of the girls from Agnes Scott College, an all-women's school down the street, look like monkeys. The night seemed to be picking up speed. I remember a patrol car cruising by, and I remember talking to the officer, who said, "Football is a very important part of the academic life. If anyone's complaining about noise from the parties, it's probably just some students who are trying to study or something." By midnight, there were so many parties going on simultaneously that it had the same effect as seeing a tape loop shown on a row of television monitors, or having one of those dreams when you walk through a room and open a door and find yourself in another room with another door and so on.

Toward the end of the night, which was actually the beginning of the morning, I walked to the farthest house on the street. It had a long, sloping roof and fat, striated columns. I had been told it belonged to a fraternity that attracted the sons of very rich southern families. The house was quiet and looked virtually abandoned except that seven young men—some of them wearing sunglasses—were sitting on the front lawn on furniture that seemed to have come from a prudish but once-fashionable living room. Another young guy was sitting on the life-size stone lion that guarded the front walk. He was wearing a crumpled button-down white oxford shirt, big tan shorts, and black sunglasses, and he had that hunched-up lonesome skinny-boy look that southern boys identify with northern boys, and northern boys identify with James Dean. Behind him was a sizable bonfire. I could make out the shapes of a few chairs and a coffee table in the blaze.

"We're on probation," the one on the lion said to me. "We can't participate in any parties. We have a problem with our grades. We *certainly* do. So we're cleaning the house instead." He dismounted the lion and took a few steps back. Two of the men sitting in the living room furniture picked up bottles and threw them at the lion. A few of the bottles missed, and the rest smashed and landed with a tinkle on the lawn. Someone poked at the fire with a table leg and the furniture in the bonfire started to crackle and collapse. "So what's a two-point-five grade average, exactly?" he went on, and then he ducked as someone threw another bottle. "If we don't do better we might get our charter revoked, that's all. That would be *such* a shame, wouldn't it, and the alumni do hate that sort of thing. But we're having a growth experience here, right? Now we know that a party is just a state of mind. At least we're having a nice fire and we have this nice lion. We're having a pretty good time." He pushed his sunglasses back and smiled to himself.

It occurred to me then that even though Nan would not have done this party quite this way, it still proved her theory that if you have thought ahead and organized the details, the rest of the party will take care of itself.

Praying

Lower East Side,
New York, New York

The Bowery Mission, the second oldest rescue mission in the country, is on a Lower Manhattan street called Bowery, which is the main drag of a neighborhood, called the Bowery, that used to cater to a rough class of workingmen but is now mainly the center of the restaurant-supply business in New York. You can buy milk-shake machines, grills, toasters, oven shelves, cake platters, pie racks, meat tongs, electric mixers, espresso makers, eggbeaters, saucepans, and pepper grinders at a dozen different stores on Bowery, but the only place you can get a meal these days is at the Bowery Mission.

The mission is a small building, fairly unremarkable to look at, except that it has three bright red doors and a crowd of anxious-looking men on the sidewalk just outside around mealtime. People on their way to the mission for a meal tend to employ a quick and purposeful stride. Very few people stroll at leisure in this section of the Bowery, although occasionally someone will roll by in a wheelchair. The street in front of the mission is sooty. Black grit regularly kicks up off of the curb and swirls around in the wind. There are often twisters of grit in front of the Bowery Mission when the climate on the rest of the street appears calm. The Sunshine Hotel, a single-room-occupancy hotel, is a few doors down from the mission. CBGB's, the punk club, is a few blocks up. The closest art gallery is three blocks away, on West Broadway.

I heard many stories during my visits to the Bowery Mission, and they all had a similar structure: the willing but unwitting innocent led by fate and God's hand into something new and marvelous. One of the stories was about how a woman named Fannie Crosby was noodling around on the mission's piano one afternoon about a hundred years ago and ended up writing what have since become some of the world's most famous Christian hymns. Another was about how a few years ago, a New Jersey police officer had put a .357 Magnum to his temple, cocked the trigger, reconsidered, and now comes to the mission every week or so to play his saxophone for the men.

Another was about how, years ago, an elder of a Mennonite Church in Lancaster, Pennsylvania, was passing through New York and somehow chanced upon the Bowery Mission. Its efforts to feed the hungry and save the wretched so impressed him that he determined that when he got back to Pennsylvania he would have his church adopt the mission as one of its charitable ventures. A ride from Lancaster to the Bowery would cover about two hundred miles and some sociological diversity. Most Mennonites had never taken that ride before this incident, just as most habitués of the mission had never before come into contact with members of this pacifist, agrarian, strict Protestant sect. Nonetheless, the elder's enthusiasm for the place eventually spread from his church to many other Mennonite churches in the Lancaster area, forging a connection between the sect and the Lower East Side of Manhattan that would probably strike many people as unlikely. The new and marvelous part of this story includes the Mennonites' donations of food, clothing, and money to the mission, and it also includes the decision by the Mennonites to make regular visits to the mission part of their largesse. As far as anyone at the Bowery Mission now seems to remember, Mennonites have been coming to Manhattan on almost every Saturday night to bear witness and speak the Word.

Of course, most of the stories about the Bowery Mission are about the despairing men who have come for the prayer services and meals that the mission offers to anyone on the street, and about how some of those men find themselves enrolling in the mission's rehabilitation program and leaving a few months later with a right relationship to God, having been unburdened of a wrong relationship to drugs and alcohol. Kenny Haisley, who was my escort at the Bowery Mission on a Saturday night not long ago, is one of those men. Kenny is tall and broad shouldered, and has smooth dark skin, close-cropped hair, dark eyes, a worried-looking smile, and a rolling, long-legged gait. He is twenty-five years old. On any street in New York, you would come across someone who looks like him probably a dozen times. Some of the times when you would have come across someone like Kenny you wouldn't have liked it. Armed robbery and attempted murder in service to his crack addiction have resulted in Kenny's experiencing some interludes in prison. During one of those interludes, a prison counselor told him about the Bowery Mission, about how it offered religious services and meals to street people and also had a residential rehabilitation program, which stresses Bible study and prayer and discipline as an antidote to drugs and alcohol. A short time later, Kenny found himself in front of the mission's red doors.

At the time of my visit, Kenny had been in the rehabilitation program for thirty-three days and didn't want to venture yet how many more he'd be staying. "When the Lord tells me it's time to go, that's when I'll go," he said. "Until then, I'm staying here, because no way am I going to mess up again." When he makes such pronouncements, he usually gazes at the ground and shakes his head, as if he were in the middle of some private internal argument. If he is standing up as he speaks, he shoves his hands into his pants pockets and sways back and forth. These bashful gestures are curiously at odds with his size, which is vaguely menacing. Overall, his manner is that of someone who has measured up his life and figures he has a lot of apologizing to do. "I used to think I was really tough," he says, shrugging and glancing down. "Now I realize I was just stupid."

At six o'clock on the Saturday night of my visit, Kenny met me at the door of the mission. It was cold and drizzly outside, and a crowd of about sixty people had already gathered on the sidewalk.

In order to get a meal at the mission, you have to first sit through the prayer service. On most days of the week, you have three opportunities at the mission to pray and eat. On Saturdays, the schedule is slightly different: there are only two services and they start an hour later than they do during the rest of the week. The program men are also allowed more free time and can have visitors on the weekend, so there is a different atmosphere and often a few of a different variety of person in the chapel on Saturday nights.

On this particular Saturday night, most of the people waiting on the sidewalk in front of the mission chapel were men of indeterminate age, in beat-up clothes and coats. Three or four of them were engaged in conversation, but most of them stood by themselves, smoking cigarettes or staring across the street. There was no one else within sight on Bowery. A bus with Pennsylvania plates was parked in front of the mission with one tire up on the curb. Kenny pushed open the door and let me in, and spent a moment surveying the crowd before closing the door.

"Too early. Doors don't open until seven," he said. "Oooh, it's cold out there. I'm glad I'm inside and not outside." We walked back through the dining room, which is a large, low-ceilinged rectangle with about two dozen metal tables, reminiscent of a school cafeteria. We crossed paths with another program man named Wilberto Ramos, who greeted Kenny and then asked if he knew where the Mennonites were. "They're out for a walk," Kenny said to him.

"Around here? They're taking a walk around here?" Wilberto asked.

Kenny shifted his weight from foot to foot. "Yeah, around here. Tommy took them on a tour of the Bowery."

"Oh my God, can you believe it?" Wilberto said.

"I can believe anything," Kenny said.

"Well, God bless them," Wilberto said. "I just hope they get back alive so we can start the service on time."

We walked to a back dining area, where the program men eat— they have their meals before the service, so that they can run the soup line for the street men—and where the various church representatives who visit the mission gather for cake and coffee and the passing out of donations when services are over. While the Mennonites have dibs on most Saturdays, the rest of the week at the mission is an ecumenical free-for-all. During the week preceding my visit, services had been run by Baptists, Episcopalians, and members of a Foursquare Gospel Church. Exposed to such variety, some of the men in the program have quite naturally developed particular tastes in religious presentation. Kenny counted himself a fan of the Mennonites. "Some of the guys don't like the Mennonites as much as I do," he said, after we sat down. "Some of them like the wilder services, you know, the ones with more . . . whatever. Noise and hollering, I guess. Personally, I like the Mennonites. It's funny, because when I was growing up here in the Bronx, I never heard of no Mennonites. I didn't know what they were. But when they do the service, I like it. It's real quiet. It's like someone telling a quiet story. It's more, sort of, personal or something. I like it, especially on Saturday." He tapped his hand nervously on the table. "After all, I had plenty of excitement on Saturday nights in my life. I like a little peacefulness now."

Just then, the door opened, and a short, muscular black man wearing blue jeans and a parka strode in, followed by about fifty Mennonites. The reference point for traditional Mennonite clothing is something rural in the eighteenth century. The girls, who looked to be in their late teens, were wearing black wool coats, homemade gingham dresses with high collars, and white cloth bonnets over their hair. The handful of men in the group were wearing narrow black jackets without lapels, and heavy, round-toed black shoes. After a moment I realized that the black man in the parka was the program man named Tommy who had been leading the Mennonites on the walking tour.

"We're back!" Tommy said. "We went to Little Italy, and the Lower East Side, and a little bit into Chinatown. We went all over the place. You know, I used to be a bus driver, so this comes naturally to me." As he was saying this, the Mennonites gathered in the back of the room and started to talk among themselves in hushed voices. Wilberto Ramos came back into the room, and when he saw Tommy he motioned to them and said, "How'd they like it out there?"

"They loved it, man," Tommy said. "They found it extremely interesting. It's different from what Pennsylvania's all about. They're good walkers, too."

"What's it like outside?" Kenny asked him.

Tommy took off his coat and threw it on a chair. "Cold, cold, *cold*. And lots of brothers out on the street looking to score. Dealing with Satan. Reminds me of my former nasty self." He rubbed his hands together and blew on them to warm them. A few more program men wandered through the room, and then headed for the chapel. Someone said the doors had opened and that the street men were on their way in.

"Looking to score, score, *score*," Tommy went on, rubbing his hands again and grinning. "Those were the bad old days, right, Kenny?"

Kenny bowed his head and looked down at his own hands. "Oh, boy," he said. "Do I ever know." When Tommy left the room, Kenny watched him and then said, "He talks too much."

We got up and walked together into the chapel, and took seats in the back with the rest of the program men. The Bowery Mission chapel is a long, narrow room faced with rough, beige stone. It has many rows of wooden pews, a high, arching ceiling, a simple altar, a piano, and an organ. It seems to be unconnected, in both architecture and ambience, to the harshly lit dining rooms and the rest of the building. The pews on the right side of the chapel were filled with the men who had been waiting out on the sidewalk. One or two of them had fallen asleep, apparently just seconds after sitting down. Two women were seated in the front pew; one of them was pregnant and was missing one of her front teeth. The pews on the left side of the chapel were being saved for the Mennonites, who walked in after a moment and filed silently into their seats.

"This is how I know it's Saturday," Kenny said, nodding to the Mennonites. "For me, this is something to see."

Wondering about what Saturday night meant to people on the outskirts of society, I once spoke to a man I knew of who had spent a year traveling with hobos. He said there was no meaning to any day of the week for hobos—the only distinction that mattered was whether they had money or not. Being poor is both monotonous and weirdly chaotic. The things that structure more ordinary lives—work, future plans, obligations—are missing, and the only organizing principle is the effect of the occasional windfall. Kenny told me that being a drug addict created that same sort of detachment from time. He said an addict sees time just two ways—time when they're high and time when they're trying to get high. When he was still using crack, he spent a lot of time getting high on weekends, but it never registered as weekend entertainment, just as a lot of time getting high.

"Don't bother asking an addict about Saturday night," he said, as we watched the Mennonites file in. "They don't know one night from the next. It's all the same, only for the question of whether you're high yet or not." He said this with obvious distaste. "The thing here at the mission is now I have stuff to do, and places I have to be. The weekends are different, because we have some free time and the services are later and stuff. I'm working to get myself together. It's different when you're getting high. Everything is just about getting high. You don't even know what something like time *is*."

A thin, sandy-haired man, one of the mission's pastors, walked up to the altar and asked that everyone in the chapel put away all reading material other than the Bible. He then introduced the Mennonites and said they had come to the Bowery from the Weaverland Mennonite Conference in Lancaster. The chapel was quiet, except for a few street men who were snuffling and coughing. The Mennonites stood up in their pews, walked up to the altar, and began arranging themselves with some difficulty in the limited space. A few more minutes passed. Kenny started flipping through his hymn book and jiggling his legs up and down. Every once in a while, he would glance at me and a tentative smile would pass over his face. A few of the program men sitting near us had their eyes shut, their elbows on their knees, and their foreheads balanced on their thumbs. Some of them were whispering prayers to themselves. An usher walked down the aisle and woke up the street men who had fallen asleep. The Mennonites all finally crowded around the altar. Backlit, their faces were hard to see, but the silhouettes made by their clothes and the neat rows of the women's white bonnets had an extraordinary appearance, disjointed from this time and place. They stood still for a moment and then started to sing. There was no musical accompaniment—just fifty or so voices in close and sometimes crowded harmony, singing an austere, whispery version of "Joy to the World."

For close to two hours, they sang. At one point, the choir stood silent while a young Mennonite husband and wife sang an a cappella duet. The usher walked down the aisle a few more times and prodded a couple of street men who were dozing and one who was reading a science-fiction paperback. Kenny was now folded over his knees with his eyes cast down. Near the end of the two hours, the mission pastor came back to the altar and said in a choked, afflicted voice that anyone who wanted to come forward and pray was invited to do so, and that some of the men in the rehabilitation program would join them for moral support. One by one, about twenty street men clambered out of their pews and headed for the altar, some limping and others just walking slowly, as if something in their bodies ached, and then a number of program men came up, knelt beside them, put their arms around their shoulders, bent their heads and started to pray. In some cases, their heads were so close together that it looked as if one of them was whispering a secret into the other's ear. When the space in front of the altar was completely full, the pastor turned around and asked the Mennonites to sing something to accompany the praying. The way he said it made it sound urgent. The Mennonites clustered closer together and then began singing "Joy to the World" once again, slowly, in high, keen voices. Kenny had his eyes mostly closed and his face set in such a way that he appeared to be in pain. The dim light of the chapel, the stillness of the chapel air, the worn-out men in the pews, the men embraced at the altar, the pastor kneeling beside them, the Mennonite chorus standing above them—together, it made a tableau the likes of which I shall never forget.

The Mennonites leave early, because the ride back to Lancaster is long. They leave while the street men are still standing in the soup line, and while the program men are still dishing out supper to them. Kenny and I watched them board their bus, and then went back into the dining room and stood behind the soup line for a few minutes. He soon saw someone in line he recognized from a drug program he had been in a number of years ago. He greeted the man with a nervous wave and asked how he was doing.

"Okay, man, I'm okay," the man answered. He had a perturbed look on his face, and as he was talking, he dug around in a huge basket for a piece of bread.

"Are you still messing up, you know? Messing around?" Kenny asked him.

"Well, I'm getting under control. I'm in Narcotics Anonymous, and I'm still getting my high, you know, but then that's it. I'm trying to get my life together. You know what I'm saying? See, I'm working to get some stuff together and get my life back together. I'm on my way to a meeting after this. You ever been to the Midnight Miracle?" Kenny said he hadn't. "It's over on St. Marks Place," the man went on. "It's this whole house, and it's filled with all the Anonymouses, the narcotics, the alcoholics and whatever. Saturday night at midnight. The whole place gets full. You feel it. You know what I'm saying? Really, brother, it's very spiritual." Abruptly, he walked away and sat at one of the long metal tables, where the street men were hunched over trays of food.

"Whew," Kenny said to me, watching the man negotiate his way to a table. "I knew him a *long* time ago. He's still on the street, messing up, you know?" He looked out across the room, which was now entirely full. Every chair at every table was taken up by someone eating dinner. Then, in six or seven minutes, it was suddenly empty. Having eaten without anything more than the slightest conversation, the men had gotten up and walked out the mission doors and onto the street again.

Kenny hung his thumbs on his pants pockets and said, "They leave pretty quick, don't they? Doesn't matter what night it is. You think they're going to hang around more because it's Saturday night? No one hangs around just because it's Saturday night. They come here because they're hungry and they leave when they're not hungry anymore." A few of the street men, it turns out, had gone back into the chapel, where names were being drawn to see which of them would get to sleep that night in one of the fifteen beds in the mission basement. In the dining room, I could hear the program man who was drawing names call out, "Alfred Lopez. Lopez, the Lord blessed you tonight—you got a bed."

At ten o'clock, the pastor announced that he was leaving for the night and reminded me and the men of their curfew. Some of the program men had already gone upstairs to sleep, and a few were waiting in line at the pay phone to call their wives or mothers or girlfriends. Kenny had told me that he missed his mother but she had forbidden him to call her until he had made his way through more of the program, that he was trying to stay away from an old girlfriend because she was still using drugs, and that he had children but he wasn't that close to them. The sight of the men lined up at the phone seemed to affect him like a quick punch in the stomach. We walked downstairs again. The building was still. The part of the street you could see through the windows was dark and empty. It was spooky. Kenny saw that Wilberto and some other men were sitting in the dining room eating a snack, so we went over and joined them. Many restaurant- and grocery-supply stores make food donations to the Bowery Mission. The donations are often large and usually haphazard—two hundred Number Ten cans of clam chowder might come one week, two thousand banana cream pies the next. This week the donations had included Weight Watchers products and hundreds of Entenmann coffee cakes. The men had piled food onto paper plates and then gathered around the table, where they fell into a discussion about whether Satan was in one's mind or in the world at large. Before any satisfactory consensus was reached, another man came over and sat down. He had bristly blond hair, some acne, and fresh-looking wounds on his wrists. He looked younger than most of the other men at the table. On his plate, he had six cookies from the batches the Mennonites had brought, one piece of pie, one piece of coffee cake, and two Weight Watchers ice-cream bars.

"You're new, right?" Kenny said to him. His voice was low, almost a mumble.

"Yeah, I just got here," the guy with the blond hair said.

"Michael is your name, right?" Wilberto said.

"Yeah, Michael," Michael said. "Do you guys always have snacks? Do you always have the back thing open, the pantry? I haven't had a cigarette in twelve days. I had the weirdest dream last night, I couldn't believe it."

"Dreams," Wilberto said, and snorted for punctuation. He twirled a paper clip between his thumb and forefinger. "Hey, brother, we all got dreams."

"No, really," Michael said. "You want to hear? I mean, do you want to hear this dream?" He looked around the table excitedly. There was a long silence. Kenny finally said, "Sure, what was your dream?"

Michael began a long and colorful narration that included a tank, his mother, someone carrying a gun, his old neighborhood, another tank or big car, him in imminent danger several times, and a strange man with a weird face. "Satan," Wilberto interrupted, when Michael mentioned the weird face. "That was Satan trying to take you away again."

"Nah," the man next to Wilberto said. "That was a drug dream. I've been there. It's the leftover drugs working out of your system."

Someone else scraped his chair back, stood up, and said, "I've heard enough of that shit. I'm going to bed."

"Well, I'm sorry," Michael called after him. "That's not shit. That was my dream."

Kenny, who had been staring at Michael for a few moments, said, "You can use that, man. You can think about that and think about yourself. That's a story about you. Pastor Dooley says that your dreams are about yourself." Michael ignored him and started eating a Weight Watchers bar. The table grew quiet. The curfew for the evening was only a few minutes away, and a few other program men walked through the dining room on their way upstairs to bed. Two men at the table then began talking about their wives and how much they missed them, although one of them mentioned that his wife was the person who had introduced him to drugs.

"Nothing like a little family life," the other man said.

"Yeah, well, I'm getting that together, too," the man said.

"Well, for now, the program is your family," Wilberto said to him. "You got to get used to that. Look, here we are on Saturday night, and we're your big date—the other drug addicts at the Bowery Mission."

"Hey, shut up, man."

"I'm just kidding, man! You got to learn to lighten up a little! I've seen it all, nothing bothers me anymore. I've used drugs for fifteen years, stole ten thousand dollars worth of merchandise from Bloomingdale's, I've lived the gay life-style, and now it's all the past to me. You just move on, you know? Now it's God's will, and I'm just with God."

"You gay?" Michael asked, and then whistled as if he were impressed.

"I lived that life," Wilberto said. "That's not important anymore, though, you know? What's important is the word of God."

"You're all talking too much," Kenny said, in a quiet voice. He stood up to leave, and then looked around the table and said, "You'd be better off talking less and thinking more about your lives."

A few months after I spent the evening at the mission, I was driving down Bowery for other reasons and I saw the Mennonite bus pull up beside the mission's red doors. It was, obviously, a Saturday. I didn't know which of the men who had been in the program at the time of my visit were still living at the mission, who had moved into the job-training program, who had gone back to using drugs, who had left town, who had stayed. The sensation that had come over me during the night I had been at the mission—the feeling that I had dropped out of real time and into something completely removed— seemed surreal in retrospect, and looking at the rather blank facade of the mission now, I could barely believe that any of it had happened. A few men were already on the sidewalk waiting to get into the chapel, and through the window in the red door, I could see the top of someone's head. It was probably a program man who was hanging out downstairs before the start of the Saturday-night service. A lot of them hang out near the door early Saturday evening, as if they were testing the urge to just open it up and leave. After a few minutes of watching the top of the man's head bobble up and down, I started my car up again and drove past the mission, past the restaurant-supply stores, and past the big junkyard at the corner of Bowery and Houston that is filled with things that appear to have been tossed in at random, old bathtubs on top of sinks on top of window screens on top of window frames on top of a pile of hubcaps, ovens, metal cabinets, shutters, radiators, tables, and toilets. Most of what's in the pile are useful things that might be useful again someday.

Socializing

Houston, Texas

Like everything else in Houston, St. Anne de BeauPre Catholic Church is right beside a six-lane freeway. The church itself is small and plain, a mauve brick building with brown trim, set at an angle to the street; the church hall, which is made of corrugated metal, is a few yards to the east. The immediate neighborhood is Polish, black, and Mexican, and by turns crummy and nice. One time, when driving through, I noticed a whiskey-drinking party under way at a broken-down house, next door to a pretty bungalow which had miniature topiary and thirteen inflatable Easter bunnies on the front lawn. St. Anne's is built on a foundation deep in the soft Houston soil. The nearby houses are small, wooden, and rectangular, set on cement blocks. To anyone accustomed to houses being attached to the ground, these look as if in a strong wind they would simply fly away.

Jane Champagne lives close to St. Anne's. This turns out to be a significant convenience, since she drops by several times a day. Besides attending morning mass, Mrs. Champagne goes to St. Anne's for meetings of the Altar Society, to run the St. Vincent de Paul chapter, and often in the early evening to cook dinner for the parish priest. Inevitably, her role as chairperson of the church's regular Saturday-night dances, which feature the zydeco music she first fell for during her Louisiana youth, calls her to the church many other times. The zydeco dances are sometimes called by the old slang name, "lala dances," by people who attend them regularly. Being chairperson of the dances requires an amount of time and attention many people would begrudge a paying job. Mrs. Champagne begrudges nothing when it comes to lala. She has run the dances at St. Anne's for nine years, so she has had plenty of time to mull this over. "I'm always ripping and running and ripping and running," she likes to say. "Here and there, to the church and back, ripping and running, all day, every day. But that's what it takes to do it right."

Mrs. Champagne often says that she considers this excess of ripping and running worthwhile because she gets so much pleasure out of producing a top-quality dance for her family and friends. Her husband, Wilfred, a retired city mechanic, says he thinks all the ripping and running is worthwhile because it keeps Jane Champagne foxy. She is, in fact, a lively and attractive woman. Compact and fit, she has three children, six grandchildren, a strict policy against revealing her age, and a devotion to making it impossible to guess. Her face is oval, dark skinned, unlined, and mobile. She has black hair with springy curls, a flirtatious smile, and a genuine-looking wink. Her voice is soft and a little sleepy; her accent is rounded and loopy Creole—Texas by way of the Louisiana bayou by way of eighteenth-century France. She is quite short; perhaps to compensate for what she seems to consider a disadvantage, she spends a lot of time balanced up on her toes, pitched forward, ready for takeoff. On days when she knows she will be doing a lot of her ripping and running, she wears pastel sweat suits and matching athletic shoes. To church dances, she wears print dresses with colorful sashes and lace collars, saving her nicest ones for the dances at St. Anne's.

Some people date the beginning of great Saturday nights in Houston to 1971, with the founding of Mickey Gilley's, one of the original, archetypal citified-cowpoke bars, where pipe fitters and data processors—new Houston—could dress up in ten-gallon Stetsons and two hundred dollars Tony Lamas and drink toasts to a Wild West they never knew. Others would say that the true Houston weekend began on the night of Saturday, February 3, 1967, when a promoter named Paul Boesch presented girl wrestlers and a pro tag-team card at the Houston Coliseum: It was the first such Saturday night wrestling extravaganza in town, and it has continued every Saturday night in the twenty-some years since then, forging a permanent association between Houston, wrestling, and Saturday night and proving the earliest and most enduring glimpse of what mass-market Sunbelt end-of-the-century leisure entertainment would be all about.

Jane Champagne believes that the era of great Saturday nights in Houston began in 1958, when a man named Clarance Gallien, Sr., left his farm in Opelousas, Louisiana, and moved to Houston, settled in the parish of St. Francis of Assisi, and started hiring musicians to come from Louisiana to play in the St. Francis church hall every Saturday night.

Opelousas, a small town in the southern cotton-farming tier of Louisiana, is often described as being a very nice place to live. During its heyday in the 1950s, there was always plenty of socializing going on in Opelousas. All the members of all the extended families in town hung around together. Everyone belonged to the same few Catholic churches. On weekends, a lot of people around Opelousas would get together at someone's house, move the furniture out and stack it on the porch, and then dance all night in the empty rooms. The accompaniment at these house parties was the chattery accordion-based zydeco music that the French-speaking blacks of Louisiana—Clarance Gallien's and Jane Champagne's ancestors—had made up out of Caribbean syncopation, French folk melodies, and rhythm and blues. The French part of zydeco had been borrowed from the Cajuns, the Nova Scotians who had been deported to Louisiana in the eighteenth century and who eventually taught their language and customs to local slaves.

In the 1950s, almost no one else in the world had even heard of zydeco music, while in Louisiana it figured so much in the course of things that people used the word "zydeco" as two nouns and a verb. According to how and when you said it, zydeco meant either the kind of music itself, or the kind of zesty dance party where the music got played, or the kind of two-step touch-dancing that you did at the parties to the music. In theory, this meant that you could zydeco to zydeco at the zydeco. The slang term for zydeco—*lala*—enjoyed the same linguistic multipurposefulness. In Opelousas and the neighboring towns, zydeco had also produced its own nobility. There were lesser royals, such as Fernest Arceneaux, known to fans as the New Prince of Accordion, and then there was the king, a dashing and masterful accordion player from Lafayette Parish named Clifton Chenier.

Clarance Gallien was a personal friend of Clifton Chenier's—they had cut sugarcane together as kids—as well as a two-nouns-and-a-verb kind of zydeco fan. At one point Gallien was so moved by his affection for the traditional weekend zydeco parties that he built a little nightclub in the front yard of his farm and held dances there every weekend, often with Chenier on the stage. The club was a sound success, but in 1953, Mrs. Gallien—a zydeco devotee herself, but a woman possessed of the sort of quiet dignity offended by having a nightclub in her front yard—prevailed upon Clarance to close it. With the closing of the club, some of the charms of the Opelousas social life began to dim. For that matter, the business of farming weedy patches of land in bayou country was also starting to lose its capacity for exciting the imagination, while Houston, only a few hundred miles from Opelousas, was coming into its own and beckoning.

In 1953, when the Galliens arrived, Houston was as yet a relatively unformed place—cattle still grazed where the tallest building in Texas, the Transco Tower, now stands—but the city was also starting to toss up the first of dozens of tall, glassy buildings and to attract money from all over the world and to capitalize on the oil business and to have thousands of good jobs for the asking and to pop up out of the swamp. Houston was beginning to look an awful lot like the future. By the end of the decade, many people with excitable imaginations were converging on the city. The new settlers were from Iceland, Chile, Japan, Ecuador, China, Mexico, and Manhattan, from places so far and wide that the movement of many Creole blacks, including Clarance Gallien and family and later, Jane

Champagne, a mere two hundred miles from western Louisiana to northeastern Houston went largely without notice. For the Creoles, though, the move was dramatic. After all, they had left quiet country towns where people knew one another and still farmed with mules for a huge, fragmented city with an economic stake in landing a man on the moon.

Many of the Creoles settled in the Fifth Ward in northeast Houston. A black neighborhood full of plum orchards, dairies, plots of old cotton farms, and hundreds of flimsy shotgun shacks, the Fifth Ward was a place unto itself, cut off from the rest of Houston on the south by muddy Buffalo Bayou. The Creoles came to the Fifth Ward but did not assimilate. Set apart by their French language and their Catholic religion, and by the fact that many of them had white and Indian blood, and by the distinctiveness of their Louisianan culture, the Creoles lived in a world within a world within a world: a section of the Fifth Ward called Frenchtown, which had its own social organization (the Creole Knights, composed of the original Frenchtown families) and clubs (the Continental Zydeco Lounge, the Silver Slipper, Pe-Te's Cajun Barbeque) and music.

Clarence Gallien happened to settle just outside the boundaries of Frenchtown, but he still stayed close to his Louisiana people. He had been a popular man in the social universe of Opelousas; he was a popular man in the social universe of Opelousas-once-removed. In Houston, he became a leader in the community and in his new church. In 1958, when he asked his pastor at St. Francis whether he could hire some of the zydeco musicians from back home to play on Saturday nights at the church hall, he pointed out that it might be a way to raise funds for the church. But people now say that it wasn't just that Clarence Gallien loved his church—it was that he was also always one to deplore a wasted weekend, always one to remember the pleasures of life in Opelousas, and always one to instigate a better way to have fun.

To the surprise of anyone who assumes that churches would not be on the list of venues where one might find a raucous dance party on a Saturday night, the pastor of St. Francis liked Gallien's idea about bringing musicians in from Louisiana, and he encouraged Gallien to set up a dance. Gallien did so, and what seemed like the whole of the relocated Creole community showed up. More dances followed. For the next few years, Clarence Gallien re-created at St. Francis of Assisi the Saturday-night zydecos he used to have back on his Opelousas farm. Many of the same people who had been patrons of his Louisiana club showed up for the dances in Houston. The fact that the zydecos were taking place in a big city instead of a little farm town didn't seem to expand the universe of people in attendance: the dances still attracted almost only Creoles, and for that matter, mostly those Creoles who grew up in the same smallish section of Louisiana. Just as in Opelousas, Clifton Chenier often played at the church hall, driving in from Louisiana on Saturday afternoon and staying the night with the Galliens after the show.

Fans like to say that Clifton Chenier "brought zydeco out," a turn of phrase that makes it sound as if he had physically carried it from an unreachable place and deposited it in public view—which, if you think of your culture as different and even unimaginable to an outsider, is probably a reasonable way to describe the popularization of a music that had sprung up and flourished within it and had seemed to be exclusively your own. Chenier did, in fact, bring zydeco to Houston and in time to many other parts of the known world, where it was eventually appreciated as a remarkable kind of hybrid folk music. Even after he could command a situation more consequential than a little church meeting hall, Chenier would come to the Houston zydecos and play.

In time, many Creoles in Houston prospered enough to leave Frenchtown. They resettled throughout Houston. They joined Catholic churches all over the big city. As soon as the number of Creoles in a congregation got large enough and expressed enthusiasm for it, those churches also started holding zydecos on Saturday night. St. Anne de BeauPre was among them. Each church would appoint its own dance chairman, and every dance chairman was trained by Clarence Gallien. He would show each of them how to get the posters printed, how to advertise the dance in the *Texas Catholic Herald*, how to negotiate with the musicians, how much gumbo to cook for the concession stand. Mr. Gallien's policy of raffling a bottle of whiskey and letting other chairmen announce their up-coming dances at intermission was also widely adopted. When the number of zydeco-hosting churches reached twelve, the chairmen convened and decided to set up a schedule so that they wouldn't overlap or have to compete for musicians, and to ensure that there would be a lala dance every Saturday night in some church in town.

When Clarance Gallien died this fall, there were a few people in Houston who wondered whether any Saturday zydeco dance they attended might turn out to be their last. His family now says that it gave him great pleasure to know that the church dance circuit was in hands as good as the likes of Jane Champagne and the other dance chairpersons, and that he would leave a lasting impression on the city. Gallien's son Clarance, Jr., who happens now to be chairman of the zydeco dances at St. Francis, once explained this to me in passionate terms. "I know we'll carry the zydecos on," he said. "In my youth, I had nothing to do with the zydecos. I had strayed away. But now I'm back. Now I understand what it's all about. I want to follow what my father did. Zydeco was *in* him, and he loved bringing it to Houston. He liked how it kept us all together like a family. We're all devoted to it. We all plan to carry it on."

The week I was in Houston, it was St. Anne's turn in the zydeco rotation, so Jane Champagne was doing even more ripping and running than usual. On Thursday, when I caught up with her, she was shopping with a pensive-looking woman she introduced to me as Miss Guillfrey. Miss Guillfrey is St. Anne's designated gumbo maker and her services were about to be required. The two women had conferred in the morning and decided to buy their ingredients that afternoon at a supermarket near the church where Jane Champagne likes to do her shopping. The store is called Fiesta Foods, and it has the kind of eccentric inventory induced by the luxury of space—ten steps through the door, you've walked past potatoes, lawn chairs, gobo root, socket wrenches, catfish, inflatable kiddie pools, and lo bok. To get what you need for gumbo, you would have to traverse all four far-flung corners of the store.

After picking out a shopping cart with good wheels, Mrs. Champagne mentioned to Miss Guillfrey that she was expecting a large crowd on Saturday night because she had managed to book Boozoo Chavis, one of the musicians contending for the musical throne since Clifton Chenier had passed away. Boozoo, who is fifty-eight years old and lives in Lake Charles, Louisiana, had actually retired from zydeco many years ago after some bitter business concerning a record company and a copyright, then spent decades training race horses for a living, and then was coaxed out of musical retirement over the last couple of years. Although he returned to the church circuit in Houston, he also started playing in clubs across the country where zydeco had gotten popular with people from places other than places like Opelousas. Boozoo once told me that he preferred playing at the church dances to playing anywhere else because he thought they attracted the most intelligent people. Apparently, public demand for him has made such choosiness economically unsound. Boozoo's last appearance at a church dance had been months ago, and Mrs. Champagne said she was very happy that she was the chairman who had gotten him back into town.

"You know how it is with Boozoo," Mrs. Champagne said, putting six bunches of scallions in the cart. "Mr. Boozoo Chavis. Some people call him 'Bozo.' I say 'Boozoo.' Anyway, we have got to be prepared. Everyone in town is going to want to come hear Mr. Boozoo play." Miss Guillfrey, her brow furrowed, counted the bunches of scallions. "Miss Guillfrey, I really think we're going to have a lot of folks on Saturday," Mrs. Champagne went on. "I'm expecting a lot of people. I think we need all those onions. I think we better get a lot of everything, onions, bell peppers, and *everything*. I don't want to run out of gumbo and get people *mad*."

Miss Guillfrey put a few peppers into the cart. "I hate when I run out of gumbo," Mrs. Champagne said. "They ran out of gumbo last week at St. Philip." We walked on, passing piles of melons and kiwis and pecans and window-cleaning spray, until Mrs. Champagne stopped and scrunched her mouth up in thought. She looked at the cart, then looked up at Miss Guillfrey, then pushed the peppers around in the cart.

"Oh, let's see, now," she said. "Let me think a second." She tapped Miss Guillfrey in the shoulder. "Grab a few more peppers for me, would you now, Miss Guillfrey? I want to make sure we have enough. I want my dance to be *nice*."

As we picked up the rest of the ingredients, Mrs. Champagne said that she had been dance chairman of St. Anne's for the past nine years, that she had been trained by Mr. Gallien, that when Mr. Gallien died this fall everyone knew it was up to the dance chairmen to keep the zydecos going in his name. She then said that she had grown up on a farm close to the town of Lafayette, near Opelousas, and that her mother spoke only French, that she wished she'd taught her own children French but that she hadn't gotten around to it, and that she had barely spoken French since she moved to Houston almost thirty years ago to live with her sisters and brothers after her mother passed away. She met her husband, Wilfred, in Houston. He grew up in Opelousas.

"*Comment ça va?*" she said to me, cocking her head to the side. "See, I still speak my French. But here I am in Houston now, and all the time I see folks from back home. Isn't that funny? We're like family. It's just like a family. We stick together. You know, a lot of people come to the big city and they want to go with the ways of the city, but I don't think that's really right. I think you should stay the way you want to be. I really do. You know, to this day, I remember my mama used to put on the zydeco when I was a little girl, and I loved it. I really loved it. It's almost the first thing I remember hearing. This was back in Lafayette. My brother and I would dance to it sometimes. I loved zydeco since I was just a little, little girl. We used to listen to Clifton Chenier. He was the king. Clifton Chenier died a few years ago, and oh, do we all miss him. My husband and I go to the zydecos just about every single weekend, even when it's not at St. Anne's. I love to go hear the band, and sometimes I have to announce my dances, and mostly I like to see everyone. Wouldn't you say that's why we like it, Miss Guillfrey?"

"I would."

"Zydeco's the thing I loved when I was just a little girl," Mrs. Champagne went on. "Just imagine, here I am getting to hear zydeco every week, and I'm not such a little girl anymore."

She and Miss Guillfrey counted out twenty-eight lemons and put them in the cart. The lemons rolled around for a minute and then settled among the peppers. We went down the rice aisle, and Mrs. Champagne hoisted a saggy twenty-five-pound sack into the cart.

"Miss Guillfrey's quiet today, isn't she?" Mrs. Champagne said. "Now tell me, Miss Guillfrey, what else do we need?"

"Shrimp?" Miss Guillfrey asked.

"We got that back home."

"Boudin?"

"That butcher made us a lot of boudin. That's in the freezer. I've got all the boudin we need. I'm concerned about our gumbo. Do we have everything for the gumbo?" Miss Guillfrey raised her eyebrows and didn't say anything. After a moment, Mrs. Champagne snapped her fingers and wheeled the cart back to the produce, stopping in front of a heap of garlic. "Oooh, almost forgot garlic," she said, *tsk*-ing at herself. "I like a lot of garlic. Two pounds, don't you think, Miss Guillfrey?" Miss Guillfrey gave the garlic a baleful look and dug her hand into the pile. Mrs. Champagne then dug hers in, too, and said, cheerily, "Let's get some nice ones, please."

We grabbed dozens of chubby garlics out of the heap, dropped them into the cart, and headed for the cashiers. The cart, filled to the top with large portions of lots of things, wobbled down the aisle. A casual observer might have guessed that we were successful contestants in Supermarket Sweepstakes or very big eaters. Mrs. Champagne surveyed the food with a satisfied look on her face, and then said, "Oh, my God, all this food and I didn't get anything to feed Wilfred! Oooh, he's going to have nothing at all to eat! I have to run back and get a frozen food or macaroni or he's going to be starving tonight. Can you imagine, here I am at the grocery store forgetting my own husband? See, that's what happens when all I have is zydeco on my mind."

On our way home from the store, Mrs. Champagne drove through Frenchtown and pointed out where she had lived as a young woman new to town. In the thirty years since then, Houston's indigenous ground-cover of fast-food shops, muffler centers, and strikingly uninteresting low windowless tan-colored office buildings had spread to the edges of Frenchtown but not into it; it is still mostly a neighborhood of rows and rows of little houses, crowded together on streets narrow as wagon traces. Many of the houses in Frenchtown are hard of paint and windows. The lawns are dust, flowers, weeds, and car parts. A few businesses are open and a few are closed. We drove by a squat wooden building, bleached out and boarded up, and Mrs. Champagne pointed a finger at it and recalled that it had been either a zydeco club or a chicken coop. "I don't exactly remember now. Anyway, it doesn't look like much now," she said. "It really was nice back then, though. This whole neighborhood, I mean. It really was. It was just like family. Everyone was from back home."

As we drove along the streets, talking about the way Frenchtown had been, we passed a lot of churches. Baptist. Seventh Day Adventist. Gospel Hall. Another Baptist, in a grove of toothpicky pine trees. A Kingdom Hall. "You can't avoid getting your soul saved in Houston, can you?" Mrs. Champagne said, winking. "You won't find zydeco in these, though. These aren't Catholic churches. All of us French people belong to the Catholic churches. You know what I think about that, though? I say there isn't but one God, so we're all in this together." Another Kingdom Hall. She pointed to it. "I went there once, when I knew I was going to miss mass at St. Anne's and there was no Catholic Church around. Like I said, there isn't but one God, whatever way you look at it."

She sighed and slowed down at a light. "Sometimes, some other people, not French people, will say to me, 'How come you dance and drink in your church hall? That's awful!' You know what I say? I say there's nothing wrong with people having fun. Lord, they work all week, they're entitled to have some fun on the weekend, and better to be doing it in the church hall than in some . . . some . . . *nightclub* or something, don't you think?"

The light changed. We crossed a railroad track and drove a few miles west, close to the home of a school-bus driver named Mary Zeno who is the zydeco dance chairman at St. Gregory the Great. Once, when I visited Mary Zeno's house, she had showed me a display she'd made out of album covers—two Clifton Cheniers, and one Buckwheat Zydeco and the Ils Sont Partis Band—and then she had mentioned with great sadness that one of her daughters had become a Baptist and refused to dance anymore. I told this story to Mrs. Champagne, who shook her head in sympathy.

"Can you imagine?" she said. "Well, everyone's got to be the way they got to be. A lot of the young people love zydeco. More and more they do. Two of my kids don't like zydeco too much, but my daughter Wanda does. She loves it. She'll be there on Saturday night." Suddenly, she looked at her watch and gasped. "Oh my goodness, it's getting late. I've got to go to the church and feed Father and get the gumbo ingredients home and feed Wilfred and then call my other little helpers who are going to work at the dance! Ripping and running! I'm always ripping and running! I was up at five-thirty this morning for mass and I've been ripping and running all day. I think I need a little vacation."

She peered over the steering wheel at me. "Oh, goodness, oh, I shouldn't be telling you this! Maybe I shouldn't. Well, I'll tell you. Tonight *is* my little vacation. When I'm done with all this ripping and running, I'm going to scoot on over to the VFW Hall to play a little bingo. Just a little bingo. That's my vacation. And I feel lucky tonight, too." Saying that, she drove out of Frenchtown, under an overpass, past a cowboy-boot shop, past a half-deserted shopping mall, past a church and then another church, toward home.

Someone—compelled by malice, mischief, or greed—had recently stolen all the air conditioners out of the church hall, so on the sweaty, swampy Saturday night I was spending in Houston, there would be no cool air at St. Anne de BeauPre. The prevailing opinion around the church was that it had been a mercenary incident. This happened to be a time in Houston's history when things were getting stolen. The day I got to town, the Federal Reserve took over twenty-six local savings-and-loans. There were so many blank-looking empty stores and buildings throughout the city that Houston struck me sometimes as looking like a face with its front teeth punched out. Spring was overripe and getting sticky. In this sort of economic and meteorological atmosphere, an air conditioner can become a medium of exchange.

"Oh well, let's not bother worrying about those air conditioners," Mrs. Champagne called out from the church hall kitchen. "Everyone'll be dancing so much that it just won't matter. I wonder, though, who would go taking an air conditioner from a church? My goodness, that really makes me wonder."

It was now Saturday, late in the afternoon. Mrs. Champagne had come to the hall so she could get an advance feel for how things were going. Those things included the gumbo, which Miss Guillfrey had prepared at home earlier in the day and then had dispatched by volunteer to the hall. A box of snakey-looking boudin sausages retrieved from the Champagnes' freezer sat on a counter nearby. Three women, Mrs. Champagne's helpers, were already bustling around the kitchen when we arrived, setting out soup bowls and drinking glasses and carrying on a detailed discussion of how long you should wait to have sex after having a baby. It was several hours before the zydeco would begin, but there was plenty to do.

The night before, Mrs. Champagne had discovered that she had forgotten to put posters up around the church to advertise the dance. They had been printed up a few weeks ago, but the furthest they had gotten was the trunk of Wilfred Champagne's car. We were just going into the bingo hall and had been putting our coats in the trunk when the find was made. Mrs. Champagne had riffled through the posters and groaned. "Boozoo's going to *kill* me if he finds out," she said. "Oh, now, don't tell anyone. The thing is, we're going to have a huge crowd no matter what. Everyone knows it's at St. Anne's this Saturday."

The discovery of fifty unused posters in her trunk and the subsequent fact of losing flat-out at the bingo game did not affect her spirits then or today. "Nothing like a zydeco to put me in a good mood," she explained, stirring the gumbo. "If you don't know about zydeco, you don't know. It's something we can't get out of us. It really is just like that. After ripping and running around all week, it's what everyone looks forward to every Saturday night."

A man named Earnest Broussard, late of Opelousas, still fluent in his French, plumber by trade, zydeco dance volunteer by personal appointment, strolled into the kitchen and said, "Well, Champy, what can I do to help here? Besides finding those stolen air conditioners, I mean."

Mrs. Champagne slapped him playfully on the forearm and then directed him to a mop and a stack of folding chairs. "Let's get this place looking good, Earnest," she said. "I don't want to hear anything else about those air conditioners." I followed Earnest and the mop around the church hall. The hall was as plain on the inside as it was on the outside. Besides the small kitchen in the back, there was practically nothing in it. The walls were covered with thin, dark paneling. Over the center of a small elevated stage at one end hung a foot-long crucifix. On another wall was a small plaque honoring the people who contributed to the building fund—among them three Broussards, three Baptistes, three Jolivettes, two Babineaux, two Simians, Wilfred and Jane Champagne, and several men with the first name of Curley.

"This looks like nothing now," Earnest Broussard said to me, sweeping his arm around. "Wait a couple hours. You won't want to ever leave. Oh, my God, once you hear zydeco, you'll never be able to leave. That's one thing we brought with us from Louisiana." He suddenly put down his mop and began to pantomime driving a team of mules. "We had a lot of nice things back in Louisiana. Wonderful mules! I loved those mules, and I loved being on the farm. And we had zydeco. Now we don't have the mules anymore and we sure aren't on the farm, but tonight we're going to have zydeco."

Outside, the church parking lot was filling for evening mass. Zydeco dances last until two or three in the morning. Sunday mass is soon thereafter. A lot of people who are going to the zydecos attend weekend mass on Saturday night so they don't have to get up early on Sunday morning. Sometimes, people who live far from whichever church is hosting that week's dance will go to mass at that church instead of their own so they can be at the hall on time.

Several hours before the dance, people were already drifting in and taking a look around the hall at St. Anne's to see what there was to see. Most of them paid compliments to the gumbo, greeted Earnest Broussard, and then on their way out the door attempted to coax Mrs. Champagne into reserving a table for them, which is something she is loathe to do. Most of them gave up and left. Two of them persisted, arguing that they were having birthday parties at the zydeco tonight and wanted to decorate their tables before everyone came in. A lot of people celebrate their birthdays at the church dances. It is rare to go to one of the zydecos and not see at least one of the tables decked out with crepe paper and balloons.

Mrs. Champagne relented. Within a few minutes, two of the long tables that Earnest was setting up were stacked with presents.

Mrs. Champagne watched with her hand on her hip and displayed a practiced look of exasperation. "Brenda, I'll tell you one thing," she warned one of the table decorators. "You're not here at eight, *I'm* going to take that table and all the presents. Don't say I didn't caution you, now. I'm mean and nasty when I have to be."

If the Polish and Mexican members of St. Anne's congregation— that is, the 50 percent or so of the congregation who do not speak French, who didn't grow up in bayou country, and whose own personal musical monarch probably hails from Memphis with a guitar rather than from Louisiana with an accordion—find the occasional Saturday-night goings-on at the church hall off-putting, it is not apparent. At St. Anne's, there have been zydecos four or five times a year for nine years. On occasion, a few of the parishioners who are not Creole will come over to the hall for a few minutes or even a few hours to hear the music. More often, they will drop by just for a moment to see what else there might be for them to enjoy. In any case, they seem to consider it a windfall to some lesser or greater degree. When Mrs. Champagne and I went over to the church for mass at five o'clock, we sat in a pew in front of a woman with gray-green eyes and a white-blond beehive who nodded enthusiastically as soon as we sat down. Then she pinched Mrs. Champagne and said, "Hello, doll, good to see you. You have any gumbo tonight?"

"Sure we have gumbo," Mrs. Champagne whispered. "You just come on over as soon as mass ends and get some."

"I just love when you have your dances," the woman said, sounding filled with appreciation. "Means I don't have to cook on Saturday night."

Mrs. Champagne winked at her and told her to come early before the gumbo ran out. Then she took a piece of paper out of her pocketbook and wrote "We will have Gumbo and Boudin and Zydeco Dance at the Hall tonight." She then did some minor editing to the text. Toward the end of mass, she passed the note to the priest, a weary-looking man with longish white hair. He read it to himself and then announced that everyone was invited to the hall for gumbo. A few black people in the church who were dressed in clothes that suggested zydeco more than mass turned and nodded in a comradely don't-we-know-it manner at Mrs. Champagne. At the same time, several white people craned their necks and gave her eager looks. A few minutes later, when we were back in the kitchen, some of those eager people were lined up to buy gumbo to take home.

"Going to stay for some zydeco?" Mrs. Champagne said to the first woman in line.

"I'd sure like to, Jane," she said. "I got to get home. I'll just get a couple of gumbos. You all have fun tonight. Maybe I'll stay next time."

Next in line: "Just three gumbos, please. My husband's in the car. Oh, it looks good. Hope you all have fun tonight."

Next: "Two gumbos." This woman was stocky and was wearing an embroidered dress. She said her name was Rosita Hernandez. She kept sniffing in the direction of the gumbo and drumming her fingers on the kitchen counter. Finally, she said, "You know, Jane, I'm just going to call my husband and tell him a story. I'll tell him some kind of story, I don't know what. You need someone to help back in the kitchen? Need help with the gumbo? I could help out with the gumbo for you. I think I'll stay."

Just then, the back door of the hall opened, and Boozoo Chavis stepped in, followed by four immense young men who were carrying musical equipment. Boozoo is a beefy, sad-eyed man who is well known for his trademark cowboy hat, his classic zydeco compositions, and his cantankerousness—the latter quality being one he is rumored to be indulging all the more since Clifton Chenier died and boosted Boozoo's musical standing. It just so happens that Boozoo is not the only zydeco musician to have been stimulated, sometimes to excess, by the sudden absence of zydeco's dominant figure. Rockin' Dopsie, leader of the Cajun Twisters and one of Chenier's most popular rivals, lost only three weeks after Chenier died before persuading the mayor of Lafayette to crown him King of Zydeco. A few months later Boozoo was named King of Calcasieu Parish by the mayor of Lake Charles. Buckwheat, of Buckwheat Zydeco and the Ils Sont Partis Band, has been wearing a crown—for fashion purposes, at least—since he left Chenier's band and started his own in 1979. In the wake of Chenier's much-mourned passing, all this scrambling for a position that had always been just a spontaneous proclamation on the part of fans has struck some people as kind of tacky. Others argued that it is a good sign, proving that the scepter would be passed and that zydeco could and would outlast its most famous practitioner. Whoever is wrong would still probably agree that zydeco is enjoying a new flowering these days.

Mrs. Champagne walked through the empty hall toward Boozoo, stopped and sat down at one of the tables, pulled a pencil and piece of paper out of her purse, put them beside her, put on her glasses, and then folded her hands on her lap. She was wearing a black-and-white print dress with a white lace collar and a large sash around the waist. "Boozoo, you come over here," she announced. "You get over here right now. I have to talk to you." Boozoo put down the accordion he was fooling with, stomped over to the table, and sat down beside her. Mrs. Champagne smoothed the lace on her collar and then picked up her pencil. "Boozoo, I don't remember what I said I was paying you," she said. "Honest to God, I don't remember."

"Champagne," he said, thrusting out his lower lip, "you don't remember? For real? Well, I remember. You're paying me . . . you're paying me . . . two thousand dollars." He shot her a glance that was all at once saucy, friendly, and full of effrontery.

Mrs. Champagne countered with an equally complicated look and then burst out laughing. "You're crazy, Boozoo. Now you listen to me. I've been running around all week to get this zydeco ready for my church and my family and all my friends and now you're giving me a hard time. I think I'm paying you fourteen hundred. Wasn't that it? Fourteen? Maybe even twelve?"

"Two thousand, Champagne."

"I'm giving you fourteen hundred, you devil. And I got you booked for July, don't I?"

"No, you don't. I'm already booked for July. You never sent me any money and I already got booked for July."

There are no rump zydecos to speak of in Houston. The circuit is the church halls, and the chairmen run the circuit in engaged cooperation. Even clubs like the Silver Slipper usually book their zydeco bands on Sunday rather than Saturday night so they won't overlap with the churches—a case of acknowledged defeat as much as cooperation. It is also true that any chairperson who couldn't make it to another chairperson's dance some weekend—pleading a prior engagement or even a certain surfeit of zydeco in their lives—would probably be forgiven. Nonetheless, it rarely seems to happen; in fact, the other chairpersons are often the first people to show up at the hall. This particular night, some of the first people at the door were Clarance Gallien, Jr., and his wife, Deberia, who share dance chairperson duties at St. Francis; Nolan Thibodeaux, who runs St. Philip Neri; Genevieve Robertson, who used to run the dances at St. Francis; Ruby Baras of Our Lady of the Sea; and Mary Zeno of St. Gregory.

Mrs. Champagne greeted them as they came in with more delight than I had expected considering that she'd spoken to most of them a couple of times in the course of the week. There is always business to take care of on the zydeco circuit, so the phones are going all the time; Mrs. Champagne is one of those people who is always being hounded by her call-waiting beep.

She beamed at each of the chairpersons as they came in. "Didn't I tell you?" she said to me in a low voice, after directing Ruby Baras to a good seat near the stage. "I told you everyone was so nice. Everybody in the whole zydeco family is real nice, and we're all so supporting of each other. We all go to each other's dances. That's a nice kind of family, isn't it?"

There is ulterior purpose to the chairpersons' punctuality, since they usually come with flyers advertising their dances and the intention of stirring as much interest as possible in advance of the date. That night, even before Boozoo started playing, conversations about upcoming zydecos were under way and the tables were papered with flyers. In one pile of flyers, the next few Saturday nights of your life would be taken care of. St. Francis of Assisi Parish Hall on Saturday, March 18, Music by John Delafose and the Eunice Playboys. Big Zydeco Dance featuring Lil Brian and the Zydeco Travelers, April 8, St. Monica. Zydeco Dance at St. Patrick's Parish Hall on Saturday, April 29, Music by Sam Brothers 5, Sponsored by the Holy Name Society.

Mary Zeno was helping someone spread flyers around, and she passed near my table. "I'm going to book Buckwheat soon," I heard her saying. "You know, I'm crazy about Buckwheat Zydeco and the Ils Sont Partis Band. Aren't you, too? I like everyone, I love all zydeco, but I especially love Buckwheat. You should mark it on your calendar: Buckwheat. He hasn't played in Houston for a while. You should be sure to make it. Buckwheat, coming up. Buckwheat's real zydeco but he's also a rock-and-roll man. Did you know he's kin to me? Really! That's right, me and Buckwheat. I'm not lying."

Then the hall filled—totally, suddenly. First the birthday-party tables; then every table of the forty or so that had been set up, and then every square foot of the open space by the kitchen and the door. The drab, empty, highway-bound, new Houston suddenly seemed one or two million miles away. The hall was lively and crowded and noisy, exactly the way I had begun to envision the zydecos had been in Opelousas—I had been, of course, imagining Opelousas the whole time I had been in Houston, because it seemed so much more real to the people I was talking to than did the city they lived in now.

For a while, Mrs. Champagne disappeared in the crush, making good on a warning she had made to me earlier—that she was so short that she would be hard to find once it got crowded at the zydeco. Wilfred Champagne, a stocky man with a mildly melancholy aspect and a whispery voice, stood his ground near the kitchen door, his hands on his hips, advancing and then dropping a bid to keep some open space for the people working in the kitchen who were scooting around. It was hard to walk back and forth in the hall. No one seemed to go more than six or seven steps before running into a cousin, sister, old next-door neighbor from Lafayette or Frenchtown, brother-in-law, mother-in-law, or friend, so walking around became a process of threading through, in the manner of a pinball working around the bumpers in a pinball machine. The people buying tickets had formed a thick, hyperactive line that started near Wilfred and ran out into the parking lot. At a few minutes before nine, it was no longer possible to look out of the door and see the pointy top of St. Anne de BeauPre.

At nine, when Boozoo began playing, there were probably three or four hundred people in the smallish hall. The ages were various. I saw young girls and teenage boys, middle-aged couples, parents with children, thirtyish singles. Everyone was mixed in together. I squeezed through the aisles and passed quite a few interesting groups of people: elderly twins in identical straw boaters and striped ties, sitting with a youngish woman with ratted hair, a red dress in someone else's size, and a peevish look on her face; a huge man who looked about thirty or so, sitting with an elderly woman who appeared to be asleep. Attempting to find Mrs. Champagne, I got stuck, for a while, in a crowd of people near the kitchen. The young woman near my elbow turned out to be one of the birthday celebrants. Her name was Brenda Fitch. It was her thirty-fourth birthday. As we were talking I realized that Brenda had twenty-two dollars in cash pinned to her dress. She said it was a good-luck custom to pin money on someone celebrating a birthday, and then she counted the money with an expectant look on her face. "Okay, I'm not rich yet but I'm doing pretty well so far," she said. "I've got a lot of family here, so I might even clean up if I'm lucky."

I asked her what she meant by a lot of family.

"Well, you've got to define that," she said—or, more exactly, she yelled, since Boozoo had just begun a thumping loud version of "Zydeco et Pas Sale." Brenda looked around the hall. "Really, I'm probably related to about half the people in this whole room. I'm serious, I probably am. But I'm most specifically related to just the people over there." She pointed in the direction of her table. "Just those. That's my fourteen brothers and sisters. We get together on almost every Saturday night wherever the zydeco is, just to see each other. So that's all the absolute relatives I could claim. But when it comes to my birthday, I'm not so choosy. I'd take money from anybody."

Zydeco music has a rhythmic pace that is chunky and insistent. Many of the songs are lovesick or full of admiration for women, and some are funny, but the sound of zydeco music mostly reminds me of bluegrass—vigorous but also sort of sad. That night, Boozoo first played a tiny, diatonic Cajun accordion that made whiny noises, and then switched to a large Italian one with a fatter sound. He wore his usual cowboy hat, a belt that had his name stamped in the leather, a white cowboy shirt, and a clear-plastic butcher's apron to keep his sweat from warping the accordion. His son Anthony stood to his right on the stage, playing a traditional zydeco instrument called a frottoir, a corrugated metal thing that you wear like a shirt and rub with a spoon handle to create a loud buzz. Another of his sons, Wilson Chavis, Jr., plays backup accordion, and another, Rellis, is the band's drummer. Zydeco dancing is formal in structure and spontaneous in content: hands go on shoulders and waist, as in a waltz, and feet go all over the place, as in a jitterbug. There were a lot of couples whose dancing was precise, complex, and beautiful. Quite a few others just swung around. The dance floor had filled the minute Boozoo walked on stage, and until he left at two in the morning, there was never more than a square foot or so that wasn't filled.

In the middle of the dance I found Mrs. Champagne again. She happened to be in the kitchen, checking in on the operation, just as the kitchen volunteers announced that all the gumbo was gone. Mrs. Champagne groaned. She was already hoarse from yelling over the music. "Oh, and I forgot to save you any boudin," she said to me. "It got all eaten up already. Maybe I should have got more. Oooh, my voice, and I got to still do the raffle. Maybe Wilfred will do it. No, I'll have to do it. Everyone having fun?" The volunteers nodded at her. One of them was her daughter Wanda, a slim, buoyant woman in her early thirties who had come to help Mrs. Champagne with the dance. Wanda was overseeing the "setups"—buckets of ice and fruit that are sold to accompany the bottles of liquor the dancers bring from home. Setups are a piece of almost-lost Texas history. State law used to forbid the sale of mixed drinks, so bars and dance halls could only sell drink fixings and let patrons bring a bottle from home. Occasionally, in certain poor neighborhoods and disreputable-looking pool halls in Houston, you can still see signs advertising setups for sale. Otherwise, you see them nowadays only at church halls. Almost everyone I saw coming into the zydeco was carrying a bottle of Jack Daniel's or Crown Royal and was buying a couple of setups. The profits from everything at the zydecos—the setups, the gumbo, the tickets—go back to the churches. For them, the importation of a rather unique form of music from an unusual part of the country has proven to be quite a good deal.

Mrs. Champagne's face took on a fretful expression. "Gosh *darn*, I knew we should have made more gumbo! I'm too old to learn anymore, isn't that the truth?"

Rosita Hernandez, who was manning the cash box in the kitchen—after, I assumed, a successful phone call to her husband—said, "Oh, Champagne, you did fine. Whoever didn't get gumbo didn't get it, and that's their trouble, I say."

"Everything's great, Mom," Wanda Champagne agreed. "Everyone has what they want. Go have fun."

Mrs. Champagne hopped on one foot and then the other and started to smile. "Oh, everything's going fine. My dance is turning out nice. Everyone came and everyone's having a good time. Ripping and running! That's what I did all week. I was ripping and running to get the dance together. I'm going to be exhausted tomorrow. I'm going to stay in bed all day, I swear."

"Do it, Mama," Wanda said.

"Do it, Champagne," Rosita said.

"Don't push me, I swear I will," Mrs. Champagne said. She was radiant. "After all this ripping and running to get my zydeco together, I *need* to sleep all day."

Toward the end of the night, several people hollered for Boozoo to play his hit "Paper in My Shoe," a sweet lament about being by yourself and not having someone to love. As he began to play it, the dance floor filled up with more people than I thought it could possibly hold. Even in the jam, the better dancers still managed to keep their intricate, elegant moves intact. The rest of us just rocked back and forth, almost in place. When the song ended, there was agitation for Boozoo to play a song of his called "Deacon Jones," of which he does a clean version and a dirty version. The audience seemed to be calling for the dirty version. He played the clean one.

Watching Television

When Ron Simon told me that videocassette recorders made him sad, I immediately knew what he meant. Simon is the curator of the Museum of Broadcasting, in New York City. He has an office in midtown Manhattan where he is surrounded by old television scripts, posters advertising an "I Love Lucy" retrospective, and a few thousand books on popular culture. He had been digging through museum files to give me an overview of Saturday-night television when he realized that the whole notion might soon be a thing of the past.

"Now everyone has VCRs," Simon said to me, sounding a little grim. "That means that everyone can just tape shows whenever they want and watch them whenever they want. The notion of a show feeling like part of a particular day may soon be a thing of the past. That whole sentimental attachment might just disappear." He shook his head. "It makes me a little sad," he said. "It used to be that certain days of the week were really associated with certain shows. I *liked* growing up with the idea that Saturday night was 'Gunsmoke' night."

The thought in my mind when I came to talk to Simon was that watching television on Saturday night has always been—and seems destined to always be—a little different from watching television any other time of the week. For instance, no one even likes to admit to watching television on Saturday night. Many people claim that they never do. This is, evidently, a myth. Quite a few people—millions of people—do watch television on Saturday night; Nielsen ratings over the past decade show that the size of the Saturday-night audience is only slightly smaller than audiences during the rest of the week. It just happens that the nature of Saturday night makes watching television something most of us would rather not be doing then—or at least not own up to it if we do.

It has been blamed for it, but television did not create a nation of stay-at-homes whose idea of nightlife consisted of a glass of Bromo and a remote-control unit. Before television even existed, radio thrived on the big Saturday-night audience at home. Many of the most popular radio shows in the 1930s and '40s were scheduled for Saturday night. In New York, for instance, the 1946 Saturday night schedule included "Interview with a Star," "Your Hit Parade," "Stump the Authors," "The Answer Man," "Life of Riley," "Twenty Questions," "Roy Rogers," "Saturday Night Dance Parade," "Can You Top This?," "Dick Tracy," "Famous Jury Trials," "The Green Hornet," and "Leave It to the Girls." From 1936 through 1948, Pet Milk's popular "Saturday Night Serenade," starring the singer Jessica Dragonette, was also on the air. Still, television networks were leery at first of scheduling any programming for that night. "The assumption was that Saturday was strictly for going out, and that no one would stay at home to watch television," Simon says. "There was nothing on the air on Saturday night at all, for the first several years after network television debuted."

By 1948, though, television was already so successful that the networks were eager to fill every bit of time they could. In spite of being skeptical about the likelihood of developing a Saturday-night audience, the networks scheduled odds and ends: basketball games; a country-music show called "Saturday Night Jamboree" featuring a yodeler; something called "Blues by Bargy"; "Paul Whiteman's TV Teen Club"; a quiz show called "Spin the Picture"; and a talk show, starring Studs Terkel, which was set in a bar. There was nothing as odd-sounding as the 1946 Friday night staple "I Love to Eat," but there was finally something on the air.

From the beginning, it seems that Saturday-night television carried a stigma. For generations, girls without dates on Saturday night would carefully draw their curtains so that no one wandering past their house would see the telltale light in the window—the social equivalent of a billboard on the front lawn saying I AM HOME ALONE ON SATURDAY NIGHT. With the advent of television, these girls had something to do, but they had to be even more careful to shield the blue light of the Zenith from the eyes of passersby. One woman in her early fifties recently told me how excited she and her friends were when their families first got television sets. "We thought that there was finally something to do on weekends when no dates materialized," she said. "But then we started considering how much light a television generates, and how easy it was to see even through curtains, and how *obvious* it would be to anyone walking by that there was a girl without a date inside the house, and just like that, our excitement over Saturday-night television died."

Television on Saturday night really began not with "Paul Whiteman's TV Teen Club" but in 1950, when NBC's Sylvester "Pat" Weaver decided to acknowledge that there were maybe even millions of people who *were* home doing nothing much on Saturday night. NBC was reluctant to invest anything in Saturday-night shows until he made a specific proposition, but he came to them with the claim that he could create shows that would actually take advantage of the myths of Saturday night, rather than trying to fight them. He described his pitch to me. "I said I would make shows that would take everybody out to see those things that only people of privilege who lived in the right places could normally see," he recalls. "Things like a Broadway show, dinner theater, performances."

Weaver concocted a block of programming he called "The Saturday Night Revue." The revue would start at 8 p.m. with "The Jack Carter Show." At nine, it would offer "Your Show of Shows," starring Sid Caesar, Imogene Coca, and Carl Reiner. Both shows were live comic extravaganzas, indebted to the vaudeville and Broadway revues from which their performers were drawn. The Carter show was broadcast live from Chicago. "Your Show of

Shows" originated in New York. Anyone watching a full evening of "The Saturday Night Revue" would see two hours of performance, and, according to Weaver, would feel as if he or she were out on the town, seeing the best of what was happening across the country on that Saturday night. If they watched "The Saturday Night Revue," Weaver felt people could stay at home and still do what they really *wanted* to do on Saturday night: go out. Weaver's calculation proved accurate; "The Saturday Night Revue" was an enormous hit, and Saturday-night television was born.

"On any given night a majority of the population stays home. But in fact [few of them] consider Saturday night psychologically 'like every other night.' [People who feel Saturday is ordinary] may be aged, or have very young children, or are new in the neighborhood, have to work Sunday, or are simply not very social." This is the conclusion of a 1955 study, commissioned by NBC, which was trying to determine what sort of radio and television programming would be viable on the weekends. The study made the point that everyone—with a few exceptions—feels that Saturday night is special, even if they spend it at home. Most people were probably willing to turn the television or radio on, especially if there were something distinctive provided. The network read this not as a referendum on the significance of Saturday night in American popular culture but as a green light for the pursuit of rating points. Saturday night would never be neglected again.

The most ferocious competition for the Saturday leisure audience was the one between television and the movies. Since the birth of the movie industry, a night-out-at-the-movies date had been a staple of Saturday night in America. Theaters have always made most of their ticket sales on Friday and Saturday nights, and weekend box-office receipts were the most important indicator of a film's failure or success.

Going to the movies has always entailed more than just watching the movie—the ritual of leaving the house, standing and talking in line, sitting in a darkened room with a few hundred other people, hearing their reactions and chatter, being with a companion, made it an event. This was particularly true in early movie houses—Bijoux and Palaces and Regencies and Grands. To go to the movies was to experience a private pleasure in a special public setting; it was something of an occasion. Television was an entirely different creature. To begin with, it was free, always available, and offered a comfortable and reliable continuum week in and week out. But most importantly, television was at home—a fact that perfectly suited the time. Besides gutting cities and altering nearly all facets of urban life, the move to the suburbs that occurred after World War II changed American leisure. The prewar taste for gathering in social groups outside the home—dance halls or bowling alleys or movie theaters—was lost. To suburbanites, these social centers of the cities were remote and inconvenient and part of a world they had eagerly left behind. If anything, Americans in the suburbs were house-proud, and fascinated by the pursuit of how to have fun at home. Television, attendant at this birth of suburbia and the assertion of single-family life, was perfectly suited to the new world. By the 1950s, television had drawn off much of the movie theater audience. In 1946, Americans spent $1,692,000,000 on movie admissions—nearly 20 percent of the country's total recreation expenditures. By 1958, that amount had dropped in dollars to $992,000,000. In percentages, 1958 movie admissions represented only 6 percent of what Americans were spending that year on recreation. A survey done later that year showed that Americans' favorite activity to do in a family group, besides eating, was watching TV. Television had taken hold.

According to Ron Simon, the people in charge of the movie studios were nervous about the trend to television. Eventually, they would capitalize on its success by filming shows themselves, but until then, the studios saw television as the enemy. They resisted the networks' attempts to buy feature films to show on television. The only films they would release to the networks for television use were ancient material or low-budget junk that couldn't get an audience in the theaters anyhow. But by the end of the decade, the studios could see that their battle with the box was useless. Television was everywhere. A social watershed of sorts occurred in 1952, when the TV Dinner was invented. Created by dieticians at the Swanson Company, a turkey-freezing concern in Omaha, the TV Dinner was the very first of what marketing people have come to call "life-style" products—products designed to enhance the way modern Americans spend their time rather than servicing standard notions of need. Of course, the heat-and-serve dinner in its partitioned aluminum tray (modeled after Japanese lacquered dinner boxes, and now enshrined in the Smithsonian) was ideal for using in front of the set. But calling it a TV Dinner had more interesting implications—it suggested that television had become so popular and fundamental to contemporary life that it had marketable cachet just as a label. The family television room was standard in the homes of the 1950s; there were hit shows on every night of the week. Television was even creating its own stars. No amount of resistance or obstruction by the studios could impede television's success.

It was not long after that the studios realized that it would be more profitable for them to join forces with television than to continue the effort of trying to beat it down. A few studios made deals with the networks in the late 1950s—notably, Walt Disney and the British producer Sir Alexander Korda, who sold many of his films to television in 1958 and 1959. And on Saturday, September 23, 1961, television's war with the movies was over for good. That was the night that NBC's "Saturday Night at the Movies" was broadcast for the first time. Unlike any network movie showcase before it, "Saturday Night at the Movies" was in color and featured current films. It had for a logo a movie marquee dotted with blinking lights, drawn at an angle that made it look enormous. It had a roiling musical theme with an upswelling of drumrolls and strings, a stirring sound, more majestic than most of what came out of a television set.

" 'Saturday Night at the Movies,' with its tricked-up grandeur and drama, tried to duplicate a Saturday night out at the movies," says Tim Brooks, a network executive who has published complete television schedules from the year of TV's debut. "But in some ways, if you use the standards of the house-proud fifties and sixties, it was even better than going out to the movies, because it was available in the comfort of home, and it permitted us use of our own La-Z-Boys, which we had gotten on credit, and we could make our own popcorn, which we'd bought at the new supermarket." This would make it seem that "Saturday Night at the Movies" appealed to people who didn't want to spend money for movie tickets, but the show actually found its biggest audience among the affluent—probably the people who owned their own homes and loved to languish in them. A 1968 *TV Guide* survey showed that the program was highest rated among people with incomes over $10,000 and with at least one year of college. On the other hand, it didn't even rate in the top ten with lower-income and less-educated people, who preferred "The Lucy Show."

Beginning with its initial offering of *How to Marry a Millionaire*, starring Marilyn Monroe, Lauren Bacall, and Betty Grable, "Saturday Night at the Movies" followed with the big hits of the day, including the likes of *Bridge Over the River Kwai* and Alfred Hitchcock's *The Birds*, for seventeen years. If television was loser nightlife, then with "Saturday Night at the Movies" it had finally become full-color, sophisticated loser nightlife.

Once television was entrenched, it was obvious that a certain number of people could be counted on to watch anything anytime, even a test pattern—a sort of bottom-line vote of devotion to the medium itself. That meant it was no longer necessary, as it had been in the early days of television, to design shows just to lure people into turning on their sets. People now watch television constantly—according to the A. C. Nielsen Company's 1987 survey, at least one television is turned on for an average of seven hours and five minutes each day in the typical American home. Two-thirds of the people polled by the Los Angeles *Times* in 1981 said they got most of their information about "what's going on in the world" from television.

With an audience so devoted, networks no longer need to worry about the special nature of any particular night to have reasonably successful programming. Their real concern is to corner the largest share of television's steady audience. The whole idea of leaving Saturday night dark—without any programming at all—because people might be at the theater or strolling through the town square, has seemed, for at least thirty years, as quaint a notion as candle snuffs.

Even so, there is still something different about Saturday-night

TV. I suspect that because most people are so resistant to the idea of staying home on Saturday night, they get the feeling that Saturday-night programming brings out a bit of the sadist in network executives. Certainly, some Saturday-night programs were pitched so low that they even shamed the rest of the marginally intelligent television schedule and made anyone watching feel even more pained by their lack of social alternatives, adding insult to injury: it's bad enough having nothing to do, but you feel even worse when you find yourself spending Saturday night watching something as asinine as "Holmes and Yo-Yo." Since Saturday's ratings are somewhat lower than the rest of the week, its commercial time is the cheapest, so the networks always look to fill the night with programs that don't cost much to produce. That accounts for Saturday-night shows like "The Dating Game" and "The Newlywed Game." From 1967 through 1970, these two game shows (the highest-rated Saturday-night programs before "All in the Family" and "The Mary Tyler Moore Show" aired) ran back to back on Saturday night from 7:30 to 8:30 p.m. They made trashmaster Chuck Barris—the man with the curly-brown hair helmet—the indisputable king of Saturday-night television as it is in our collective memory most feared and hated. "The Dating Game" and "The Newlywed Game" both had as their operational premise the idea that embarrassment is the single funniest human emotion. That the shows ran on Saturday night heightened that humiliating quality. If one can give Chuck Barris credit for creating subtext, the shows also addressed Saturday night as the ultimate date night and the night most commonly associated with sex. Their success, which was considerable, took off from that awkward point.

There were other lapses of quality in Saturday-night programming: there was "The Partridge Family," and "The Bionic Woman," and "Flipper," and "I Dream of Jeannie," and "Pistols 'n' Petticoats," and "Maya," and "Mannix," and "Mr. T. and Tina," and "The American Girls," and "CHiPs," and "Big Shamus and Little Shamus," and "BJ and the Bear," and "The Secrets of Midland Heights," and "The Ghost and Mrs. Muir." There were countless other dumb programs stacked up on Saturday night. The juvenile parameters of these programs weren't network idiocy, though—it was marketing savvy, since the Saturday audience has always had a high percentage of viewers under eighteen years old.

But real marketing genius showed itself in the late 1970s and early 1980s, when ABC scheduled two hours that made up perhaps the ultimate Saturday-night schedule: "The Love Boat" followed by "Fantasy Island." The two shows—the first, a series of fey paeans to romance on a cruise vessel, and the second a run of baroque morality plays staged by a dwarf and a dullard on a deserted sandbar—fit perfectly on Saturday night, imbued as it is with all sorts of expectations about love and social probity. The ratings were sky-high. "Maybe," a network vice president, who still finds their success fascinating, said to me not long ago, "people who stay home on Saturday night have more fantasy on their minds than those who are home watching television on a Tuesday." Maybe. Neither "The Love Boat" nor "Fantasy Island" bothered to develop or sustain stories or characters. Instead, they just let viewers dip into other loves and lives—perfect armchair fantasies. It was like having a nationally broadcast consolation prize for having no such love or social intercourse of one's own to propel one out of the house.

Some people who are quite aware of the difference between Saturday-night television and TV on any other night of the week work at WATS Telemarketing, in Omaha, Nebraska. WATS, which is what people in the marketing business call "an 800 operator," is a company that mans the telephone lines for televised advertising pitches. When Golden Hits Incorporated runs ads on late-night television for a seven-record set of Slim Whitman's greatest hits and instructs interested parties to call 1-800-HIT-SLIM to order (promising that operators are waiting for your call), chances are the calls are coming to WATS Telemarketing or another one of the dozen 800 companies in the greater Omaha area.

Susan Hanson, who is in charge of public relations for WATS, told me that the 800 operators cluster in Nebraska for a number of reasons. The work is repetitive but demanding, she explained, but Nebraskans feel that they understand the work ethic better than anyone else, and as proof, personnel directors for the 800s never have trouble finding good, steady employees for the operator slots in Omaha. Moreover, the Nebraskan accent is flat and uninflected, as close to standard American English as you're likely to find anywhere else in the country. The people at Golden Hits and Popeel Pocket Fishermen and Cubic Zirconium Inc. and Craftmatic Beds and New Generation Hair Growth products and Diet Plan and Ginsu Knives like that, because they prefer callers to feel comfortable, and perhaps even think they're dialing somewhere familiar and close to home. According to telemarketing wisdom, this means they're less likely to reconsider the order or worry that it'll never arrive. Above all, Omaha offers the telemarketers proximity to the United States Air Force Strategic Air Command, which is headquartered just outside the city. When SAC located in Omaha, it upgraded local phone service to handle the kind of radar and military communications such an operation would require. Though it wouldn't seem that the two businesses—war-monitoring and the marketing of such items as Painter's Pal—would have much use for each other, the 800 operators also need extremely sophisticated phone service, and Omaha was one place in the country they could get it for free.

Calls come in to WATS Telemarketing from all around the country all times of the day and night. Hanson says WATS answers anywhere from 30,000 to 60,000 calls each day. Last year, WATS answered 28 million phone calls. The volume is highest in the late afternoon, when people who work at home tend to take a break and turn on the television, and a special offer might just catch their eye. The calls slow down in the evening. They pick up again very late at night.

There's nothing notable about the number of calls that comes in on a Saturday night, Hanson says, but it's the *type* of call that's unusual. WATS operators have told her that they find that many people who call on Saturday often begin by claiming some interest in an ad they just saw on the TV, and then, right after they ask a few questions about the product, they just start to talk. The operators say that the talk is innocent—"What's going on? Where are you guys located? Doing much business tonight? What other sorts of things do you sell? How many calls do you answer in a night? What's it like to get all these calls? What's the weather like out there? What time is it? Do you always have to work on Saturdays?"

The operators at WATS say that the chatterbox calls don't really bother them. "They figure that after all, it is Saturday night," Hanson says. "Out in the world, outside WATS Telemarketing here in Omaha, it is still Saturday night and all that, so anyone who's doing nothing better than calling about ads they saw on TV must be pretty lonely. The operators will talk to them for a few extra minutes. Maybe they figure that it can't hurt to exercise a little charity."

Being bored and forlorn watching Saturday-night television is now almost as much an institution as is going out and having a ball. Still, I found most of the facts about Saturday-night television viewing contradict the way it feels. For instance, it's a little surprising to note that Saturday has had more top-ranked shows than any night other than Monday. And in fact, in spite of Chuck Barris and his spawn, Saturday-night television actually has a history of quality. Ron Simon pointed out that Saturday night has had many critically acclaimed programs, starting with "Your Show of Shows." "Texaco Star Theater," "Checkmate," "The Joey Bishop Show," "The Outer Limits," "Get Smart," "Mission Impossible" (for three seasons), "Gunsmoke," "The Defenders," "M*A*S*H" (for two years), "Perry Mason," "The Jackie Gleason Show," "Leave It to Beaver" (maybe not critically acclaimed, but definitely well loved), "The Carol Burnett Show," and "The Bob Newhart Show" were all Saturday-night programs. "All in the Family," which was on Saturday nights for five of its twelve years, was so popular that the size of the total television audience on Saturday night during its run grew noticeably. The audience usually stays constant, and a hit show simply attracts the biggest percentage of it. That means that people who normally were going out, or were home but not watching television, made a point of watching just to see "All in the Family." Not only have there been good programs on Saturday night, those shows have often been the quintessence of their genre. "Gunsmoke," for instance, was the most popular and best-regarded TV western, "Perry Mason" considered the ultimate lawyer show, "The Defenders" the embodiment of TV noir.

Saturday traditionally is an "hour" night—its shows have been full-length programs with developed ideas, rather than the quick snippets characteristic of half-hour programming. And because audiences are usually a little smaller on Saturday, the networks have allowed Saturday-night shows somewhat wider range. On Saturday night, there's less to lose. The shows can be a little riskier, and in some cases they've been better. Archie Bunker's plainspokenness, for example, set a television precedent; before that, "The Defenders," with its highly charged, dry-eyed look at dark issues, pushed television out of vaudeville and into the realm of drama.

"The Mary Tyler Moore Show" graced Saturday night for its entire seven-year run—1970 through 1977. Not only was it the quintessential sit-com, the show was also the first to portray a single woman with a double bed, which was considered pretty dicey in its day. In contrast to gooey fantasy-romances like "The Love Boat," "Mary Tyler Moore" was a meta–Saturday-night show. Its star was a single woman (not unlike many Saturday-night television viewers) working for a television station, whose life and loves and problems were funny but not ridiculous. For many lonesome souls curled up on their couches picking at frozen dinners and wondering what in the world they were doing at home, Mary Tyler Moore was something of a patron saint. Many people now in their thirties remember it as the first show they ever watched on Saturday night that didn't make them feel embarrassed for having nothing more interesting to do. In her *Esquire* farewell to "The Mary Tyler Moore Show" in 1977, Nora Ephron wrote, "It was a lovely time, not at all like the first time I was single, when there was nothing to watch on TV on Saturday nights but something called 'I Dream of Jeannie.' I actually used to watch it, too. Every week. In those days I was somewhat more idiotic than I am now about things like Saturday night and New Year's Eve. . . . All I want to say, without being too mushy about it, is that it meant a lot to me the second time I was single and home alone on Saturday night to discover that Mary Tyler Moore was at home, too. . . . Okay, Mary. I'll keep it short and sweet. Thanks. You made it possible for millions of Americans to stay home on Saturday night and not feel they were missing anything."

On February 11, 1975, Herbert S. Schlosser sent a memo to Robert T. Howard concerning a peculiar new idea he had. Although there was nothing in the past to suggest this could work, Schlosser wanted to launch a new comedy show late on Saturday nights.

"With proper production and promotion, 'Saturday Night' can become a major show in television that people will talk about. It can carve out its own audience and increase sets in use if we do a good job," wrote Schlosser, who was then president of NBC. He went on to describe his concept for a "young," "bright," "distinctive," "new," "exciting," "fresh" program for late Saturday night. He ended the memo by stating, "Saturday night is an ideal time to launch a show like this."

Why Saturday night? It didn't seem to be a natural choice for a show that Schlosser envisioned as a prestigious showcase for new comic talent. In spite of its past successes, Saturday-night television still had that reputation for being leisure for losers. What's more, the networks were still less involved with Saturday-night programming than any other night of the week, and except for prime time, they had more or less let it go wild. Saturday is the only night of the week that television isn't uniform across the country—it's the only time that the medium has a haphazard, homemade look. The network evening news doesn't run, or if it does, it's anchored by second-stringers. The familiar faces of Johnny Carson and David Letterman are missing. Big blocks of time are left for local affiliates to fill however they can. Saturday afternoon and early evening is when local stations often run locally produced programs and syndicated shows—"Putting on the Hits," "Solid Gold," "Soul Train," "Candlepins for Cash." In Cleveland, where I grew up, Saturday night was ushered in by a polka variety hour and a talent program hosted by a popular local master of ceremonies named Gene Carroll. (I still remember one Saturday evening, I saw some colleagues of mine from elementary school, the Hollander sisters, on the show doing a dance routine and singing "You've Got to Have Heart." For me, weaned on high-tech, expensively produced TV and accustomed to seeing stars in good costumes and sophisticated sets on every show, the sight of those girls, who rode the same bus as I did to school, was depressing. I preferred television to be a neat illusion, broadcast from somewhere remote and inaccessible and different from my hometown. Frankly, I wasn't crazy about being forced to realize, as

I was only on those Saturday nights, that television did not come directly from outer space, and in fact, only a few miles away from my house, some guy with a camera was taping my prancing school-mates and projecting the picture through the air.) Saturday night is the least desirable time to work anywhere, but especially at television stations, where the show must go on whether anyone's watching or not. Consequently, Saturday-night crews are usually inexperienced or elderly or part-time, as well as tired and bored. They're often unsupervised, too. Night workers in all industries make the most mistakes of any shift of workers; in television that translates into mistakes like running reels of movies out of sequence or leaving them on during commercials or showing them out of focus or without sound. Since commercial time is priced according to audience size, Saturday-night spots are bargain basement, to the delight of certain advertisers. As a result, Saturday-night commercials have become the domain of cheaply produced Veg-a-matic-style sales pitches (fielded by the likes of WATS Telemarketing) you'd never see during prime time. And even at that price, stations often can't sell all of their Saturday night commercial time, so they plug strange old public-service announcements or armed-forces recruitment come-ons into the unsold commercial slots.

With that kind of Saturday-night standard, local affiliates had come to expect little from the networks on Saturday—there just wasn't enough money or prestige to be had, especially late at night. So in 1975, when Schlosser and NBC offered them this new late-Saturday-night show, they were surprised and even skeptical. It was as if the network were trying to colonize the wasteland's real waste-land. Naturally, NBC had its own agenda. Before "Saturday Night Live," all that NBC offered its affiliates for late Saturday broadcast was Johnny Carson reruns, and its ratings were rock-bottom. Some local stations skipped Saturday's *Tonight* show altogether, using the time instead to run movies they dragged out of their vaults. The network was anxious to keep the affiliates in line, and to try to attract an audience to TV at a time no one ever had. Enough of the affiliates agreed to try the show, and in October 1975, NBC's "Saturday Night Live" debuted.

The show was immediately and completely associated with the

night it was on the air—starting, of course, with its name. It wasn't the first show to have "Saturday" or "Saturday Night" tacked onto its title—in fact, NBC's "Saturday Night Live" was thirteenth on that list, after "Saturday Night at the Garden," "Saturday Night Dance Party," "The Saturday Night Fights," "The Saturday Night Hollywood Palace," "Saturday Night Jamboree," "Saturday Night Live with Howard Cosell," "Saturday Roundup," "The Saturday Sports Final," "Saturday Sports Mirror," "Saturday Square," and, of course, "The Saturday Night Revue" and NBC's "Saturday Night at the Movies." Unlike other television shows, these shows couldn't be juggled to another night of the week, a practice so common in network scheduling that it's rare for a show to play many years on the same night. "Saturday Square" couldn't be shifted to an open slot on Tuesday without looking more than a little odd.

NBC president Schlosser worried about this when christening "Saturday Night Live." "To the extent that we do not affect clearance [get the affiliates to run this show] on Saturday night," he wrote in a memo to other network executives, "stations could play it on Sunday night." Then he added, "But under what title would the show play on Sunday night? Would we have separate titles for those stations who play it on Sunday night?"

There was a reason to put up with that inconvenience, and why so many shows have had "Saturday night" in their name. All of them have been programs that were immediate, topical, playful—a quality telegraphed to the audience by using "Saturday night" in their names. Calling a show "Saturday Night Something" is in effect sort of like affixing it with a Good Housekeeping Seal of Fun. Naturally, if "Saturday Night Live" had instead been named "Comedy Playroom" or "Post-Vietnam Humor Workshop," it would have still been the success it was. But the show relied on cultivating an image of irreverence edging on danger, and naming it for the night when, in popular theory, *anything* goes, brought the point home.

Schlosser told me recently that he had always considered Saturday to be the only night appropriate for his show. No weeknight, and not even Friday night, was ever considered. Now a corporate executive at a Manhattan investment bank, but still hatching new television plans by the dozen, Schlosser talks about "Saturday Night

Live" the way a teacher might describe the beloved class brat. "I wanted it live, young, sassy, smart-alecky. Saturday night was the right night," he said. "It just *was*. It was relaxed. It was fun. It was ideal."

Saturday was also the night when Schlosser figured that the people in NBC's Standards and Practices Department might tolerate such a frisky undertaking. Schlosser also says that he was counting on the audience for the show to be a little looser than a typical weekday one. "We were right," he said, smiling. "We could tell the audience was pretty loose by the fact that we never received more than a very small number of complaints about the show's propriety."

Running the show on the weekend also meant that NBC's other powers-that-be were long gone to their country homes and beyond the reach of any panicky Standards and Practices factotum by the time the show would air. That ensured that the show's irreverence, and dicey political and sexual commentary, would be safe from too much immediate meddling. On Saturday, the show was essentially insulated from the chill of network interference even more than it would have been on a Friday or Sunday night. Schlosser believes that there is no question that this influenced the way the show evolved.

"Saturday Night Live" launched a dozen comedy careers, and it proved you could be cheeky on TV, and it brought Elvis Costello glaring into American living rooms, and it made a myth of John Belushi, and it made lots of money for the network. But what it did that seemed impossible to do was to make it socially safe—and even desirable—to watch TV late Saturday night. This was a historical first. The show sometimes attracted an audience on par with a prime-time show; given how tiny late-Saturday-night audiences tended to be, those numbers were astonishing. Rather than Saturday's traditional "bi-modal" audience (children and elderly people, who happen to be television marketing executives' least favorite groups of viewers), "Saturday Night Live" had an audience of educated eighteen- to forty-nine-year-olds, who were exactly the kind of people who used to avoid television on Saturday night as if it were the measles.

"Saturday Night Live" was the first time the members of the baby boom had coalesced around a television show since the Watergate hearings. As it happened, these were both programs people wanted to watch in groups; both gave the viewer the feeling that news was being made; both were live shows, which meant that anything might happen. At the time "Saturday Night Live" debuted, nearly 70 percent of all Americans were too young to remember life before television. Television dominated every sense of news, style, and popular culture. Americans born after World War II made up the first generation to have its childhood examined and sanctified and uniquely serviced by television. This was also the first generation to have the events that transfigured it—political assassination, the Vietnam War, Watergate—played on television. Now television was affecting the well-established notion that cool people didn't watch television on Saturday nights. Especially during the show's peak in the late 1970s, the social earth, as it was known by people of this generation, would stand still at 11:30 p.m. on Saturday night. I remember being at parties on Saturday night that would be going strong; at 11:30, they would stop, and everyone would crowd around the set to see the show. Before "Saturday Night Live," I'd never been at a party where this happened. But watching "Saturday Night Live" was like joining a better party that happened to be broadcast from NBC's Studio 8H. I knew people who were reluctant to go out anywhere they wouldn't be able to watch the show. Eventually, getting together with friends to watch it became a social ceremony in itself. This was a strange new protocol for Saturday night, and a radical one for television, and it turned the usual logic about both on its head.

In 1983, the Roper Organization surveyed the general public about "a machine called a videocassette recorder." Twelve percent of those asked had never heard of them. By the next year, 64 percent of the people Roper polled said they would rather watch movies at home on their VCRs than in movie theaters. By that year, forty-five thousand VCRs were being sold each day, and video rental stores had become more common than post offices.

One Saturday night before I met Ron Simon, I spent a few hours

watching the crowds come in and out of a video store in a suburb
of Cleveland, Ohio. Video Adventures is in a strip of shops on a road
that is lined with strips of shops. This particular strip happens to
be on a corner and at an angle, so the parking lot in front of the
store is wedge-shaped and congested—a condition worsened by
the fact that many people pull into the lot and wait to see if anyone
walking into the store is returning a movie they'd like to rent. Like
most video stores, Video Adventures's decor runs to cardboard
advertising cutouts of Tom Cruise in *Top Gun*, promotional posters
for movies like *Monster Dog* ("The Fear . . . The Terror . . . The Night-
mare!!!!"), a popcorn machine, saloon doors separating the adult
section from the rest of the store, and racks of movie tapes—by one
manager's reckoning, five thousand movie tapes. That night there
were four bored-looking young people behind the counter ringing
up rentals. They spoke only to one another, except for occasional
breaks during which they would dispense capsule reviews ("It's sort
of like *Jaws*, but happier"), apologies for movies they recommended
("You should try this—it sounds stupid, but it's about this guy who
gets to be friends with this rat, and it's really great"), and grim
reports about movie availability ("*Jagged Edge*, are you kidding?
You're about three hours too late").

The first people in the store that night were mothers with children in tow, most of whom had to reassure their children at some
point during their stay that *E.T.* would be on video soon. By eight,
the mothers were gone and the demographic skewed to couples,
who spent most of their time arguing over movie choices. A few
single women drifted in, wandered through the Adult, Moderate
Adult, and Classics sections and then left. Nearly everyone picked
up and examined copies of Woody Allen's movie *Interiors* but no
one rented it. One couple wearing matching suede outfits rented six
movies, mentioning in a loud voice that they had three VCRs. Business peaked at nine, and most popular movies were gone shortly
after that. Earlier in the day, one of the managers had estimated that
on Saturday, the store's busiest night, eleven hundred movies are
rented, most of them by nine o'clock. A few people rented X-rated
movies. One of them, a middle-aged woman in a polka-dotted shift,
took a copy of *Wrestling Meat* and held it behind her back while she

waited in line. As she was waiting, someone came up to her and said, "Lois dear, how are you? What are you renting?" Several people who knew each other met in the store unexpectedly. At eleven, two women who had been in earlier with their children came in and walked back to the Drama section. One of them picked up a box with a picture of Tom Selleck on it. "Here we go," she said. "Now something for *Mommy*."

Many people would say that the advent of the videocassette recorder and the video-rental business has finally made staying at home on Saturday night an engaging option. It is easy, inexpensive, diverse, and available. People with babies and no baby-sitters are great advocates of the form. Anyone who is lazy, single, overworked, housebound, or broke is likely to argue that there has been no greater development in this century. For a while, I had begun to think that because of their popularity across all social lines, video stores might become the new town squares—that is, that everyone would make a trip to their local Video Adventure on Saturday night to see friends, talk about movies, jostle for copies of *Top Gun*, and meet people. From my limited survey, I would say that has not been the case. The atmosphere in video stores is friendly but no one lingers. Some stores have even begun to deliver. According to one Long Island video-store owner I spoke to, the new wave in video rentals is the on-site outlet, which, he explained, meant mini-stores inside supermarkets and malls. "People want to get their movies and go home," he said. "I stopped turning on my popcorn machine in the store. No one really wanted to hang around the store, and no one was even eating the popcorn. I had thought people wanted the movie-going experience, even if they were renting something to take home. But I was wrong. They wanted to get a movie and go home and watch it."

Which brought me, finally, to Ron Simon at the Museum of Broadcasting. Among the other things that videocassette recorders do is record television shows so that they can be played whenever the viewer has time or inclination. Time-shifting, as it is known, allows you to watch Johnny Carson for breakfast if you wish, or see "thirtysomething" on Friday instead of Tuesday. This has made television a malleable medium that anyone with a VCR can custom-make. The time of programming something special for Saturday night—something that could make Americans feel as if they were at a burlesque performance or at the theater, so they wouldn't mind that they were home on Saturday night watching television—is long past. Some people would consider this a fortunate development. Ron Simon isn't sure.

"I don't know," he said, the day I visited him at the museum. "It used to be that some shows were on some nights and that made the night feel a certain way. I still remember specific shows on specific nights from when I was a kid." He shrugged. "I even sort of liked the awful feeling I used to get on Saturday night when some dumb show came on. It seemed like it was part of the experience of Saturday night. It was one of the things that made Saturday night different from other nights. Now the week is just a blur. Everything is time-shifted. I wonder whether it will affect the way television shows are made, or programmed. I don't think it matters as much about shows that are on weeknights, but the weekend shows seem special. That kind of thing might disappear now that these VCRs have become permanent fixtures in our lives. I just don't know how I feel about it. It really does make me feel a little, oh, *sorry*, I guess." After a moment, he smiled and then said, "On the other hand, wouldn't it have been great to not have been stuck watching Lawrence Welk every Saturday night?"

Sitting

Pleasantville, New York

According to the United States Bureau of Vital Statistics, there are 12,608,609 potential baby-sitters in this country, and Allison Suzanne Cohen is one of them. Before she achieved baby-sitting potentiality, which she defines as the twelfth through the sixteenth years of life, Allison was one of many small unemployed children living in a pleasant town called Pleasantville in Westchester County, New York. As soon as she turned twelve this year, she became highly sought-after among the mothers of Pleasantville, who pine for a Saturday-night baby-sitter the way prison inmates might pine for a metal hacksaw. Allison now works most Saturday nights tending to Pleasantville's Camerons, Jennifers, Jasons, Chloes, Dustins, Alexandras, and Adams, and she often reflects with enthusiasm on her job.

"I'm sure at some point, I'll know it's time to stop," Allison said recently as she got ready for an evening sitting down the street at the home of Jim and Debbie McLoughlin (James Junior, age five; Devon, one and a half). "That point will probably have something to do with boys. I'm sure that will happen but it hasn't happened yet. I'm at that stage where I love kids and babies, so I really like to baby-sit. I really do love kids. They're so neat. Have you heard of Allie's Corner? I thought you might have. Well, Allie is me, and Allie's Corner is something I do one afternoon a week on my street. The littler kids come over to my house and I play games with them and watch them and take care of them until their mothers want them for dinner. It's a good deed. We learned in Sunday school that it's important to do a good deed, so my deed is Allie's Corner. I'm not sure that sitting for people on Saturday night when they go out is the same kind of good deed, but I can tell that I'm very appreciated. I love it. At the moment, I'm a very happy baby-sitter."

Allison's mother, who was out on the back porch having dinner with Allison's father and younger brother, called in through the screen door, "Allie, come see me before you go, sweetie."

"I don't feel like the money is that important to me, but I do like earning it," Allison went on. "And I'm not really qualified for very many other jobs."

Allison is four feet eight inches tall and weighs eighty-nine pounds. She has thick chestnut-brown hair which she wears parted on the side, a round face, bright eyes, a winsome grin, a husky voice, and an abundance of kinetic energy. Her manner is by turns achingly mature, flaky, commanding, and sweet. Her mother describes this as "Allison's in-between phase." Allison describes this as being on the verge of grownupedness. Like many people on the verge of grownupedness, Allison dresses for action. She is also color-sensitive. The night she was sitting for the McLoughlins, she was wearing a pink sweatshirt, pink sweatpants, a pink hair ribbon, pink socks, and puffy white athletic shoes. Another time I visited her, she was wearing a yellow sweatshirt, yellow sweatpants, gray and yellow socks, and the same white athletic shoes. A few months after I went baby-sitting with her, she told me that she had had a revelation and had forsaken pink and yellow altogether and was now "a total green person." When I arrived at her house on this Saturday night, she was in the middle of packing a plastic bag with provisions for the evening—crochet needles, yarn, a hairbrush, and a barrette. "Let's see, needles, yarn, brush, okay, I have everything I need," she said, rummaging through her bag. "I'm crocheting a scarf for my mother for her birthday, so I like to take it with me so I can work on it. It's good to have a hairbrush, wherever. Now I'm ready, so let's go say good-bye to my parents."

The Cohens live in a big, airy, modern house with interesting angles that sits on a large lot on the side of a hill in Pleasantville, a town about thirty-five miles north of New York City. The center of Pleasantville dates to the mid-eighteen hundreds and a now-vanished dairy-farming economy. Lately, many thousands of Manhattan commuters have fallen for the town and moved onto what were, until recently, fallow fields and vacant tracts. The Cohens' immediate neighborhood is called the Estates of Pleasantville, and it is dotted with about eighty stylistically compatible, big, airy, modern, interestingly angular houses. Two years ago, this neighborhood was woods and empty pastures with sugar maples, slippery elm, clover, dandelions, sumac, alfalfa grass, and dirt. The town of Pleasantville offers a pub and a video store for entertainment, which some of the sophisticated new residents consider cruelly limited. Many people drive to White Plains or Manhattan for a night out.

"When I was a baby, we lived in Brooklyn, but then we moved to the Estates of Pleasantville," Allison told me once. "Everyone who lives in the Estates of Pleasantville lived somewhere else before they lived here. Before they were here, there was nothing here. Now there are families and houses and kids. That's why it's a nice place to live."

Pleasantville does seem like a nice place to live. I had decided to include it in my Saturday-night agenda because I wanted to determine how a twelve-year-old who thinks of herself as a regular kid in a regular town spends Saturday night these days, and I knew Allison to be such a kid and Pleasantville to be such a town. I found out that if the regular kid in question is at all enterprising, the short answer is made obvious by the mathematics of the current birth rate. After several years of slump—in fact, the very years in which today's baby-sitters were being born—birth rates have surged to their highest level in twenty-five years all over the country, the Estates included, making the baby–to–baby-sitter ratio highly favorable to baby-sitters and a source of panic for many new parents. There are now many families and many kids residing in the Estates, and many of the families with the younger kids feel a profound sense of gratitude toward the families with older kids when Saturday night rolls around. Another baby-sitter I know who lives a few miles from Allison in another fertile Westchester County town told me that her all-time record (New Year's Eve not included) was six baby-sitting requests for the same Saturday night. Allison mentioned that she's busy, but she has not yet faced this kind of glut, probably due to the discretion with which the McLoughlins have promoted her work.

"The thing about us baby-sitters," Allison says, "is that we know we're always needed. You could call practically anyone and say you'd like to sit, you're in the mood to sit, and they'd say, 'This Saturday? Well, great! Then we'll go out!' You feel very needed."

"The thing about Allison," Debbie McLoughlin says, sounding moved to the outer limits of emotion, "well, I don't really know what to say. I don't. When we moved here from Connecticut last year, we lived in fear of finding a baby-sitter. I was nervous. I didn't know if the kids here were into sitting. I thought baby-sitting had gone out of style with kids. Kids have so many social options these days, and there just aren't that *many* baby-sitting–age kids. Let's just put it this way: baby-sitters are at a premium. We first met Allison's parents because they live right in the neighborhood, and then we found out about Allison, and we felt like we'd found a treasure. She's wonderful. I wouldn't have been out of the house all summer if it weren't for her. I hope she's happy with her job. It's very important to me that she stays happy, and I hope it's a few more years before she discovers boys."

The walk from the Cohens' to the McLoughlins' house is short but steep. The street, which curves around the contours of what probably used to be bigger hills, was sprinkled with gravel and crisscrossed with muddy tracks from construction equipment. The curbs and sidewalks are as rough and white as chalk. We passed several estates-in-progress on the way down the hill. Some foundations had been laid and the mud chewed up many feet in every direction around them; the bulldozers were parked nearby, looking like dinosaurs at a mud bath. A few driveways had already been staked out. A couple of cars passed us, but there was no one else on foot anywhere in sight.

Allison said that she didn't expect to baby-sit forever. "I'm thinking of being a lawyer," she said. "My dad's a lawyer, and he thinks I'd be pretty good at it. I'd like to have my own kids, too, but that might be because I'm in a phase where I really like babies." I asked her whether the rest of her friends were starting to baby-sit. She said some were, but many of them only handled house accounts— namely, they had younger brothers and sisters and had to sit for them when their parents were out. Allison's own enterprise is similarly limited by her younger brother, Michael, except on those weekends when her parents stay home or Michael is sleeping over at a friend's or grandparent's house. She also mentioned that no one she knew personally ever went on anything that resembled a date. "There are some people who have sort of like boyfriends, I guess," she said, swinging her bag. "They're kind of the exception, though. Dating is not the big thing. Sometimes my friends will have a sleepover at someone's house or maybe a party on Saturday night or maybe some kind of Girl Scout thing, but mostly we don't really do that much. We either sit for our own little brothers and sisters or we go out sitting or we stay home or we go to the Teen Center in town. Some of my friends are just starting to baby-sit for money. I think that baby-sitting will be the big thing for the next three years or so, unless the homework situation gets really bad and we're all too busy."

Just then, as we walked around a corner, the McLoughlins' house came into view. It was big, airy, and modern, and appeared to have fresh sod laid in the front yard. By this time, the sun had dropped close to the horizon and it gave the Estates of Pleasantville an amber and slightly blinding glow. The McLoughlins were standing in their driveway, shading their eyes with their hands and squinting in the general direction of Allison's house. As soon as they saw us, they started waving and smiling jubilantly. Jim McLoughlin, a lean, pleasant, red-haired man who looked about forty, lunged after his smaller son, who was crawling toward the sod. Debbie McLoughlin, a pretty blonde woman in a fluttery blue-and-white dress, looked about eight months pregnant. After a moment, a late-model American car came around the other corner and pulled into the driveway, and another young couple in nice clothes stepped out.

"Hi, everyone, hi, we'll be one minute, hello Allison! Jim, get Devon *please*, come on in, Allison, watch the grass, it's got icky fertilizer on it, that's fine, fine, let's go inside for a second," Debbie McLoughlin said, as she walked backward to the house.

"Wow," Allison said. "Your grass looks *nice*." We walked into the kitchen behind Debbie, who crossed the room and opened the refrigerator.

"Allie, here's some Pepsi for you, and milk, or anything you'd like," she said. She reached across the counter, picked up a large bag, and smiled at Allison. "I bought you some popcorn, too. You like popcorn, don't you?" Allison nodded and looked pleased. "And we have some Pepperidge Farm cookies, too. The boys can have one cookie each before bed. Here's the number where we'll be. We're just going for dinner, so we won't be late. The boys can play outside for a while, but don't forget the grass has fertilizer on it and they can't go on it." She walked slowly around the kitchen with her hand on her belly. "All right, now is that everything? Let's see, oh, I think so. Don't forget to enjoy the popcorn. I gave you the number where we'll be, right? Okay. Have a nice time, and thank you so much for coming tonight."

Allison said, "Oh, I love the boys. I love popcorn, too. Okay, have a really, really nice dinner and everything! Don't worry about anything here, okay?"

The main agent of discomposure among baby-sitters is the creaking house. This outweighs even the absence of HBO or any other pay channel. Not having cable at all is a problem, but compared to house creaks it is only a secondary or tertiary one. Since everyone has television—or at least, anyone who has ever successfully hired a baby-sitter—the question of whether there is a television at all is never raised. Color and at least nineteen inches of screen are also *a priori* on most jobs. Other botherations: bad or limited food, or food such as cakes and pies which give evidence as to exactly how much the sitter has eaten; having to be driven home by weird heads of households; having to look directly at the money as it is being offered in payment; large, aggressive family pets; diapers; stated limits on telephone use; any noises other than creaks coming from anywhere in the house.

Allison's tenure as baby-sitter has been mostly uneventful. When pressed to remember moments of anguish or excitement, she cited one time when Devon had a dirty diaper; one time when the father at one of her jobs came home early and she didn't realize who he was at first and she had taken out a butter knife and had prepared to stab him to death; and one time when the McLoughlins' toaster sort of caught on fire. Otherwise everything has gone fine.

"This house does make a *lot* of noise," she said, as we walked around the place, followed by Devon and James, Jr., both of whom were adorable boy children cast in the mold of Dennis the Menace. The McLoughlins' house smelled like carpet glue and fresh wood. There was almost no furniture, so the high-ceilinged rooms seemed cavernous. Allison jumped up and down in the corner of the living room. "See, it's settling. Mr. McLoughlin told me that. It makes a lot of loud, creepy sounds, *which I hate*, but I try not to be scared because I know it's just the house settling or something. It is kind of scary, though, because you do hear all these gross stories about baby-sitters. Otherwise, I like being here. They don't have cable, which is too bad, but this is a new development and there's no cable yet in any of the houses. That's okay. I usually just watch 'The Golden Girls' on Saturday night anyway, and that's not on cable. Do you ever watch it? It's like . . ." She rubbed her chin and pondered for a second. "It's like . . . *funny*. It's like . . . a sit-com. All my friends watch 'The Golden Girls' so even though I'm working, I don't miss out on my usual Saturday-night show."

James, Jr. grabbed her knees and said, "Allison, I want to go outside and catch some ants." Allison looked out of the window at the setting sun, and then said, "Okay, James, we can go out for a little bit. Why don't you get some of these Pepperidge Farm cookies? I bet the ants like those." Devon, the smaller boy, climbed up on a kitchen chair and grabbed his bottle while James found the bag of cookies. A moment later, Devon fell off the chair and sat in a heap on the floor, silent and surprised. As Allison picked him up and brushed him off, she said, "Okay, let's go outside and get the ants right away."

We sat in the driveway for about forty minutes, trying to coax ants into a bucket using Mint Milanos and Tahitis, and during the breaks when the ants were deciding whether to pursue the cookies, we swatted at gnats with a Wiffle bat. Every once in a while, someone would ride by on a bicycle or a car would roar by, but otherwise, the Estates of Pleasantville, on this early summer Saturday night, was serene. Eventually, Allison got bored with the ants and gnats and suggested we go back inside. The boys ate the remaining Pepperidge Farm cookies and then toddled upstairs to bed.

"You guys are so *good!*" Allison exclaimed, after they brushed their teeth. "I'm really impressed. You're about the best kids I know!"

James, Jr. looked up at her and said, "Allison, when I grow up, I'm just going to stay home and baby-sit all the time."

Allison says this about the Wild Baby-sitter Phenomenon: "I don't really believe in that. First of all, I don't have a boyfriend, so I can't invite him over, because, like I said, I don't *have* one. Secondly, I think it would be weird and not really great to do that. Because I think it's not something I would consider right to do. As far as me having girlfriends over, they're all too busy sitting at their own jobs or for their little brothers and sisters. I know some sitters swap numbers of where they're going to be with other friends and then sit on the phone. I wouldn't do that unless someone has call-waiting on their phone, because it would be really, really bad if they called and the phone were busy for a couple of hours."

About the pleasures of being a valued employee: "I like potato chips, popcorn, chocolate, cookies, not pretzels as much, cake I guess, and anything else that I'm not allowed to eat at home. I think it's really nice when people go out of their way to buy something nice for the baby-sitter to eat."

About working on Saturday night: "Oh, it's fine with me. I just like to make sure I get to see 'Golden Girls,' and also 'Amen,' which I don't like as much as 'Golden Girls,' but I like it a lot. I don't feel like I'm missing that much by working, because the kids are usually asleep by the time the shows are on. When my friends and I start going out with boys, I'm sure that will be different. I probably won't see 'Golden Girls' at all."

At a quarter of nine, the phone rang. Debbie McLoughlin was calling to see if everything was proceeding without incident. Allison assured her that it was, and hurried off the phone to get upstairs to the television. The only television in a room with furniture was in the master bedroom upstairs, so we climbed onto the McLoughlins' bed with the remote control and some cookies. Allison doesn't consider herself a television critic as much as a television enthusiast, and our viewing was punctuated by regular expressions of those enthusiasms. "Oh, look at this," she said at several different points, followed by an appreciation such as "She's so funny" or "This is *such* a cute commercial" or "That is such a *riot*." She was rapt throughout "The Golden Girls." I couldn't get used to the idea that the young girls of America who are now in the middle of their baby-sitting phase were avid watchers of a sit-com about four elderly women, but the ratings of the program would seem to bear this out. We giggled at the show, then watched "Amen," and then Allison pulled out her crocheting and made a few desultory attempts to add to a scarf that appeared to the naked eye to be about seven feet long. She started to look sleepy. After a while, she turned to me and said in a soft voice, "I guess this isn't really that eventful, is it?"

The McLoughlins pulled into the garage at ten-thirty, and entered the house making a lot of we-aren't-robbers kinds of noises. As soon as she heard them, Allison hopped off of their bed, turned off the television, and went to the top of the stairs. Debbie McLoughlin appeared below us, and she waved and asked how the evening was in a hoarse whisper. Allison fluttered her hands and said, "Oh, great, just great. The boys are so cute." She started to walk downstairs, and then said, "Oh, Mrs. McLoughlin, you won't believe this—James told me he wants to be a baby-sitter when he grows up!"

Debbie widened her eyes and laughed. "That's just a phase," she said to Allison. "It's his baby-sitter phase."

Mr. McLoughlin drove us the several tenths of a mile back to

Allison's house, and Allison sat in front and asked him about the baby on the way.

"More sitting for you, Allie," he said. "All these pregnant mothers are good for business, right?"

Allison nodded. "Really good," she said. "I just don't exactly know what next year's going to be like, with homework and that kind of stuff. I've heard that seventh grade is like . . . the worst. It's like . . . murder. This might interfere, or maybe not." In a minute, we were in front of her parents' house. When I stepped onto the curb and looked up, I could detect the Cohens sitting in the living room, glancing out of the window at the McLoughlins' car. The rest of the Estates of Pleasantville was dark and quiet. The summer sky was milky gray and pierced here and there by stars. Allison was about to run up the driveway to tell her parents how the evening went, especially the part about James, Jr.'s interest in the baby-sitting business, but she decided to first devote some of the last moments of the evening to her duties as chief financial officer of Allison Suzanne Cohen, Baby-sitter. She reached into her pocket and pulled out her pay, which she had taken pains not to look at as Mr. McLoughlin was handing it to her. She counted it and determined that she had made twelve dollars, which she said she intended to put toward either a few new sets of barrettes or law school. "That's success!" she said, sounding buoyant. Then she headed up the driveway toward home.

Missileering

Pleasantville, New York

By all accounts, the easiest way to get to the United States Air Force nuclear missile launch facility known as Papa One is to head north out of Cheyenne, Wyoming, on Interstate 25. The interstate is a broad, four-lane highway that cleaves Wyoming's eastern third—an endless stretch of dusty, khaki-colored, pancake-flat prairie—from the western part of the state, where high, toothy mountains and wrinkled rock break the land into savage and dramatic vertical plates. The two sections of the state are very different. To say that western Wyoming is more theatrical, geologically speaking, than eastern Wyoming, would be a little like saying that Cher is more theatrical than, say, Donna Reed. A person choosing postcards of Wyoming would be better off with one that showed the western part of the state. Even so, there are people who think the eastern section really is the nicest, even though it does have the kind of treelessness, grasslessness, bushlessness, and generally featurelessness that can make you rather anxious to find out what happens next.

Interstate 25 cuts into Wyoming at the Colorado border about forty miles west of Nebraska, then swings around Cheyenne and heads toward the dry high plains. Just past the city, the road runs beside a neighborhood of boxy redwood houses set on one-acre backyards and garnished with split-rail fencing and above-ground swimming pools—a style that the developers who invented it like to call "ranchette," and the owners who have invested in it like to call something like Windy Acres or Our Four Corners or Prairie Paradise. The interstate then passes a group of flat-topped postwar chicken-coop–style bungalows and, beyond that, the entrance to Francis E. Warren Air Force Base. If your mind were somewhere else, you might drive by without even noticing F. E. Warren's low, red-brick front gate, if it weren't for the empty chassis of a Minuteman I, a Minuteman III, and an MX missile—each close to seventy feet tall and as skinny and pointy-topped as asparagus—standing upright beside it. On the extremely horizontal landscape around Cheyenne, the missiles are hard to miss, and the people I met in Wyoming who find the display a disturbing show of belligerence were easily outnumbered by those who told me they were thankful for having something around that makes giving directions in the greater Cheyenne area a little less of a chore.

Beyond F. E. Warren, I-25 cuts through empty land and then passes a cluster of low, flimsy-looking structures that house a few of Wyoming's many fireworks stores. While not as universally admired as some of Wyoming's other noteworthy features—Yellowstone National Park or the King Ropes Store in Sheridan, for instance—the stores have achieved their own moderate fame, because the type of fireworks they sell happen to be legal in only a few states across the country. According to a few people I know, this has made the stores and, by association, the state, as renowned among the explosive-minded as Louisiana probably is among people who would like to marry their thirteen-year-old cousins. Most Wyoming cities, including Cheyenne, still ban fireworks sales within the municipal limits, forcing the stores to locate in out-of-the-way places. Considering that many people would call the entire state of Wyoming an out-of-the-way place, you can imagine that the stores end up in magnificently desolate spots—in other words, traveling across Wyoming, you come across many thousands of square miles containing one snow fence, one polled Hereford, one empty oil barrel, some vast and awesome Slough-of-Despond-style nothingness, and one fireworks store stocked with Screaming Rebels, Big Bombs, Thunder Bombs, Small Whistling Missiles, Small Screaming Missiles, Air Travels with Report, Mini Mag Missiles, Saturn Missiles, Air Craft Carriers, MX Missiles, and Opening Flower Happy Birds.

Just beyond the fireworks stores, you leave Interstate 25 and turn onto Route 85, a straight two-lane road that cuts across acres of arid ranchland that spread out around it like big yellow rugs. There are some signs for local ranches—J. Berry, Berry Brothers, and Circle J—stuck in the patches of grama grass and flowering mustard and lupin and larkspur that line the road, but otherwise, there is no evidence of human commerce or recreation until you drive twenty miles down Route 85, to the gravel path that leads to the gate of Papa One. At that corner is a single-story yellow house; pieces of engines and dismantled tractors are scattered in the yard. Tacked up above the front stoop is a crooked sign that says FIX-IT SHOP.

If you were about to spend your Saturday night working at Papa One—that is, if you were about to spend Saturday night isolated sixty-five feet below ground in a fully sealed, attack-hardened launch-control capsule, monitoring ten Peacekeeper intercontinental ballistic multi-warhead MX nuclear missiles that are in a state of constant launch readiness, which two Air Force officers have to do every single Saturday night of the year—the little yellow Fix-It Shop is the last evidence of the outside world you would see.

One recent Saturday, two members of the Four-hundredth Missile Squadron at F. E. Warren—United States Air Force First Lieutenant Roger Juntunen and United States Air Force Captain James Otteson—kissed their babies and their wives; drove to the base; attended a prealert briefing covering current maintenance conditions, weather outlook, missile readiness, and upcoming distinguished visitors; signed for custody of an official vehicle; handcuffed their briefcases to their left wrists; drove an hour through the great plains to Papa One; passed a small metal sign with two buckshot holes in it that says P-1 use of deadly force authorized; checked in with the facility security police; signed typewritten statements saying "I accept custody of ten mated rocket systems/reentry vehicles"; ordered lunch and dinner from the launch facility cook; and then rode an elevator down a shaft in the earth and locked themselves into a small rectangular room—the launch capsule, in Air Force parlance—where they would stay for the next twenty-four hours.

Working on a Saturday night is not an extraordinary thing for the missile crews. A missileer I met at a barbecue in Cheyenne suggested to me that everyone would love to be able to just *turn* the missiles off once in a while—Super Bowl Sunday was the specific instance he had in mind—but that as far as he could tell, that option has not been engineered into the national defense master plan. Instead, the missile business is what management analysts call an "incessant organization"; that is, it has to be staffed and monitored constantly and continuously, day in and day out. Like most launch control crew members, Roger and Jim are assigned about eight twenty-four-hour alerts each month, and at least one or two of those end up being on Saturdays. Unless someone's weekend-alert assignment falls on an especially choice weekend, the attitude at the base when the monthly schedule is posted is something in the neighborhood of business-as-usual.

The missileers have a habit of dismissing the circumstances of their schedule by invoking the phrase "What's a weekend?" I heard this so much when I was in Cheyenne that I started to wonder if it was something you learn in missileer school between Emergency War Order Verification class and lunch. I suspected that it was meant to show military toughness by suggesting that weekends are for sissies. This suspicion was furthered when a colonel I was introduced to at F. E. Warren eyed me and said, as his salutatory statement to me, "You want to know what the missile crews will say to you about Saturday night? They'll say, 'What's a weekend?' You wait and see. For that matter, you'll probably begin to wonder about it yourself." Not incidentally, one of the first things Jim said to me when I asked him about working on Saturday night was "Well, actually, what's a weekend?"

"I give up," I said. "Just tell me why everyone always says that."

He shrugged. "I guess because once you're in the military, you have to learn to forget about things like weekends. The week doesn't mean anything to us, either. For us, it's days you're on and days you're off, period. You know, you can't just leave the missiles for the weekend, or on Christmas, or whatever. For the rest of the world, working Saturday night is some sort of taboo. For us, it's something that has to be done. Someone's got to be out here all the time, weekend or not. Some of the time, it's going to be me."

It was my intention, in Wyoming, to see what it feels like to work on a Saturday night. There are, according to most accounts, seven million people in the United States who work at night. These night workers are a source of continual fascination to people who study them, and of worry to anyone who relies on them, ever since it has been shown that an unconventional work schedule has a less-than-desirable effect on the human animal. Apparently, besides disorientation, fatigue, alienation from family and friends, and lack of visual acuity and judgment, night work has little to recommend it. Spectacular disasters have been blamed on night work and its liabilities—the chemical spill at Bhopal, India, and the nuclear accidents at Three Mile Island and Chernobyl come to mind.

It is safe to guess that of the seven million people on the job at night, most are at work on a Saturday night as well. Some of them—waitresses, bartenders, baby-sitters, actors, and musicians—have to work so that everyone else can enjoy Saturday night; the payoff is that they usually make more money on Saturday night and, according to a number of waitresses I know, really don't miss the crowds and bustle of a Saturday night out. Millions of people also work on Saturday at nonstop organizations—police and fire departments, hospitals, communications businesses, prisons, utilities, oil rigs, diaper services, and all-night gas stations. Even in a place that never shuts down, working Saturday night is different, because there are usually no supervisors around and ordinary protocol goes out the window. I once heard of a round-the-clock HoHo bakery in Washington state where on Saturday the night workers allow themselves to take unlimited HoHos off the production line for snacks.

Missileering struck me as being one of the more sensitive nonstop operations. World civilization depends on there being very little of Saturday night's lively abandon down in the silos. Moreover, knowing what I already knew about Wyoming—namely, that the practice of lively abandonment is a near art form there—it seemed that spending a Saturday night several dozen feet underground in an isolated and inaccessible and lonesome spot would be a notable and maybe extraordinary work experience. After a few days wandering around Cheyenne, the question I'd been hearing all week—"What's a weekend?"—began to get under my skin. The colonel was right. It was exactly what was on my mind as I rode the elevator down into the launch capsule.

Roger Juntunen, who is twenty-six years old, came to the Air Force by way of Duluth, Minnesota, and a scholarship for a bachelor's degree in math. He has thinning blond hair, large blue eyes, the conscious gentleness of someone who was probably a clumsy kid, and a wide, upturned mouth that gives everything he says a touch of drollness, intentional or not. He is self-deprecating to the very verge of aw-shucksism. When asked what he intends to get out of his Air Force career, he says, "Well, I want to do something realistic, of course. I'd love to make colonel, *of course*. I'd like to command a missile squadron, *of course*. But I'm just hoping to get a little ahead—something realistic, of course." He delivers the explanation of how he landed in missileering with a recurrent grin: "I never had any aspiration to be a flyer. When I joined the Air Force I requested missiles." [Lips purse.] "My feeling was that to be a flyer you have to have three qualities. You have to be perfect, you have to be a genius, and you have to be lucky. These do *not*" [grin completed] "describe *me*."

His partner, Jim Otteson, is thirty-one. He has a wheat-colored crewcut, a barrel chest, and a surprised look on his face. Sometimes, when he is in the middle of a sentence, he looks as if he just remembered that he left something on the stove. This, amazingly enough, does not interfere with the general impression he gives of resolved steadiness. He grew up in Orem, Utah; went to Brigham Young University; married the daughter of a Navy man and now has four children. When he counts off his obligations in life—one, missiles; two, children; and three, church—he clasps his hands in front of him as if he were holding a rock. Then he shakes the rock hard when he points out that the worst thing about Obligation

Number One is that he can't always take Obligation Number Two to Obligation Number Three.

Jim and Roger both wear glasses and look at ease in front of large pieces of electronic equipment. They are both tall, generously built, full-sized adult males possessed of the body type that could inspire a doting aunt to describe them as Big Boys. Even when they are wearing their Air Force missileer jumpsuits and black ascots and Smith and Wesson .38 pistols, they look like two big, bright, and slightly bemused engineering students.

As it happens, the Big Boys take up a considerable percentage of the square footage in the launch capsule, which is about six feet wide and fifteen feet long, and has the vastness of a suntanning booth. The ceiling is low and tangled with cables and pipes, like a construction site. Two of the capsule's four walls are lined with electronic gear. When I first stepped into the capsule I found myself almost reflexively counting pieces of equipment—I stopped when I got up to twelve analog gauges; two computer monitors; four control boards; ten anonymous metal compartments with big handles; two notebooks marked "Top Secret"; one black vinyl notebook marked "Papa One Movie Selections"; and one red metal box, secured with a Master lock and a Sesamee. I found out later that it is the red box that holds the Emergency War Order verification codes and two keys that, when turned in proper sequence with two launch control officers in another capsule, would send the ten MX missiles that Papa One monitors toward their targets in the Soviet Union.

I had a much easier job counting creature comforts—the capsule offers only a toilet, which can be separated from the rest of the room by a gray curtain, and a cot with stiff sheets, a pillow with the squishiness of porphyritic granite, and a rough gray blanket. Some missileers told me that the cot represents what they refer to, with piquant irony, as "The Strategic Air Command One-Man Bed Policy," which means that the bed deployed for capsule use is small enough to make it highly unlikely that more than one missileer would be asleep at a time. This is said to be beneficial to national security. As far as I could tell, though, a king-sized bed with Magic Fingers would be just as effective, because it is so noisy and cold and unpleasant in the capsule that it is highly unlikely that anyone would sleep in it ever.

Jim told me later that Strategic Air Command has designated this "The Year of the Alert Force" and has instituted an incentive deal called "The Glowing Patriot Program" to encourage missile crews who want to cheer up the capsules to give them a fresh coat of paint (Air Force–issued Doeskin or Gray Latex) or hang posters (tasteful only). Some of the crews had even taken the bait. That said, it is still understood that launch capsules, as places go, have limited appeal and that MX capsules have the most limited appeal of all. When I was nearing the end of my visit at F. E. Warren, in fact, a member of the Four-hundredth who was trying to give me an idea of how much the crews like the MX capsules gave me a cartoon called "The Big Difference" which had been hanging in the squadron locker room at the base. The cartoon compared an MX capsule to the capsules that were built for the now-obsolete Titan missiles. "Sentimental" is a word that does not fall easily into any sentence that also includes the phrase "nuclear missile," but the cartoon depicted the old Titan capsule (called "The Titan Country Club") in adoring detail—four crew members, three floors, a bowling alley, a private bathroom, a television set, and a kitchen complete with a table, a bud vase, and something burning on the stove. The MX capsule, by comparison, was depicted as a cramped room with two officers staring, bleary-eyed, at a computer console. I am told that the Titan bowling alley is a bit of an exaggeration. I can tell you that the rendering of the MX capsule is not. It is not a charming place. That didn't surprise me, but I had expected that the capsule would offer every electronic comfort imaginable.

"Do you get great television?" I asked Roger.

"Oh, please don't ask," he said, looking glum. It turns out that unless the original capsule construction included a nuclear-attack-resistant television antenna (a few MX capsules do, but Papa One doesn't), the missileers can't set up a television. And telephones—well, there is a telephone, but it is an old-fashioned one with a rotary dial.

"It's incredible when you think about it," Roger went on. "I can launch a nuclear missile or radio anywhere in the world in a second, but because we only have a dial phone in here, I can't use my MCI card."

The week I spent in Wyoming before going to Papa One, the air was hot enough to pop corn. The persistent, greasy aroma of overheated asphalt rose off the streets of Cheyenne, and in the middle of the day, the few people I saw outside skittered from shady spot to shady spot as they worked their way down the street. Downtown Cheyenne is naturally scenic. If they removed the old iron hitching posts from Main Street or passed a law limiting the amount of turquoise-and-silver jewelry any one citizen could wear at any one time, you would still know by its wide sidewalks and numerous saddle-and-chaps stores and low wood-shake buildings that you were in a righteous western town. In the middle of the heat, it was a righteous and mostly empty western town. At night, when it cooled off, there were more people outside, and by Saturday night, pickup trucks loaded with men wearing tractor hats and plaid shirts were roaring up and down the streets, and the sidewalks were loud and crowded.

I made note of quite a few traditions in Cheyenne when I was there. One of them is an interest in and affection for armaments, new and old. One day, I realized I had driven past the missile chassis in front of F. E. Warren four times, shopped in a western-wear shop that was decorated with muskets and arrows, and eaten all my meals at a coffee shop near the highway that has on its walls a collection of Indian arrowheads in homemade shadow boxes.

It is also kind of a tradition in Cheyenne to get drunk and unruly in the downtown bars. Some people consider it a genuine part of local heritage, since the formation of Cheyenne as a real town was marked by the establishment of its first bar. In 1867, the Union Pacific Railroad had laid tracks as far as Cheyenne; when they reached Sheridan Hill, just west of what is now downtown, winter set in and work on the railroad stopped. The railroad workers were sheltered in tents for the season and thus the town was born. One of the first things established here, and one of the first that gave the town any distinction among the dozens of newly formed western railroad-track towns, was the Cheyenne Social Club, which catered to Wyoming cattle barons in easy circumstances and set the standard for plush western barrooms. A number of less plush examples soon followed. Cheyenne ended up being a town with many bars.

That same year, the United States Cavalry was given a permanent post two miles north of downtown—the post eventually became F. E. Warren Air Force Base—and another tradition, the affiliation of enlisted people with local bars, began. This tradition has as its hallmark the tendency, every few years or so, for one of the young men from the base to either kill someone or get killed in one of Cheyenne's more notorious drinking establishments; but overall, it is a tradition viewed charitably even by local law-enforcement officials. A police captain I got to know, a mild, balding man named Pat Seals, told me one day when I stopped by the Cheyenne police station that he really missed the 1950s, because back then, F. E. Warren was a communications base that seemed to attract an enlistee who was, overall, wilder and woollier than the missileers. "It was a *hell* of a good time," Captain Seals had said. "On weekends, everyone in town would be pretty well oiled by two in the afternoon. It would get so wild that we had a unit of officers that patrolled the bars on Saturday nights."

I wondered if he had trouble staffing on the weekend because of that situation. "Oh, no!" he said, looking at me with surprise. "It was a whole lot of fun! All the guys on the force loved working on weekends. We'd *rush* to the bars whenever there was a disturbance, we'd *rush* to a street scene when there was a fight. It was a *kick*. It used to be a *hell* of a good time." The best time of all, Captain Seals added, was the last Saturday night of Cheyenne's Frontier Days, the town's week-long rodeo and fair held late in the summer; even judged by the considerable standards of Cheyenne high life, the last Saturday night of Frontier Days established a reputation for boisterousness that is unmatched.

Captain Seals said, "Oh, talk about tradition, well, that's a hell of a tradition. It is famous as a night to raise hell. I remember when I was younger, still on patrol, I'd be surrounded by people, I got my shirt ripped off, I had wild kids swarming all around me. Frontier Days used to be a whole lot of fun. It still is, but back then, it used to be sort of a *battleground*. It was the cowboys versus the hippies.

The guys from the base fit in there somehow, too. It was just a lot of good fun, fights, and rowdiness. Now, honestly, we kind of miss the hippies."

The cowboy bars, as distinct from Cheyenne's many biker bars and tourist drinks-with-little-umbrellas bars—there are no extant hippie bars in town—are clustered downtown near the railroad station. That Saturday, before I was taken by Air Force escort to Papa One, I spent some time in the Cheyenne Club (it has no relation to the Cheyenne Social Club except through myth), which is situated on a nice piece of real estate on an animated downtown block, and happens to be the sort of bar that you hear well before you see it. When I walked in, a band of four skinny men wearing jeweled cowboy shirts was going full throttle at a Merle Haggard song, and the dance floor, the tables, and the space in front of the bar were filled. The population looked to be equal parts oil-field roughnecks, cowboys, and enlisted men from F. E. Warren, who I could pick out by their polo shirts, their white pants, and their habit of running their hands over their Air Force haircuts. From what I had been told, the missile officers clock very few hours in bars like the Cheyenne Club. The restrictions on their drinking—no alcohol twelve hours before a missile shift—made participation in the Cheyenne Club ethos cumbersome at best, and it was understood that officers were better off not consorting with enlisted men in the livelier bars in town.

Lively I had expected, but the Cheyenne Club seemed to me to radiate a particularly antic energy. There was a hum of shrieked conversation throughout the place. A group of airmen seated at a table near mine were engaged in a contest that either had rules too arcane for me to decipher, or no rules at all except that everyone had to slug back beers and then immediately pound the table with both fists. One then mouthed something to the other two and they collapsed laughing. Shoving broke out around the bar like a rash and then subsided and then broke out again.

I observed to the man standing next to me that the exhilaration level was impressive. He looked at me and said, "Oh, the poor little kids. You know, this is it for them." The man—his name was Kevin, and he said he worked for a stamp manufacturer in Cheyenne—

observed that this was the last Saturday night before Wyoming's drinking laws changed, and that as far as he could tell, something like a feeding frenzy was under way. The last state in the union to serve nineteen-year-olds and the first when it came to liberal interpretations of what being nineteen really means, Wyoming, it turns out, had finally collapsed under federal pressure and passed legislation raising the drinking age to twenty-one. This night turned out to be an important, even momentous occasion in Wyoming history; it marked the end of a self-defining tradition, just as the opening of the first Domino's Pizza would mark the end of an era in Rome.

"I just look at them and feel sorry," Kevin went on, shaking his head and beer in time. "I mean, look, you're in the middle of the whole wide world out here, and there's nothing to do but come to these bars and have a big time. This is it. This is what's going on in Cheyenne, and here this is, the last big night before everything changes." He squinted into his beer bottle and then put it back on the bar, and said, "The poor little suckers. Now what's left for them here?"

One legacy of Wyoming's juicy, high-living heritage is a neurotic condition called the "Gillette Syndrome." The syndrome is a condition of anxiety and depression associated with extreme isolation and a feeling of disconnection from the world. The fact that Wyoming's alcoholism, suicide, and divorce rates are among the top five in the United States is sometimes credited to the Gillette Syndrome. The condition is said to occur most often among women brought to Wyoming by husbands chasing jobs in the oil and mineral industry. One big strike of oil or uranium could attract thousands of workers to a barren spot that previously hosted little more than, maybe, a fireworks store. Gillette, a town two hundred and forty miles north of Cheyenne, is exactly that kind of place. In its first incarnation, Gillette had been a scratch village, a supply stopover for ranchers in the area. Then ten years ago, low-sulphur coal was discovered nearby; a city made up of strangers, trailer parks, gas stations, and virtually nothing else erupted within months. Land was ripped out in huge chunks in the pursuit of coal. Money was around. The few social outposts in town were hard-drinker bars of the sort many wives would not have found inviting. One bar in a town near Gillette called for police assistance seventy-nine times in the first ninety days of 1980. Excluded by choice or discretion from the overly eventful social world of local barrooms and stuck in the middle of nowhere with no one around, the women of Gillette slid into pronounced depression in numbers great enough to astound mental-health experts and eventually constitute a nameable syndrome. Ultimately, Gillette became shorthand for any rootless jerry-built town swamped with social problems. The syndrome became synonymous with the depression that afflicts the dislocated and disowned.

One day I met a woman named Anne Wagner, who heads a mental-health clinic in Cheyenne. I had come to ask her about how living amid the MX missiles had affected the mental health of Cheyenne's residents, and specifically, how working underground in remote outposts, cut off from social interaction but tied in directly to global apocalyptic possibility, seemed to affect the missileers at F. E. Warren. I had just read about the Gillette Syndrome, which made me think about what it would be like to live somewhere like Gillette or work somewhere like Papa One. Anne Wagner mentioned that none of the missileers could risk seeking any kind of mental-health counseling because it would automatically disqualify them from missile duty, and that if a missileer is even known to be having problems with his wife, he is temporarily suspended from working in the launch capsules. She said some missileers see counselors secretly anyhow, and that their complaints were not as much about the awesomeness of their responsibility with the missiles but about the conditions of their lives. Their problems were a little like those of the wives in Gillette—that they felt isolated and out of synch with the rest of the world, because of the solitariness of their work and the unusualness of their schedules and the strange, flat distances they had to travel all the time.

"Wyoming is a lonely place," she said. "A place like this attracts and allows eccentricity and individualism, and it attracts transients, and people without roots, but it can be hard on people. There's the boom-and-bust phenomenon of the mineral industry, where people will one day have a lot of money and the next day they will have no job and no community to turn to. There is the fact of all the missiles here, the fact that if there ever were a war, we in Wyoming would probably be vaporized. Wyoming is a very, very isolated place. There is so much isolation, and that isolation can bring out the real difficulties in someone's personality."

When my escort first led me into the launch capsule, Roger and Jim were huddled in front of a printer reading a coded message. Another printer, which looked like an old Royal manual typewriter, was tapping away, and the radio chattered at intervals. The sounds bounced around the capsule and seemed to multiply. Roger waved and said, "Welcome to our little underground world."

Jim looked around and said, "Yeah, little. And when we say little, we mean *little*."

Roger grinned and swept his arm out, as if he were a maître d' at a cheesy restaurant. He offered to give me a tour of the capsule, and then began a spirited narration: "This is the Air Force Satellite receiver. We don't use that one too much. This, here, this is the SLIFIX—the Survivable Low-Frequency Communications System. Okay. Now, this is SACDIN, the SAC Modified Digital Information Network. We can use this to communicate with anyone in SAC. They like us to use it so that we get some practice on it. We send messages to our friends, that sort of thing. . . . Okay. Now, this is the Command Message Processing Group Printer. Okay. My clothes? This is a crew jumpsuit, and we call them crew blues. The ascot is black because our squadron is nicknamed the Black Pirates. That's our name. So we wear a black ascot to go with the name. Okay. Here is the bed, obviously. . . . The red box, you probably can guess, is the box with the Emergency War Orders and the keys. The locks belong to us. When we take over from the previous crew on alert, they take off their locks and we put on ours."

He paused and held up his hand. "Oh, I must tell you that we might receive a warbletone while you are down here," he said. "You know, do you know what a warbletone sounds like? Let's see, uh, '*weeeeoohweeeeooohweeeeeooooh*,' sort of. Well, you'll know it if you hear it. If we do receive the tone, we will have to ask you to turn around while we receive the code."

The radio started to make noise again, this time with a message from the security police upstairs. Earlier in the evening, there had been an Outer Zone Violation—that is, the sensors at one of Papa One's ten missiles had detected movement of an unspecific nature around the missile blast door. The alarms around the missiles are sensitive, but they have no discretion. A tumbleweed or pranksters or a terrorist would trigger the same alarm.

The missiles are planted in a lopsided circle around Papa One. Most of them are on the edge of a sixty-five-thousand-acre ranch owned by Alan and Lindi Kirkbride, members of a family that has raised longhorns, Herefords, Angus, and Gelbvieh cattle on this land for one hundred years. On the Saturday night I spent at Papa One, Alan Kirkbride and the Kirkbrides' children were spending the night at a 4-H camp near Laramie, and Lindi was home with a house guest, a Carmelite nun who is a friend of the family's. Many years ago, an elderly great-aunt of Alan Kirkbride's drove into an unmarked ditch the Air Force had dug while building the missile silos, and was permanently disabled from the accident. Now Lindi is a member of a group called Wyoming Against MX. The land was taken from the Kirkbrides by eminent domain. The trade-off was that their ranch roads, which had been soft dirt and gravel, were substantially improved by the Air Force, which needed roads that could support the weight of the trucks carrying the missiles to the silos. The MX weighs two hundred thousand pounds.

The closest of Papa One's missiles is three miles from the launch capsule; the farthest is about seven miles away. Some of the missileers have never touched, smelled, or seen an MX missile. The missileers do not tend to give the missiles pet names or feel personal affection toward them, except that they all tend to call the missiles "he"; when explaining the function of the computer that examines missile status at thirty-second intervals, they tend to say, "The computer says to him, 'Hey, how're ya doin'?' And he says either, 'Fine' or 'Not fine.' " In the past, bomb crews have had no knowledge of computers but more literal hands-on exposure to their weapons, and probably as a result, had more sentimental attachment to them. The bombs dropped over Nagasaki and Hiroshima were nicknamed Fat Man and Little Boy. "Papa" isn't a nickname; the launch capsules and missiles are given number and letter designations but are then referred to by the universal radio and military phonetic alphabet, like "Alpha" and "Bravo" and "Delta."

A modern-day MX silo is an unremarkable sight—a chain-link fence, a radar dish, and a round cement door that looks like a thick manhole cover. Anyone driving by a silo in a hurry would think he were passing something no more spectacular than an underground sewage-disposal tank. If the missile were ever enabled and launched as that same person were driving by, it would explode through the door and within a flash of seconds shoot nearly seven hundred thousand feet into the atmosphere, for the driver a somewhat more remarkable sight.

The Outer Zone Violation had occurred at the missile known as Papa Six (Papa One, the launch capsule, controls the ten MXs known as Papas Two through Eleven), and Roger had dispatched two security police a few minutes earlier to inspect. I would have imagined that such an incident would have also triggered Roger and Jim, but they registered only mild interest.

"Big excitement for a weekend," Roger said. "They're usually quiet, because they don't do missile maintenance on weekends unless it's an emergency. We get fewer messages from SAC on the weekend, which means we have fewer things to decode and fewer practice exercises. Some people like working weekends because you can get a lot of homework done, if you're in school."

"Did anyone tell you that most of the officers are working on graduate degrees?" Jim said. "Maybe that's why we like it when we pull a weekend alert. It's sort of like . . . baby-sitting when the baby is asleep. There's a lot less pressure, especially with the Peacekeeper missiles, since they're so new, and they're always having big maintenance jobs on them during the week to get them on line. Some of the guys, especially the single guys, they feel very deprived if they work on the weekends. They feel that's their only time to date, go out, that sort of thing. For me, it's different, because it means I get to see my kids during the week, which I like."

"I'm in school," Roger added. "I'm studying for my MBA. I like working weekends because I do have a lot of homework, and if there's less to do here, I get my studying done."

"Less to do with the Peacekeeper is just a figure of speech, though," Jim said to him. He tapped a pencil on the palm of his hand. "It's typically much busier with MXs than where I was before, Little Rock, where I worked Titan missiles. With the Peacekeeper, you're in charge of ten missiles. With Titan, you only had one missile to worry about."

"Did it make that much difference?" Roger said.

"Oh, a *lot*," Jim said. "A Titan weekend was a real weekend. Titan alerts were a lot . . . funner. There were four guys, and two people were always awake at a time. You could play cards if you wanted, which was nice. When I'd come off a Titan alert, I could go out and do something. When I come off a Peacekeeper alert, I'm kind of . . . all drug out."

"Are you? Me too," Roger said. He turned to me and said, "It's a long night down here. The worst thing is boredom. I can tell the night is long when I've already watched *The Guns of Navarone* on the VCR, and read all the new issues of *Newsweek*, *Time*, and *Business Week*, and my wife's already called, and I'm done studying, and the radio is totally quiet. Weekends are actually the worst that way." He sat on the edge of the cot and traced a pattern in the blanket.

Jim walked along the computer consoles, noting numbers to himself and then writing on a clipboard. He had a look of deep concentration on his face, like a judge at a pie contest. For a moment, the capsule was silent. Even the printer had stopped clicking. The quiet was absolute—much as you might expect if you were behind a two-foot-thick steel door sixty-five feet underground. A feeling swept over me that I can only compare to being deep underwater. I looked over at Roger and Jim, but they both had their faces turned away, toward the longest row of dials.

After a minute, Jim looked up and said to Roger, "What's your wife doing tonight?" Roger said she was visiting her family in Ohio, and then he asked what Jim's wife, Katie, was planning for the night.

Jim waved the clipboard. "She's home with the kids," he said. "She told me she was going to be refinishing furniture tonight."

"See, that's what's become of Saturday night if you're married to a missileer," Roger said to me. "We miss a lot of stuff. All the missileers are in the Personnel Reliability Program, which means we can't drink for twelve hours before we get out here so I don't like to go out if everyone's going to be drinking. I don't go out that much to the cowboy bars in town, because they're so, oh, wild I guess. We can't really do that sort of stuff. So it's like we start being out of the normal world twelve hours before we even leave for the alert. You know, we miss a lot of events. Concerts, that sort of thing."

Jim said, "You know what I miss? I miss 'Saturday Night Live.' "

"It's not as good as it used to be," Roger said to him.

"Well, I still miss it. I also miss the 'New Generation Star Trek' or 'Star Trek: The New Generation,' whatever that is. I never get to see it."

The voice on the radio said, "Security patrol returned from investigation at Papa Six." Roger got up and stood over the radio.

"And?" he asked, into the radio.

"Rabbit over there."

"Uh-huh."

"Disposed of same over fence," the radio voice said. "He or she was not harmed."

Roger and Jim are a team. All the missileers work in teams of two, one being designated as the commander and the other the deputy, and they pull alerts together until something like a promotion disturbs their partnership. In Roger and Jim's case, the usual logic of rank doesn't apply, because even though Roger is the lower ranked of the team, he has pulled more MX alerts than Jim, so he has been ranked commander of the capsule. Jim transferred to F. E. Warren this year from Little Rock Air Force Base, where he spent three years and pulled one hundred and fifty-two Titan missile alerts. Before this Saturday night, he had pulled only one MX alert.

Fooling with rankings—this is something that doesn't sit lightly with a military man, but Jim seemed to be stoic about it. That is a good thing, because the idea of the missile crew not having completely harmonious relations is slightly disturbing. There is not enough room in a capsule to air out even a low-level dispute. The Air Force screens applicants for quirks and mental imbalance before, during, and after their stints as missileers. Anyone who seeks counseling, has marital problems, develops a fondness for medications, nurtures a weird streak, resents working unusual hours, or is not willing to sign the Final Certification of Personal Commitment—which says "I understand the responsibilities of a missile combat crew member and realize what actions this duty may entail. I certify that I have no reservations over my ability and conviction to perform in such capacity"—will sail out of the program on board the Personnel Reliability rules.

Roger and Jim, as it happens, are steady men. Being both mild in manner and accommodating in style, they seem to have a rapport that is, on the whole, mild and accommodating, ventilated with a little breezy ribbing. The ribbing seems to be as much a time passer as it is a method of nonhostile display, the way monkey-to-monkey preening confirms good will. Early in the evening, Jim pointed out that he is older than Roger but looks younger. Roger conceded that he is younger than Jim and yet has less hair. Jim then mentioned that he had to pester Roger all night, since he didn't know a thing about MX missiles, and Roger nodded his head and chuckled.

"I've got to help this guy out," he said. "Who knows what trouble he could inflict if I weren't around?"

The commander of the launch capsule is also the ranking officer at the facility, which means he is also in charge of the four security police, the site manager, and the cook, who work upstairs in a small building over the launch capsule. As military configurations go, one that places the commanding officer in a locked box sixty-five feet below ground—which he cannot leave without permission of the lower-ranked site manager—is unique, if not extraordinary. The commander of a launch capsule has to feel that he can lead his troops by means of the capsule-to-topside telephone. He has to be able to ring upstairs and suggest, say, preparing for nuclear attack. Being commander has few distinct advantages, besides the fact that it is a step toward other promotions, except that the commander gets first choice of sleep shifts and movies to be played on the capsule VCR that night.

While Jim responded to a voice poll from SAC Air Command headquarters in Omaha, Roger said, "Well, we're going to miss church tomorrow. We just won't be back in time. We're lucky, because Papa One is closer to the base than any of the other capsules. Some of these guys—they drive two hours or so, to Nebraska or Colorado, to, like Romeo One and Tango One. But we all miss church. The base chaplain comes to the predeparture briefing, so we have a chance for some, you know, religion, but I don't like missing it. We don't keep a calendar down here, and we don't keep a normal clock, but I always know that Sunday is church. We're on Zulu Time, that's military time, so we can be coordinated with SAC all over the world. We can wear our watches if we want but they don't really mean anything."

Jim stepped over to the cot. "Roger, come look at this just for a minute. I don't quite see . . . something."

Roger stood up and shifted over to the console where Jim was standing.

"This is fine," Roger said. "You've got it."

"I'm still thinking Titan," Jim said, grinning. "I'll get over it."

"Yep," Roger said.

"When are you sleeping?"

"I'll sleep, uh, three to eight."

"So I'll take nine to three? Okay." Jim stared absently at a clipboard and then began to write in bursts. A message came over the radio: another message from SAC, followed by a poll of launch capsules to see who had received it.

"Radio games," Roger said. He stood up and stretched. A cheery look crossed his face. "You know, maybe I'll watch *War Games* tonight, Jim. I mean, even considering how unrealistic it is."

A colonel I know once told me that back when he was still standing alert, he could get hamburgers or steak only on Saturday nights, because the cooks refused to get their grills dirty on an ordinary weeknight. "The rest of the time, we just ate what was in the food packs," he said. "But Saturday was grill night, and we were happy as could be." Apparently, the Air Force cooks of this era are more forgiving when it comes to their grills, and, except under extraordinary circumstances, they will produce a hamburger on demand. As a result, the on-site hamburger has lost its rare, Saturday-night status; these days, a nuclear-missile-site hamburger is just another lousy dinner. When I went upstairs at Papa One, the cook,

Airman First Class Reginald Kelly, was preparing a meal to send down to the capsule crew, and one for the security officers, who were lounging in the living room. Airman Kelly took a census of everyone in the living room, made a few notes on a clipboard, and strolled back into the kitchen. In a moment, the sound of meat patties on hot metal cut through the living room.

"Siteburgers," someone said. "Yum, yum, yuck."

The topside building, which sits over the underground launch capsule, is a small rectangular structure. It has the proportions of a large toolshed, with big rooms and right angles. In the back are several bedrooms for the crew; in the front is an industrial kitchen, and a big living room with several randomly upholstered pieces of chunky wooden furniture. Toward the front door is the elevator that goes to the capsule. When I came upstairs that night, the three security police, Staff Sergeants William McMillion, David Crane, and Richard Huber, who had investigated the rabbit at Papa Six, were in the middle of post-game analysis.

"He was just a baby."

"He was scared, too, but I really think he was okay when we put him over the fence."

"I'm just glad it wasn't another *snake.* God, I hate those things. They can really squeeze in under the blast door easily. Guy I know said he was on alert once when one squeezed in, fell into the silo, and landed all the way at the bottom. I don't know how they got it out."

"Give me a break, would you?"

"Oh, come on, they're just animals. I love animals. I love coming out on alert because in the fall out here I can do a little antelope hunting when I'm on break."

Richard Huber then stood up and said, "Color me gone. I'm going to sleep."

"Awfully early, aren't you?"

"Nope. I'm out. I always go to sleep early on Fridays."

McMillion and Crane stared at him in surprise, and then started to snicker.

"Friday, man? Today's *Saturday,*" said Crane. "You really need some sleep." As Huber walked away, McMillion said, "*Saturday?* Today is *Saturday?* I didn't realize that. I must need some sleep, too."

Over hamburgers, McMillion, who is stout and dark-haired, and had the most intent expression on his face I'd ever seen—a combination of resolve and sympathy that you might come across on a toupee salesman—started talking. He told me that this was the fifth weekend in a row this security team had been assigned at Papa One. "I'm getting to be a barracks rat," he said. "We're getting a *lot* of weekends. You forget what day of the week it is because you just don't care. We stay out here for three days at a time. The missile crew just comes for the twenty-four hours and then leaves, but we're here, just counting the days: 'First day out, second day out, day we go home.' I used to think about the weekend all the time, but I don't since I enlisted."

"I thought you were going to take a base job," Crane said to McMillion.

"I can't," he answered. "My wife won't let me. She says if I was home all the time, I'd get on her nerves, so I've got to keep working missiles. She likes having some weekends to herself, too." He shot a look around the room. "This is starting to feel like home to me. I've been assigned to six different bases—I mean, Warren is my sixth. Most recently, before this, I was stationed in Turkey. By the way, whatever you've heard about Turkey is wrong. It's an *excellent* country."

Everyone fell to their meals, and the room was quiet until the phone rang—it was Roger and Jim calling Reginald Kelly to find out if their hamburgers were ready to be sent downstairs.

"Ooooh, I wouldn't want to be down there," McMillion said, in a hoarse stage whisper. "Not me. Up here, at least we've got room to move, and there are all of us to hang out together." He formed a fist and punched into the air, as if he'd made a touchdown. "And here it is, Saturday night!" he said. "And we've got a television, and we can watch the only show that matters—'Tour of Duty'!"

After dinner, Roger read three chapters of his business textbook, watched *War Games*, which he said still looked unrealistic to him, and then leafed through issues of *People, Sports Illustrated, Time, U.S. News & World Report,* and *Newsweek.* When he got to *Newsweek,* he stopped and read all of one long article. "Jim, look at this," he said, pointing to the magazine. "You should read this. It's an amazing article about some physicist who's all crippled up. All he can do is wiggle his finger." He slapped the magazine shut and said, "Okay, time for the sack." He walked over to the cot, put in earplugs, climbed into the bed, pulled the curtain around it, put his head between two pillows, and tried to sleep. After an hour, Jim woke him when a message came over the radio that he didn't understand. Roger explained it, put his earplugs back in and his pillows back together, and tried to sleep again.

The radio was now quiet. Jim sat at the console and rattled a pencil. Then he rolled the chair over to SACDIN—the Strategic Air Command Modified Digital Information Network. He made a note to himself to ask Roger something about the other printer when he woke up. "Okay, time for a little practice," he said. "They like us to use this, so let me think, who can I message?" He leaned back in the chair and stretched for a minute with his eyes closed. Then he sat back up and typed in this message: CONGRATULATIONS ON YOUR FIRST ALERT, BUDDY. FROM YOUR OLD COMMANDER J. OTTESON. He coded the message and relayed it to a friend who had been a classmate of his at missile school at Vandenburg Air Force Base, and then later served as one of his deputies at Little Rock, when he was with Titan. He picked up a magazine and started to read distractedly.

After a minute, the SACDIN printer started clicking out a message in code. When a long strip of paper had fed out of the machine, Jim tore it off the paper and gazed at it for a minute, his pencil eraser stuck into his cheek. He then said, "It says, 'I can use SACDIN, too. My commander taught me everything I know.'" He chuckled and sat back. The printer clicked on again. Jim read the second message and burst out laughing. "This one is from another friend of mine, who is in another MX capsule. It says, 'Are you still awake, Jim? I've got the commander's sleep shift tonight. How about you?' Boy, this is getting to be fun."

Roger rolled over in the cot and groaned audibly. "Almost time for my sleep shift," Jim said. He looked at his watch. It was two in the morning in the outside world. "Two, that means what?" Jim said suddenly. "That means all the bars in Cheyenne are shutting down. It's Saturday morning."

"Sunday," Roger said, from behind the curtain. His voice sounded as hoarse as if he had been screaming all night. "It's *Sunday*, Captain." He sneezed.

Jim looked at me and winked. "You're right. I just keep thinking it's Saturday. But then again, as we say, what's a weekend, right?"

The Next Day

On my trip to Cheyenne, I asked a young man who was working in an all-night fireworks store how he felt about Saturday night, and he replied, "Considering the alternatives, I like it a lot." I thought this was an ingenious answer. If you consider them, the alternatives to Saturday—that is, Monday, Tuesday, Wednesday, Thursday, Friday, and Sunday—are, in fact, rather uninspiring. The one thing that can be said is that they are useful for separating one Saturday night from the next.

A psychiatrist I met some time ago, Dr. Ronald Pies, spends most of his time as an associate clinical professor at the Tufts School of Medicine, but for the last few years, he has indulged an interest in the psychology and phenomenology of Sundays. Dr. Pies developed this interest when he was working at the student health center at Pennsylvania State University. At the time, students were coming to the center complaining of despair, lethargy, fatigue, ennui, general unwellness, and a variety of nonspecific bodily disorders, in different combinations. They had no apparent illness or disease, but they were obviously suffering from more than run-of-the-mill baccalaureate malaise. The doctors at the center were unable to offer any diagnosis. After a few months, Pies noticed that the rate of these complaints soared on Sunday nights. After a few months of such Sundays, Dr. Pies began to suspect that this disease had something to do with the day of the week rather than a virus, and that certain people in this world are so sensitive to the emotional sequence of the week that they are prone to depression on a seven-day schedule.

Pies was so excited by his day-of-the-week theory that he wrote an article for the *Centre Daily Times*, the local paper of State College, Pennsylvania, about the epidemic of what he had begun to call "Sunday Blues." The response to the article was another epidemic, this one of people calling and writing to him to say that they also got depressed at the end of every weekend, felt a little better by Tuesday, were back to normal by Wednesday, and forgot about it Friday and Saturday, only to collapse again sometime around noon Sunday. Pies told me recently that he never expected the article to generate as much attention as it did. Besides the stacks of mail and the phone calls, the article was reprinted in several newspapers around the country, and Pies himself was anointed, rather abruptly, an authority in the field. In some circles he was getting to be known as "that Sunday guy." It is not an overpopulated area of study; Pies liked the prospect of being a pioneer and found the subject intriguing enough to provide a nice diversion from his regular practice of psychiatry, and hopes to someday publish the definitive treatise on Sunday depression. To that end, he now collects any and all data he can on the nature of the day and its victims. As an adjunct to my own preoccupation with Saturday night, I have spoken to him about Sunday now and again over the last few years.

"I was really struck by this whole thing at Penn State, when so many students were complaining to me that they felt awful on Sundays," Pies said, when I visited him at Tufts University Medical Center, an island of health care in a sea of strip joints in Boston known as the Combat Zone. "I found it quite fascinating. The people who were coming in were feeling just sort of . . . *flat*. Sunday appeared to start some sort of weekly downswing for them. As far as I knew, no one had ever done any research on this kind of depression, and I really didn't know at the time what I was getting into—I didn't realize I was about to start a major study of Sunday blues." He cleared his throat. "Actually, at that time, my real interest was in psychopharmacology."

Pies is a trim, youngish, softspoken man with a halo of reddish hair, an excited-looking bushy red beard, a pleasant smile, a vaguely melancholic air, and a slightly nervous affect that manifests itself mostly in the kneading of Kleenexes. Like a lot of psychiatrists, he has a soothing voice and a riveting glance. When I first met him, he had just placed an ad in the Sunday *New York Times* asking to hear from anyone who suffered from Sunday depression. As a result, he was again knee-deep in sufferers and eager to talk about his progress. My own motives for calling on Dr. Pies were simple. I wanted to ask him, among other things, whether he thought Saturday night had anything to do with Sunday blues. I described to him what I was finding—that the widely felt imperative to be amused on Saturday nights seems to propel most people toward the weekend the way a high-pressure hose propels water toward a burning building, and that Saturday night appeared to be, for most people in most situations, the most exhilarating moment of the week. As I was saying this, Dr. Pies leaned further and further back in his chair, smiling as he kneaded the Kleenex in his hand. He looked cheerful. I asked him how his study of Sunday matched my notions about Saturday night.

"Quite well," he said. He lifted a batch of papers off his desk. "Just take a look at my Sunday Blues survey." At the start of the survey, he said, he had looked for a modest explanation. He speculated that some Sunday depressives were people who hated the prospect of returning to work on Mondays so much that they got depressed in anticipation. To ascertain this, he asked the survey subjects about work. A majority of them did indeed hate their jobs— "dissatisfied with their current state of employment" is the way I recall him describing it—and they also felt that their careers were out of their control. But that explanation didn't account for the students he had treated, who didn't have jobs, and it didn't account for the acuteness of the reaction, or the fact that many retirees experienced Sunday Blues long after they had left their jobs. He rebaited his hook. He surveyed the group about its social habits, and was able to determine that his high-frequency blues sufferers rarely "went out" during the week, and that they went out then much less often than LFBs—low-frequency blues sufferers—did. The HFBs also told him that they found it difficult or impossible to relax during the week, and that their sleep habits on the weekend seemed erratic. Then Pies presented both the HFBs and the LFBs with this statement and asked them to agree or disagree with it:

ONE MUST GET ALL ONE'S FUN IN ON THE WEEKEND

"I needed to establish an *attitude*," Pies said. "I hypothesized that the typical HFB might not be having fun during the week, that he or she wasn't integrating any pleasure into the week and was storing it all up for the weekend. I imagined that they felt that the weekend is the only time they were able to have fun—that they *must* get all their fun in on the weekend. For that kind of person, the weekend is *it*. And that, of course, would make the end of the weekend a little like jumping into icewater." He tidied the papers on the desk and added, "I figured that the HFBs were real grinds during the week. And I guessed that they were probably compulsive fun-seekers on the weekend." To Pies's great satisfaction, the HFBs endorsed the statement in far greater numbers than did the LFBs. With the data, he produced a portrait of the usual Sunday Blues victim—a person who dislikes his or her job, finds it difficult to relax during the week, and rarely goes out except for Saturday nights. As I was listening to Dr. Pies, it dawned on me that this composite HFB was beginning to sound like a lot of people I know.

"We all feel it to some degree, but the Sunday Blues sufferer has a more exaggerated reaction than the average person who appreciates Saturday night," he said. "They are truly obsessed with fun-seeking on Saturday nights. Then, on Sunday, a dark, depressed feeling might overcome them. They might not be able to get out of bed. They feel the best part of the week is gone. They have what I call 'anticipatory dread' of Mondays. The weekend is like a drug they inject, and when it wears off, they crash. This is a serious misuse of leisure time. Sunday is fairly unpopular with a lot of people. It can be a very tense day—a lot of family fighting takes place then. Sunday also has a lot of somber, religious implications.

I once found a poem by an Englishman who apparently was a terrible Sunday Blues sufferer, and in the poem he talks about the miserable feeling that would overcome him when church bells would ring. That was his signal to start being depressed. Your friend at the fireworks stand might just be a normal person who appreciates Saturday night, or he might possibly be a true HFB, if he really hates Sundays intensely and is debilitated by that feeling."

"Are there any other days of the week to avoid?"

"We psychiatrists have known for a long time that Monday is a major stressor for most people. After sleeping late and staying out late all weekend, you have to wake up early on Monday and go to work. So you feel bad and fatigued on Monday, as if you had jet lag. The greatest number of cardiac deaths among business executives occur on Mondays, for instance. It's the day with the highest suicide rate. Saturday is the lowest. Why? We don't really know. I believe the old song that it's the loneliest day of the week, but for some reason, it doesn't drive people to suicide. There is a lot of data in psychiatric literature showing that most people identify Saturday as an 'up' day. Some even like Friday the most, because they still have Saturday to look forward to."

As he was talking, Dr. Pies's shoulders started to sag, and a mournful look crossed his face. I asked if his research into Sunday Blues was at all self-interested. He sighed and said, "Oh, I don't really have a *significant* problem. I mean, it hasn't affected my job or my life. But I do get a little, uh, *down* on Sundays. I'm not a compulsive fun-seeker type, really—I just feel a little, uh, blue. You know, I don't like the weekend to end, because the weekend is . . . *fun*. And fun is . . . well, anyway, I don't really like the weekend to end. I'm very responsive to environmental triggers that make me realize the weekend is over."

"Environmental triggers?"

"Yes—that's something else we found out about our HFBs. They react very strongly to environmental triggers that signal the end of the weekend. You know, one woman wrote to me and actually said that the smell of Sunday dinner started her depression. Church bells, of course, are a classic. Maybe seeing all the stores closed on Sunday would be a trigger for some people. Maybe it would be something like not getting any mail." He tilted his head back and closed his eyes. After a moment, he opened them and said, "You may have heard of this show on National Public Radio called 'Car Talk.' That show is on Sunday afternoons, and it's very funny and lighthearted and all that, but whenever I hear it—well, for me that's my environmental cue. I start to feel down when I hear 'Car Talk.' I hear the voices of the guys who do the show, and they happen to have very distinct voices, and that's the thing that makes me feel a little down. It's a conditioned response, like a dog hearing a bell for dinner."

We discussed "Car Talk" for a few minutes, and then I asked Pies whether he had discovered any trigger that seemed unusually popular or powerful among the HFBs. He leaned forward for a moment and rubbed his beard. Suddenly, he clapped his hands. "Yes, we *did*," he said, excitedly. "We did have one thing that came up several times. A number of people recalled that their trigger for feeling depressed that the weekend was over was the theme song to 'The Ed Sullivan Show.' Remember that theme? *Dum-da-da-da-dum-da?* Apparently that set a lot of people off. For a while, I thought we might have to call this 'Ed Sullivan Syndrome.' "

I mentioned that "The Ed Sullivan Show" had been off the air for years. "Does that mean the people with the Ed Sullivan trigger feel fine on Sundays now?" I asked.

"Unfortunately not," he said. "You see, Saturday night still ends, and Sunday still begins, just like always, so they get depressed again, just like they always do. The only difference is that now that Ed Sullivan is gone, they seemed to have moved on to a new environmental trigger. Isn't it amazing how this works on people's moods?" He shook his head. After a moment, he added, "This new trigger has the same powerful effect that Ed Sullivan did. I'm now seeing a *lot* of patients with '60 Minutes' Syndrome."

Some months after I had last spoken to Dr. Pies, I found myself at home on a Saturday night with nothing to do. I hadn't bothered making any plans; there was nothing to watch on television; all of my friends were busy. The night loomed ominously. Here I was, in a city full of things to do, on the night of the week that is universally understood to have more vitality and possibility than any other, and I had nothing to do. It was already nine o'clock, which meant nearly every movie I'd want to rent would already be out at my neighborhood video store, but that seemed to be the slippery slope I was sliding down so I figured I would settle for anything as long as it was in color. Even at nine o'clock, the store would probably still have some color movies available. I put on my jacket. Then I realized I would have some fun anyway. I had no intention of wasting a Saturday night, and the fact that it was Saturday night was bound to make anything seem special. That is the way it is with Saturday night. I would just walk the long way to the store and see the sights: the cops who were walking in pairs down the street with an eye out for their brisk Saturday-night business, and the restaurants where lines were beginning to form, and the drug dealers who would be busier tonight than any other night, and all the apartment buildings where the sounds of summer parties would be floating out of the windows, and all the people who would be hurrying down the sidewalks on their way to something, to a dance or dinner or to visit friends, with that anxious, excited, polished, dolled-up look people always seem to have on their faces on Saturday nights. It sounded like plenty to do.

Afterword

I wonder what it would be like to write this book now, more than two decades after I first began looking at Saturday night around the United States. It's a book that examines a particular slice of social time, and time has transformed into a very different entity in those two decades. In some ways, it's become as malleable as taffy, easy to mold into whatever shape we want. Things used to happen when they happened, and only when they happened; time had a stern, insistent way of finding us and stopping us in our tracks. Now it seems like things happen when we've decided we're ready for them to happen. The week used to feel like it had such an inviolable order, and within the week, days felt bound and organized and set. Days had distinct personalities. When I was in college, for instance, and banks didn't yet have ATMs, the end of banking hours on Friday was a line of demarcation, the last moment you could get cash for the weekend. The scramble to get to the bank before it closed was part of what made Fridays feel like, well, Fridays. But I haven't been in a bank to cash a check for years. These days I meander over to an ATM whenever the need for cash arises. Any day can be cash day. Part of what gave Friday its individuality has been erased. The same is true for every part of the week, including Saturday night.

When I started writing *Saturday Night*, I was convinced that those markers in time mattered; that having time feel like it had some texture, an ebb and flow, was a comfort and a necessity. The distinctiveness of Saturday night mattered most of all because it was the most electric, emotional portion of the week. Saturday night was also an ideal common denominator. It was the one moment in the week that everyone—regardless of station in life, age, hometown, or ethnicity—could agree upon as being special. For a writer like me, very interested in seeing what makes us similar and what makes us different, and eager to describe a big sweep of American popular culture, Saturday night was a perfect frame through which to view all those sorts of communities. Rich, poor, Westerner, Easterner, teenager, old—despite everything that such people didn't have in common, they did share the feeling that one night of the week had a different tinge. Even staying at home doing nothing on a Saturday night—one of the most usual ways to spend the evening, although not nearly as engaging a subject for journalism as, say, polka dancing—had a noticeable quality. Saturday night was just different. It was the happiest night and the saddest night, the most communal night and the loneliest night, the most public night and the most private night of the week.

The biggest change in Saturday night since this book was first published has been brought about by technology. For instance, in 1990, television was available on a preordained schedule. Videocassette recorders were just becoming popular. And VCRs were just the beginning. Within a few years they were everywhere, and then they came and went, replaced by even more versatile DVRs; and then DVRs were joined by on-demand programming, and by Hulu, and by TiVo, and by HBO GO, and countless other ways to watch television without regard to a schedule. In other words, it's never been easier to watch a specific show whenever you decide to watch it. The control of time, in the case of television, has been placed in the hands of the viewer. As Ron Simon, curator of the Paley Center for Media, put it, what all of these systems offer in convenience has to be balanced against what they took away—the identification of a specific show with a specific night of the week. For the first three decades of commercial television, Saturday night was a premier spot on the schedule, home to everything from the brilliant sketches of *Your Show of Shows* to the contemporary controversy of *All in the Family*. I used to rush home on Saturday nights to watch *Saturday Night Live*; now I rarely watch a show when it's actually broadcast, and much of the time I couldn't even tell you what the regularly scheduled slot for the show is. Time-shifting television shows are so commonplace now that network programmers have largely given up worrying over the elaborate scheduling of shows; they know that most of the audience will just watch programming whenever they choose to. It's wonderful to be able to watch what I want when I want, but still, there's something lost. I used to love that achy anticipation of waiting for my favorite shows to be on, and I loved the feeling that so many people were watching together. All over the country—at least as I used to picture it—everyone was sitting down at the same time to see the same show. It created a virtual community before we had even thought of the idea of virtual communities.

Community itself has been redefined in the last twenty years. Saturday night used to be an irresistible reporting opportunity because most people used it as the night they gathered with kindred spirits, making it a perfect time for me to observe them in a self-selected group. Weekdays were filled with family and with work associates, but Saturday night was saved for romance or for friends—your fellow zydeco fans, your club-hopping pals, the other people in town who liked cruising Main Street as much as you did. The opportunity to be with a community of like-minded people was rare and precious. Now that kind of gathering is not so rare and not so easy for a writer to observe. If you are a '55 Chevy aficionado, you don't have to wait for Saturday night to gather with other Chevy aficionados, nor do they even have to live in your town: you can belong to a '55 Chevy Google group and a '55 Chevy Facebook page; you can follow #Chevycruising on Twitter. Online, you can talk about cruising in a Chevy with people all over the world, at any time of day. On one hand, this has made certain kinds of communities bigger, more universal, and more diverse, which is exciting, but I sometimes wonder if it's also flattened the communities out to fit on a computer screen. What will it mean if communities with shared interests were all connected on the Internet but no one ever went outside to see what they might see? What would happen to cities, and to Main Streets, nightclubs, bowling alleys, and cafés? Is it a good thing if our real-life ways of gathering, of actually being together in real time, in each other's presence, end up withering away?

Often readers will ask me what has become of people I've written about. Most of the time I don't really know. As a writer, I'm a serial monogamist. I fall entirely in love with my subjects while I'm engaged with them, and then, thanks to a combination of necessity and circumstance, I move on. I am always interested in what has become of the people and places I've written about—in some cases more than others, of course—but the opportunity to find out often just doesn't present itself. (Again, I'll reference technology here. When I wrote this book, the ways people kept in touch were limited to letters and phone calls, both of which entail a deliberate effort. Now, with email and Facebook, it's possible to stay in touch without so much of a commitment; maybe this will usher in a new era of ongoing awareness of my subjects. We'll see.)

It's unusual that I revisit a project as I've done here with *Saturday Night,* so this was a special chance to satisfy my curiosity, to see what twenty years had wrought. Some of what I learned didn't surprise me. For instance, every one of the hot-for-a-moment Los Angeles clubs that the kids in "Scene Making" patronized has closed, their moment of Saturday-night significance passed. Stuart Anderson's Cattle Company in Portland, where bands went to die, is also closed, and the band No Means Yes never did make it to the big time, although the phenomenon of the aspiring band playing Saturday nights in midrange, midpriced cocktail lounges will surely live on forever. In Elkhart, people still cruise, but gas prices—around $1.15 when I wrote the chapter, but averaging more than $4.00 as I write this now—have made it an expensive pastime rather than one of the cheapest ways to spend Saturday night. James Perron, the mayor who squared off with Elkhart's cruisers in 1989, is now the director of project development for United Water in Indianapolis. He recently told me that he thought the cost of cruising had dampened its appeal, but so had technology. "Cruising wasn't about driving, it was about meeting friends," he said. "But social media may have taken the place of that. People have other ways of getting together. It doesn't have to be in person: you can find anyone on the Internet."

Some Saturday night mainstays have shown impressive durability. The Wellesley bus still runs on Saturday nights (and has inspired a Facebook group, www.facebook.com/group.php?gid=2200049228, otherwise known as The Fuck Truck Has Fucked Me Over Group). Quinceañeras have continued as a Saturday-night tradition in Hispanic communities, and during these twenty years the number of them has continued to grow. While quinceañeras aren't considered a sacrament, the Catholic church finally decided to formalize the tradition in 2009, after a committee of bishops, priests, nuns, and laypeople spent a decade writing a prayer book especially for them, the *Order for the Blessing on the Fifteenth Birthday*, available in English and Spanish. The Bowery Mission still operates in downtown Manhattan, still in the same location, even though the neighborhood around it has become surpassingly fancy and fashionable. On many Saturday nights, Pennsylvania Amish and Mennonite churchgoers still arrive at the mission by the busload to sing and pray. There is still polka dancing at Blob's, and occasional zydeco dances at St. Anne's; there are still many tons of steaks slapped on platters at the Hilltop Steakhouse. There are millions of teenagers taking on the time-honored employment of Saturday-night babysitting; they earn $8 to $12 an hour these days, about twice what they were earning in 1990. Warren Air Force Base is still open, having survived the round of military cuts that closed more than ninety other bases. The fact that it is still open is less amazing to me than the casualness with which my request to visit it had been treated. In 1985 or so, I had simply written a letter to the Pentagon asking for permission to spend the night in the missile silo, and after a bit of a wait, I was granted permission in what seemed to be the most nonchalant sort of way. Today, in the wake of 9/11, no such thing would ever happen.

And the people? The young ones I wrote about are grown up now; many of the old ones are gone. The social mavens of Manhattan, Nan Kempner and Pat Buckley, died a few years ago, and some people believe that their style of entertaining died with them. Some of the most popular zydeco musicians I wrote about, including Boozoo Chavis, have passed away, but Jane Champagne, the impresario of the lala dances at St. Anne's, remains devoted to her church, and just a few years ago received an award for her "spirituality and service to the community." The Wellesley students who went wild on the bus to Cambridge are serious professionals now, and in many cases, they are parents of kids nearly old enough to start riding that Saturday-night bus themselves.

It seems, in the end, to all balance out—those things that have changed and those that have remained, the factors that have chipped away at what made Saturday night so special and those that keep shoring it up, the arch we pass through in our push through each week. And I still think Saturday night remains a true through line in the jumble that is American popular culture; however we manage to mold time to our liking, we all still do experience the turn of time, and we all know when it has come around to that night that feels enduringly and magically different. I hope it will always be that way.

—S.O.
August 2011